- Foucault — Disc + Punish
  " — The Hist of Sexual / The Will 2 Know...
- Derrida — Of Gram (Struct, sign + play)

Reimagining Ireland

Volume 4

Edited by Dr Eamon Maher
Institute of Technology, Tallaght

PETER LANG
Oxford • Bern • Berlin • Bruxelles • Frankfurt am Main • New York • Wien

Paddy Lyons and
Alison O'Malley-Younger (eds)

No Country for Old Men

Fresh Perspectives on Irish Literature

PETER LANG

Oxford • Bern • Berlin • Bruxelles • Frankfurt am Main • New York • Wien

Bibliographic information published by Die Deutsche Bibliothek
Die Deutsche Bibliothek lists this publication in the Deutsche National-
bibliografie; detailed bibliographic data is available on the Internet at
<http://dnb.ddb.de>.

A catalogue record for this book is available from The British Library.

Library of Congress Cataloguing-in-Publication Data:

No country for old men : fresh perspectives on Irish literature / edited
by Paddy Lyons and Alison O'Malley-Younger.
        p. cm. -- (Reimagining Ireland ; 4)
  Includes bibliographical references and index.
  ISBN 978-3-03911-841-0 (alk. paper)
  1. English literature--Irish authors--History and criticism. 2.
National characteristics, Irish, in literature. I. Lyons, Paddy. II.
O'Malley-Younger, Alison.
  PR8753.N6 2008
  820.9'9417--dc22

                           2008038879

ISBN 978-3-03911-841-0

© Peter Lang AG, International Academic Publishers, Bern 2009
Hochfeldstrasse 32, Postfach 746, CH-3000 Bern 9, Switzerland
info@peterlang.com, www.peterlang.com, www.peterlang.net

for

Flavia Swann

because she brings out the best in everyone

Contents

Introduction

PADDY LYONS AND ALISON O'MALLEY-YOUNGER

> That is no country for old men. The young
> In one another's arms, birds in the trees
> – Those dying generations – at their song,
> The salmon-falls, the mackerel-crowded seas,
> Fish, flesh, or fowl, commend all summer long
> Whatever is begotten, born, and dies.
> Caught in that sensual music all neglect
> Monuments of unageing intellect.
>
> — W.B. YEATS, 'Sailing to Byzantium'

'Sailing to Byzantium' looked forward to a departure overseas, to emigration. From the mid-nineteenth century, and well into the twentieth century, away was all too frequently the direction in life taken by Irish citizens, most often to assure for their families some economic prosperity; and often too, away was the direction taken by Ireland's writers – Joyce, O'Casey and Beckett, for instance – seeking access to freedom and to experience not readily available at home. Taken literally, Yeats's poem is no guide to the mood of those times: there is little to suggest sensual music was in much abundance in the Ireland of the late 1920s. Times were hard, then, and for the young who stayed, it could seem as if geriatrics ruled; as if the young were doomed to be – in Anthony Cronin's notorious and erstwhile censored phrase – 'Dead as Doornails under Dev'.

But by the late twentieth century, all was changing. By the 1980s, Ireland was the European country with the largest percentage of citizens under the age of twenty-five, and their music was being heard: Ireland had a thriving new musical culture, and was – in the words of the singer Dana – 'spiritual home to the Eurovision Song Contest.' By the 1990s the economy was prospering, heading for the boom which would come to be known as 'the Celtic Tiger'; and the flow of emigration had given way to waves of migration, returnees coming back from abroad to take up work in a new Ireland, soon to be followed by waves of new immigrants from other lands.

Explanations are various. By the late years of the twentieth century, the developed world was shifting away from its old economic base in heavy industry, a shift which for many countries would be and still is painful and disruptive. Ireland, however had – relatively speaking – been bypassed by the Industrial Revolution of the late eighteenth and nineteenth centuries, its economy remaining significantly agricultural, and hence out of step with the progress of wealth. In the late twentieth century this would prove advantageous: Ireland had less industrial baggage to offload, and could readily move to the forefront under new post-Fordean economics. Irish confidence became apparent under the Presidency of Mary Robinson, whose generous emphasis on inclusiveness – inclusion of the world-wide Irish diaspora, and inclusion of new immigrants – gave a boost to Ireland's position on the world stage, and thereby too to Irish writers.

Further progressive change was to take place with the initiation of peace processes in Northern Ireland, bringing a new climate to a part of the island which had for decades been bedeviled by sectarian 'Troubles'. Under the leadership of Bertie Ahern, government by coalition had already become the norm in the Republic; when the St Andrew's Agreement of 2006 brought about a power-sharing Assembly for Northern Ireland in Stormont, this so astonished the international media that world leaders and American presidential candidates would jostle to claim for themselves some association with the achievement of this new harmony. In short, Ireland no longer appeared to be ruled by the old quarrels of old men, and is exemplary now for showing how it's possible to move forwards socially and politically as well as economically. For Ireland's writers, here is a new situation calling for response; and for those who study Ireland's culture, here is a radically new position from which to view the past.

In the year that 'Sailing to Byzantium' was written (1926), it must have seemed to Yeats that a quasi-mythical world of wonderful promise had been fully superseded by profiteering gombeens at their greasy till, whose rise he had deplored in 'September 1913', where he famously stated 'Romantic Ireland's dead and gone'. With 'Sailing to Byzantium', his imagination turned to escape from the world of the real – the natural world – away from the world which privileges youth over age – and in the manner of high modernism he celebrated instead a distant realm of art and poetry, at once imaginary and symbolic. The magnitude of his feelings of loss is betrayed through the desire to be absorbed by the eternal – and hence imaginary – 'monuments of unageing intellect'. Yeats thus voiced a yearning for, and a lament over an 'imagined Ireland', an Ireland of the mind, as he sought a divorce from the crises and turmoil which beset the country at the beginning of the twentieth century, as it was moving from subaltern colonial status towards full independence. Writers before and since Yeats have done the same, producing laments, eulogies, elegies and liebstodts, which have envisaged Ireland in guises ranging from ailing Aislings to de Valera's fantasy of a land where comely maidens danced at the crossroads. Yet, as the broad title of this series indicates, if Ireland can be imagined, it can also be re-imagined. It is now time, as Richard Kearney has argued, 'to open Irish minds to life as it [is] lived in the present that is unencumbered by nostalgic abstractions from the past or millennial abstractions about the future. Ireland [has] come of age. The moment for critical stocktaking [has] arrived' (Kearney, 1988: 261).

This volume attempts a critical stock-take of Ireland's culture as it is re-imagined in the wake of the Celtic Tiger – an Ireland which has given proof that women too can be good and effective presidents of the nation, and where women are no longer are corralled into dancing at crossroads, and minding hearth and homeland – an Ireland in which traditions are often transitional or transnational, and where identity can be evolution-ary as well as revolutionary. As Fintan O'Toole has pointed out, 'Ireland is not one story any more' (O'Toole in Boss and Westarp, 1998: 171). It can be said that the Celtic Tiger has been leaping in new directions, and reaching new perspectives. The essays in this volume address and interro-gate these fresh and still-changing stories of Ireland – taking into account that political and ideological backdrops have changed the country from a famine-ravished but invariably idealized rural idyll, to Ireland's emergence as one of the wealthiest nations in the world. Ireland has moved from a third world culture to a first world country, and the politics of peace are transforming the landscape of possibilities, which Seamus Heaney suggests are best 'appropriated by those with a vision of the future rather than those who sing battle hymns to the past' (*Irish Times*, 10 April 1998). As Chris Morash observes: 'If Irish cultural debate is to move forward, a new vocabulary must be found' (Morash, 1991: 122).

Under the heading 'New Readings' we gather a range of reconsiderations of the writings of the past. Some of the writings addressed here have not been studied previously, or have not been considered deserving of study before now: Irish women's fiction from the era of the first world war – fiction that interestingly crosses sectarian divides – comes under the spotlight, as too does science fiction, a youthful and speculative literary genre, whose appeal for Irish writers has not before been widely noticed. The obsessive dimensions of the Gothic are revisited through post-colonial perspectives. Gender issues are re-opened, and Eilis Dillon, who is best remembered for her translations from Irish and for her children's fiction, can here emerge as an adult novelist, a serious and challenging investigator of family structures. A further hidden human geography is uncovered, whereby gays were marginalised in times when terrorism took centre stage, thus inviting questions as to how far those spaces still remain to be remapped. With the healing of sectarian wounds well underway, Brian Friel need no longer be positioned as purely a champion of Catholic Ireland, and his exposé of the Catholic pseudo-aristocracy can come into the light. Irish Classics too are reconsidered – the European dimension is enlarged through a demonstration of Joyce's rediscovery and scrupulous redeployment of ancient arts of memorialisation; and it is at last possible to identify the dark side of Flann O'Brien's comedy.

Along with Irish writing from both North and South, 'New Territories' also addresses new and distinguished writing from the Irish diaspora: Colum McCann's fiction has already brought into focus the Slavic world, and here it is considered in its further turn to the world of Romany; Martin McDonagh's plays are relocated within larger theatrical tendencies that link as much to Brecht and Pirandello as to Synge and the rich past of Irish drama. The new ground for Northern writers is examined as it is scrutinised in the fiction of David Park, as it is spoken about in a hitherto unpublished interview with the novelist Glenn Patterson, and as it is reconfigured by poets who have emerged in the decade following the beginnings of the peace process. The re-emergence of history as a strand in the Irish novel is considered in relation to Roddy Doyle and Dermot Bolger; as too are the ways whereby the novels of Deirdre Madden have registered the world of visual art and visual artists. Rewritings and re-adaptations of Shakespeare by the present generation of Irish playwrights, both North and South, provide a further barometer for writing in a time of change.

The contributors to this volume are from Ireland, North and South, from the Irish diaspora in Britain and in Scotland, and from Europe and from the United States. Many of their essays originated from the international conferences of the North East Irish Culture Network (NEICN) held annually at the University of Sunderland; others result from co-operation and partnership between NEICN and the Irish Studies work now thriving at the University of Glasgow. Both Sunderland and Glasgow have long been home to large and settled Irish diaspora communities, and it is a special satisfaction to us that from these communities outside the island of Ireland we can foster study in response to what is best and new in Ireland's continually developing culture.

Works Cited

Boss, M. and Westarp, K. (1998), *Ireland: Towards New Identities*, Aarhus University Press, Aarhus.

Kearney, R. (1988), *Transitions in Modern Irish Culture*, Manchester University Press, Manchester.

Morash, C. (1991), Workshop report on 'Irish-Ireland', in E. Longley (ed.) *Culture in Ireland: Division or Diversity?*, Institute of Irish Studies, Belfast.

PART ONE

New Territories

Learning How to Live:
David Park's *The Truth Commissioner*

TOM HERRON

> The tragedies of the past have left a deep and profoundly regrettable
> legacy of suffering. We must never forget those who have died or been
> injured, and their families. But we can best honour them through a
> fresh start, in which we firmly dedicate ourselves to the achievement of
> reconciliation, tolerance, and mutual trust, and to the protection and
> vindication of the human rights of all.
>
> — *The Agreement*, 10 April 1998

The Truth and Reconciliation Commission (TRC) into the Canadian
Indian residential schools scandal that opened in Ottawa in June 2008
is the most recent example of a modern form of inquiry that, in its most
famous incarnation, came to characterize South Africa's formal transition from the period of apartheid to what is often described – heroically
if, perhaps, somewhat prematurely – as the New South Africa or, even,
the Rainbow Nation. On the opening day of the Canadian inquiry, the
Canadian Broadcasting Corporation asked how it was possible to construct an adequate 'truth' concerning events that occurred up to half
a century earlier. Further to this, it asked: even if the 'truth' of what
'really' happened is somehow achieved, then does reconciliation inevitably
follow? Since the first TRC – set up in Zimbabwe in 1984 to investigate
the Matabeleland massacres by Zanu PF forces – the possibility of reconciliation produced by such truth-finding inquiries has been encour-
aged through special measures, such as the granting of indemnity against
prosecution dependent on full disclosure, the emphasis on inquistorial
rather than adversial modes of inquiry, and, perhaps most importantly,

the adoption of legal protocols that are in important ways, extra-judicial: TRCs are not Courts of Law; there is no prosecution, there is no defence. In this sense they must be distinguished from those trials of individuals that have followed major wars and massacres, such as those held at Nuremberg (1945–46) or The Hague (into the Rwandan genocide, and the war crimes perpetrated during the breakup of former Yugoslavia).

So, in Bolivia, in South Africa, in Chile, in Algeria and many other countries,[1] TRCs have played an important, if not unproblematic, role in the establishment of new 'official' truths and, leading on from that, the forging of those processes of 'forgiveness' and 'healing' that are frequently cited as prerequisites for the development of sustainable post-conflict civil society. As yet, however, there has been no TRC to inquire into the events of the Northern Ireland conflict (1966 –1998).[2] To some extent this is surprising given the ways in which the peace process in the North – torturous, labyrinthine, and incomplete as it has been – is held up in some quarters as an example to other societies in conflict. But one only has to look at long-standing failures of truth-recovery (the farcical testimony given to Lord Saville's new Bloody Sunday Inquiry by former British paratroopers, many of whom seem to have suffered catastrophic levels of amnesia concerning their actions in Derry on the afternoon of 30 January 1972; the persistent denial by the British Government of the well-documented collusion that occurred for more than two decades between the security forces and loyalist paramilitaries; the continuing silence of the Provisional Irish Republican Army (PIRA) on the fate of the 'disappeared': those people abducted and murdered and whose bodies have never been recovered) to see the difficulty that all parties to the conflict might have in coming to a full truth concerning their past actions (both heroic and less commendable).

This is not to say that 'truth' and 'reconciliation' are somehow absent from Northern Ireland. Indeed, a veritable industry comprising academics,

1   For discussion on lessons that might be learned from TRCs in other parts of the world, see Hamber 1998.
2   I follow David McKittrick's dating of the beginning of the 'Troubles' to 1966: (McKittrick, 2000).

social workers, cross-community activists, business development officers, church outreach workers, civil servants, advertising executives, artists and art administrators, counsellors, politicians, and many others, has developed in the North devoted to the understanding of conflict and its immediate resolution, and to initiatives promoting 'peace and recci' as the panolpy of processes at all levels of the social formation has come to be popularly known. A very recent development, occuring only one week before the publication of David Park's *The Truth Commissioner*[3] was former First Minister Ian Paisley's announcement of the creation of a four-member panel of victims' commissioners and the allocation of £33 million for the 'victims' sector' over the next three years. This is the culmination of many initiatives in which the hurt caused to victims of the conflict has begun to be addressed. Such a turn to the victims – evidenced also in the new Bloody Sunday Inquiry, the Stevens Enquiry, the Eames/Bradley Commission (the Consultative Group on the Past), the Police Service of Northern Ireland's Historical Enquiries Team, the Irish Government's Remembrance Commission, the work of the Police Ombudsman, and the Independent Commission for the Location of Victims' Remains; as well as in smaller-scale campaigns, such as those fought by the sisters of Robert McCartney, the family and supporters of Pat Finucane, and the families of the victims of the Omagh bombings – is, no doubt, a manifestation of how far Northern Ireland has come since the PIRA ceasefire of August 1994 and the Good Friday Agreement of April 1998. It is perhaps only when violence has ended that trauma suffered and perpetrated can begin to be more fully comprehended. But at a moment in which the demands of reconciliation and cross-party agreement are paramount, there is a severe danger that the 'truth recovery' avowedly at the heart of each of these initiatives is in peril due to the political, economic and social imperatives of post-Agreement Northern Ireland.

Imagining the existence of a TRC for Northern Ireland, *The Truth Commissioner* is tightly but uncannily indexed (the novel's action is located in a strangely disoriented present) into the truth recovery initiatives set

3   4 February 2008.

out above. By focalizing so much of the narrative through the eponymous truth commissioner, Henry Stanfield, the novel voices for much
of its duration a weary scepticism towards the claims and rhetorics of
such commissions. At the same time – by giving such prominence to the
testimony of the family of one of the disappeared – the novel displays an
acute sensitivity to the need of victims' families to find the truth of what
happened to their loved ones. To a greater extent that any other work
of fiction produced in the North of Ireland in recent years, *The Truth
Commissioner* is an extraordinarily timely intervention at a moment when
the past, in the words of Seamus Deane 'is at the mercy of the present
moment' (Deane, 1991: xxi). For those who assert the necessity of looking forward to a bright and, no doubt, better future, Park's novel is an
uncomfortable reminder that the past cannot be escaped. Amid, or rather,
as we shall see, below, the photo-op smiles and the blandishments of the
New Northern Ireland, there is a hidden reservoir of injustice that makes
intense demands upon the present. And where official channels of recognition are blocked, other alternative and minor forms of remembering come
into force: the annual commemoration parade, vigils, campaign groups,
and, in the realm of the arts, the work of poets, film-makers, muralists,
and novelists. In bringing to light aspects of the past that find no voice
in the present – more than that, that are ruthlessly silenced in the present – artists and other advocates of memory, not only re-imagine what
has been forgotten, but also imagine a present and a future that would
accommodate that past in all its glory and shame. I want to argue in this
essay that *The Truth Commissioner*, for all its sense of disappointment and
loss, is such a work. At the same time I want to examine the ways in which
the novel's scepticism is itself overcome – albeit cautiously – by a certain
optimism, suggesting that some form of truth leading, perhaps, to some
form of reconciliation may *just* be possible in the 'new' Northern Ireland.
The fact that this reconciliation occurs only in the realm of fiction, and
has not substantially been matched in the social formation of the North
(more segregated now than at any time since the foundation of the statelet
in 1921) guards against blithe celebration of reconciliation and healing.
This is especially the case bearing in mind that the novel's suggestion of
the possibility of transformation is the result not of legal, state-engendered

process, but occurs through an entirely unpredictable haeccity of circumstances. This makes for – as several reviewers of the novel attest – an enjoyable, even satisfying sense of readerly resolution. However, the fact that just beyond the borders of the book, in the social formation on which the novel draws and to which it is addressed – albeit in visionary terms (the likelihood of a TRC for Northern Ireland is precisely nil) – there is so little evidence of ground-root societal reconciliation, of genuine social rapprochement, ensures that *The Truth Commissioner* remains an unsettling, provoking text that brushes abrasively against the highly polished grain of contemporary Northern Ireland politics.

The novel's resonant title is, in fact, the designation offered personally by British Prime Minister Brown to Henry Stanfield who, for some considerable time, seems to occupy center-stage of the novel. 'Corroded with scepticism',[4] Stanfield is closely aligned to the novel's omniscient narrative voice, and this, coupled with the fact that he is the carrier of the rather grand title, and the fact that he is the officer of state to whom all other protagonists are called to account, encourages an initially powerful identification with the character that takes the form of a strange transference, in that both character and reader are drawn for analogous reasons into the rhetorically and hermeneutically suggestive phrase – 'Truth Commissioner':

> he has to admit that it was the job's title that first prompted his acceptance. 'Truth Commissioner' has a nice ring to it and its accompanying salary is almost as generous as its scope. ... The job title has a magisterial ring to it but also a rather totalitarian, industrial edge, and he enjoys this juxtaposition of ideas. But what he enjoys most is thinking of the book that will surely come out of it and already he's batting ideas around for a title – *The Whole Truth ... Nothing But the Truth ...* perhaps even *The Freedom of Truth*. (Park, 2008: 18–19)[5]

The novel's present-time schema begins in South Africa, where Stanfield and his team of younger colleagues are based to learn lessons from

---

4   The phrase is from J.M. Coetzee's *Disgrace* (Coetzee, 1999; 102), a novel with which *The Truth Commissioner* is in close dialogue.
5   All subsequent pages reference to the novel are to this edition.

participants in the South African TRC. Any sense of idealism within the
workings of that body, and the transferability of its procedures and ethos
to Ireland, is immediately shattered by Stanfield:

> three weeks of ... suffocating, endless meetings with the smugly condescending
> ANC and their carefully chosen supporters; detailed study of legal documenta-
> tion and lengthy reports; long pointless journeys on dusty roads to the townships
> to talk to those who had participated in the Truth and Reconciliation process
> and the interminable lectures on the need for *ubantu*, the African philosophy of
> humanism. (Park: 10)

Once in Belfast – the city is rendered entirely and unremittingly in unfavourable terms by Park, as, indeed, is Northern Ireland as a whole: 'He
will spend the next two years living in a city that he considers much
the same way as he might think of a piece of dirt that he hoped he had
shaken off his shoe' (Park: 20) – Stanfield's attention is only tangentially
on the job in hand. He occupies his evenings with Kristal, a high-class
and enigmatic escort and spends much of his time worrying about the
state of his relationship with his estranged daughter, Emma. His depth
of cynicism for the process over which he presides is disturbing, but it
is a disposition shared by the novel's other protagonists who are introduced abruptly into the narrative. Park's selection of four middle-aged
men is suggestive that the novel is in large part a satire on aging, desire,
and loss. All four protagonists –Stanfield, Francis Gilroy, James Fenton,
and Michael Madden – are in the grip of anxieties that may be described
as generically male, as having little to do with the central scandal of the
novel. One-time senior PIRA leader, Francis Gilroy is now installed in
the power-sharing government as Minister of Children and Culture.
Nicknamed 'the lemonade man' (after C&C, Cantrell and Cochrane,
local producers of fizzy drinks), Gilroy secretly reads Philip Larkin in
order to raise his cultural capital: 'needs to read some books. On the
quiet. Try to crack it. Understand what it's all about' (Park: 72–73). He is
a hypochondriac and expends much energy worrying about his position
in the movement and about the forthcoming wedding of his daughter
to Justin, an English advertising executive. Retired RUC officer, James

Fenton is struggling to come to terms with, among other things, what
has happened to the police force of which he was proud:

> Like all his generation he has accepted the pension and the pay-off deals that were
> too generous to be refused, even though it stuck in his throat to have to acknowl-
> edge that he was considered part of the corporate embarrassment, part of a past
> that had to be quietly replaced. (Park: 127)

Michael Madden, now ensconced as an illegal immigrant in Florida,
with Ramona his beautiful partner who is expecting their first child, tries
desperately to forget his past in Belfast as, again, a PIRA volunteer.

Much of the pleasure of the novel lies in its perspicacity concerning
the fate and fears of men. By allotting each character his own substantial
portion of text, *The Truth Commissioner* ranges far beyond what might
be termed a 'Troubles' or 'post-Troubles' novel. The book reads, initially,
as a series of short stories, as each character's narrative is abruptly curtailed, and replaced by an entirely different character, location, and set
of concerns. These men are mourning their own lives: Stanfield, for his
multiple infidelities and 'lost' daughter; Gilroy, for the toll the political
struggle has had on him and his family (even though the family members
seem to be coping not at all badly with the hardships they had to endure);
Fenton, for the child he and his wife Miriam never had, and for the young
boy he betrayed; and Michael who, as a man of a younger generation,
seems to mourn for his future, so full of fear is he that the intrusion of
his past will destroy everything he has built in his new life. The men's fear
and disappointment is sublimated into quite desperate activity: Gilroy's
attempts to acculturate himself to poetry and the arts in the midst of a
hectic life as government minister; Fenton's lonely efforts for the orphanage in Romania; Stanfield's compulsive womanizing; Madden's attempts
to keep his head down, while fostering ambitions, in the United States.
It is part of the powerful logic of the novel – in contradistinction to
the melancholic disappointment of the 'real' – that such performances
of normality can by exposed as precisely that: performances, pretences,
deceptions. More by accident than design, the 'secret' shared by these men
will be brought to the light through the workings of the maligned Truth

and Reconciliation Commission. And it is surely no coincidence that these male performances are exposed by the promptings of two women: the mother and the sister of one of the 'disappeared' whose death and place of burial are among the first to be considered by the Commission: this is 'case number one hundred and seven, the case of Connor Walshe' (Park: 316).

In his recommendation that a TRC be established in Northern Ireland, Sir Kenneth Bloomfield suggested that the fate of the disappeared be given priority in any truth-finding process. 'There is, first of all,' Bloomfield wrote in 1998, 'the poignant category of the "disappeared".... I would voice a fervent appeal, on behalf of those whose loved ones have disappeared without trace, that those who can offer information about their fate and where bodies may lie should now do so' (Bloomfield, 1998: 38). He continued:

> Many of the relatives have faced up long ago to the probability that a loved one has been killed, but it is one of the most fundamental of human instincts to seek certain knowledge of the fate of a husband or wife, son or daughter, brother or sister. Common humanity cries out for this modest act of mercy. (Bloomfield: 38)

Like decommissioning and collusion, the fate of the disappeared has cast a long shadow over much of the optimism following the Good Friday Agreement and the subsequent improvements in so many aspects of life in Northern Ireland. Ten years after the Agreement itself, and nine years after the setting up of the Independent Commission for the Location of Victims' Remains, and following calls from, among others, former First Minister Ian Paisley and the President of Sinn Féin, Gerry Adams for those with information relating to the disappeared to make it known to the PSNI or An Garda Síochána, the remains of several of the missing are still unrecovered. In imagining Connor Walshe as among these unsolved cases Park's novel returns us with the uncomfortable but powerful return of the repressed to the darkest, and only belatedly acknowledged, days of the conflict.

In death Connor Walshe *comes to* exert a power that in life he was never able to yield. I stress 'comes to' because one of the most remarkable insights of Park's novel is that this dead boy becomes spectral, and takes on the ethical force that specters possess, only once the institutions of State allow such a becoming-spectral. Connor Walshe only begins his presencing, his haunting once the TRC begins its operations: there is absolutely no evidence presented to us that he exerts any influence (in the form of memory, of guilt, of mourning, of contrition) on the men who will eventually, and against all their wishes, be haunted by him in the most devastating manner. Scarcely invested with an identity in life, the fifteen-year-old police informant meets his end in a farmhouse in South Armagh sometime in the mid-1980s. Abducted, interrogated, executed and then secretly disposed of by the PIRA, Walshe remains, until the inauguration of the TRC, simply one of those more than three thousand victims of the northern conflict. But just as the ghost of Michael Furey materializes almost out of nowhere in a palpable and, for Gabriel Conroy, an overwhelming presence at the close of James Joyce's 'The Dead', Connor Walshe returns as a revenant to unsettle the calm surface of the world of the living just as the angel in St John's Gospel returns to trouble the waters of Bethesda. The strand of images linking each protagonist in which water is invested with restorative and, indeed, curative properties is inaugurated in the novel's Biblical epigraph:

> Now there is at Jerusalem by the sheep market a pool, which is called in the Hebrew tongue Bethesda having five porches.
> In these lay a great multitude of impotent folk, of blind, halt, withered, waiting for the moving of the water.
> For an angel went down at a certain season into the pool, and troubled the water: whosoever then first after the troubling of the water stepped in was made whole of whatsoever disease he had. (St John 5, 2–4; cited Park: vii)

Not that the four protagonists within the novel are aware of the potentially transformative, even redemptive, effects of Connor Walshe's apparition. Even after being summoned to appear before the Commission, each does everything in his power to avoid reckoning with Walshe. But when, in a remarkable *coup de théâtre juridique*, counsel for Walshe's mother and sister produces a tape-recording of the boy's interrogation just prior to his death, a supplement beyond the already-degraded protocols of

the Commission and beyond the obfuscatory tactics of the men comes
into play:

> [Fenton] hears the voice of Connor Walshe. And then he's transported once again,
> despite the resistance of his will, to all the places he heard that voice, the voice
> that is instantly recognizable, and there's the same pleading, the familiar edge of
> desperation that he heard in it the very first time, but this time there's no pretence
> of bravery, no attempt at bravado or aggression. The voice fills the chamber with
> its whimpering, broken stammer of words and it flows down through the rows
> of seats and laps round Michael Madden like the water laps and slurps round the
> jetty at the lake. (Park: 327)

Fenton, Madden and Gilroy have had earlier glimpses of the young man
in whose death they, with varying degrees of involvement, participated.
Fenton sees his ghostly face materializing out of the mist, 'swooping
towards him out of the darkness' (Park: 177), and senses a correspondence between the dead Walshe and Florian, the gifted young boy who
befriends him at the Romanian orphanage. Madden half-senses his presence in the child allegedly abused by his local Catholic priest. Gilroy,
who for most of the novel succeeds in avoiding being directly implicated
with the boy's murder, finally revisits the scene of his death as he sits with
Sweeney, his most-trusted advisor, under the stained-glass windows of
Clonard Monastery:

> 'Connor Walshe. After all this time. Who would have thought it?'
> 'You remember him, Francis?'
> 'Of course,' Gilroy says as he rubs a finger across his bottom lip. (Park: 271)

And even Stanfield senses that Walshe is somehow imbricated with his
own anxieties concerning his relationship with his daughter: 'How can
he be tied now to a boy whose photograph he's never seen? How can his
desire to see his only child be meshed with some other long-dead boy
from a Belfast back street?' (Park: 67).

In some senses the dénouement follows a conventional courtroom
drama plot. Connor Walshe's disembodied voice operates in the chamber
of the TRC almost as a *deus ex machina*, an unpredictable and uncon-
testable final ploy that puts an end to uncertainty and to game-playing

of all four protagonists. The taped voice possesses an authority – again, an authority that it lacked while it was still alive – that comes from its abyssal appearance, its arrival from an other time, its materialization out of, and across, time to (following Derrida) 'unhinge' the present, to open it up, to superimpose upon the present (which is, anyway, only a simulacrum to avert anxiety) the non-contemporaneous presence of past injustice. The fact that the 'voice' (disembodied, distorted, and virtual though it is) is captured and transmitted on analogue tape, reminds us of Susan Sontag's celebration of the photograph as bearer of authenticity, as 'stencilled off the real':

> a photograph is not only an image (as a painting is an image), an interpretation of the real, it is also a trace, something directly stencilled off the real, like a footprint or a death mask ... a photograph is never less than the registering of an emanation (light waves reflected by objects) – a material vestige of its subject in a way that no painting can be. (Sontag, 1977: 154)

The same is true of the taped voice in which vibrating air produced by the body impacts against an electro-magnetic receiver. So, while the participants in the TRC are in the presence of spectrality at this moment, there is also the shocking and almost unbearable intrusion of the 'real':

> The voice beats against the walls of the chamber like some moth trapped in a tremble of confusion and looking for release. Stanfield looks down on the listeners and sees their eyes drop to the floor as a kind of collective embarrassed shame settles on the room because they know they're listening to the voice of a boy who's about to die and they know that their presence intrudes even all these years later and that their places should be taken by a priest or his family, someone, anyone, who will put a hand on his shoulder and tell him that everything will be alright. They want the tape to stop. (Park: 328)

It is an intensely powerful moment of text. In Deleuzian terms it is a sort of plateau across which the novel's rhizomatic strands, evasions, opinions, performances, fears, desires, and lies intersect in a moment of absolute clarity. Of course, the moment will pass; the novel will not condense this moment into its own truth. But it is remarkable nonetheless that here, in the derided, compromised chamber, the workings of which even its presiding officer has precious little faith, a moment of potentiality is produced. It is spectral, yes. But it is also ethical. When Derrida exhorts us (as he most certainly *does*) to learn to live responsibly he stresses that such ethical living must include, indeed depends upon, an awareness of injustices past, present, and future:

> The time of the learning to live, a time without a tutelary present, would amount
> to this ... : to learn to live with ghosts, in the upkeep, the conversation, the com-
> pany, or the companionship, in the commerce without commerce of ghosts. To live
> otherwise, and better. No, not better, but more justly. (Derrida, 1994: xviii)

The voice of the ghost, the materialization of what is absolutely other – the trace of a long dead child – ushers in the truth, as they see it, of Madden and Fenton. This subaltern voice also implicates Gilroy, now elevated to among the highest in the land, the representative of Government:

> There's nothing [Stanfield] can do now, it's out of his control, ... so slowly he rises
> and stands waiting until there's perfect silence and then with a curiously light
> and pleasing sense of recklessness, of flying close to the sun, he says in a loud and
> steady voice, 'The Commission for Truth and Reconciliation calls Francis Gilroy'.
> (Park: 346)

Notwithstanding our readerly attachment to Gilroy, this is a delicious, complex moment. It is a moment in which truth, if not attained (there are still inconsistencies between the versions of truth proclaimed by Madden, Fenton, and Gilroy), is at least approached, not least through the men's inadvertent corroboration. Hélène Cixous suggests that 'writing, in its noblest function, is the attempt to unerase, to unearth'; it is a move-ment 'toward what I call: the Truth' (Cixous, 1993: 9). And if we are suspicious of such fulsome assertions of a singular truth, then Michael Ignatieff's qualification of the concept is extremely apt in the context on what Truth and Reconciliation Commissions may produce by way of truth. If a single truth cannot be arrived at, he argues, then a version of events that 'reduce[s] the numbers of lies that can be circulated unchal-lenged in public discourse' (Ignatieff, 1996: 113) may well provide, at the very least, some redress to the injustice perpetrated years before.

The Truth Commissioner is a contemporary fantasy. It is absolutely of its moment in ways in which novels (in contrast, say, to journalism or even, occasionally, poetry) so rarely are, and it is profoundly subversive of that moment. The fact that it *is* fantasy, that the scenario it imagines is unreal, does not exist, and will, in all likelihood, never exist produces an undoubted sense of tragedy in that it seems only in the world of imaginative writing that the dead, the utterly lost are permitted to have their say. However, the text's indexing of the contemporaneously 'real', most notably the new Bloody Sunday Inquiry, engenders, as I prefer to see it, a cautiously optative disposition towards such valiant truth-finding attempts, no matter how flawed or compromised they may appear to be. This is not to assert, however, that reconciliation, nor that even more difficultly absolute gift, forgiveness, follow on from whatever version of truth emerges in the chamber of the TRC: indeed, the novel has absolutely nothing to say on either. If Connor Walshe, described by his sister Maria as 'not an angel' (Park: 318) is, in fact, a secular, if spectral, incarnation of the angel at Bethesda, he is so only in the most attenuated and incomplete manner. The waters he disturbs produce no grand sense of healing: Madden, Fenton, and Gilroy are impelled to do nothing more than tell their truths. They may begin to feel the healing that truth may offer, but what of the family of the lost child? What of the victims? Park's novel closes with the most delicate suggestion of resolution. But no reconciliation, no forgiveness. Not there. Not yet.

Works Cited

Bloomfield, K. (1998), *We Will Remember Them – Report of the Northern Ireland Victims Commissioner*. The Stationery Office Northern Ireland, Belfast.

Cixous, H. (1993), *Three Steps on the Ladder of Writing*. transl. Sarah Cornell and Susan Sellers, Columbia University Press, New York.

Coetzee, J.M. (1999), *Disgrace,* Secker & Warburg, London.

Deane, S. (1991), 'General Introduction', *The Field Day Anthology of Irish Writing,* 1, Field Day Productions, Derry.

Derrida, J. (1994), *Specters of Marx: The State of the Debt, the Work of Mourning, and the New International,* transl. Peggy Kamuf, Routledge, London.

Hamber, B (1998), ed. *Past Imperfect: dealing with the past in Northern Ireland and societies in transition,* INCORE, Derry.

Ignatieff, M. (1996), 'Articles of Faith', in *Index on Censorship,* 25:5.

McKittrick, D. (2000), in McKittrick *et al* (eds), *Lost Lives: the stories of the men, women, and children who died as a result of the Northern Ireland troubles,* Mainstream, Edinburgh.

Park, D. (2008), *The Truth Commissioner,* Bloomsbury, London.

Sontag, S. (1977), *On Photography,* Penguin, London.

'Nothing Is Ever Arrived At': Otherness and Representation in Colum McCann's *Zoli*

JOSÉ LANTERS

Like its predecessor *Dancer*, Colum McCann's fourth novel *Zoli* (2006) is loosely based on the biography of a real person: the Polish 'Gypsy' poet Bronisława Wajs (c. 1910–1987), better known as Papusza ('doll'). Papusza's fictional counterpart in the novel, Marienka 'Zoli' Novotna, is a Slovakian Rom whose life, like that of her alter ego, is deeply and adversely affected by policies implemented against her people by the Nazi and Communist regimes. In interviews, McCann is often asked about his fascination with 'Otherness' in his work, as the characters he chooses to write about are almost invariably racially and culturally far removed from his own white middle class Dublin background. Postcolonial theorists like Abdul JanMohamed have indicated the fundamental problem inherent in the attempt to 'write the Other' by arguing that a genuine understanding of Otherness 'entails in practice the virtually impossible task of negating one's very being, precisely because one's culture is what formed that being' (JanMohamed, 1985: 65). McCann, however, argues that writers do not 'speak for people', but 'with them' (Welch, 2006), and remains largely unapologetic about exploring different cultures and ethnicities in his work. Indeed, he is careful to acknowledge that he inevitably writes from his own cultural perspective, even when creating characters from a different background: '*Zoli* is an Irish novel. How can it be anything else? I'm an Irish writer' (Hayes, 2006). Conscious that he did not, as an outsider, want to 'sentimentalize' or 'brutalize' the culture of the Roma, McCann also felt he had a social obligation to shift perceptions with his novel, to 'bring a light to what we call "the other". Having a complex light shone on "the other", I think, in the end, makes us better people' (Donnelly, 2007).

In her discussion of Margriet de Moor's 1996 novel *Hertog van Egypte*, Claudia Breger (2004) points out that representations of Romani characters in texts about 'Gypsies' by 'non-Gypsy' authors are often tainted by 'the dominant anthropological discourse which constructs "the Gypsy" as an eternal other to civilization and modernity', a discursive frame which 'is not necessarily challenged by good intentions or personal experience' (Breger, 2004: 132). The details of Papusza's life that form the basis for McCann's novel make the question of representation particularly poignant. A talented singer in a family of noted harpists, Papusza also distinguished herself by learning to read and write, in defiance of the Romani taboo against literacy. After hearing her perform, Jerzy Ficowski, a poet who had long studied the Roma and was an advisor to the Polish post-war government on the 'Gypsy Question', convinced her to write down her songs, arguing that publication of her work would help lead to a better understanding of the Roma among the settled population. The elders of Papusza's family supported the post-war Communist regime and initially condoned her celebrity among the non-Gypsy population (referred to by Roma as 'Gadjo' or 'Gadñe'), but changed their position after they were forced to give up their nomadic way of life in a traumatic process that came to be known as the Great Halt. At that point they came to regard the publication of a number of Papusza's 'songs' in the magazine *Problemy* as a betrayal of the secrets of their culture. Her attempts to undo the damage by retracting her work from the publisher were in vain: she was declared 'unclean' by the elders and expelled, and lived the remaining thirty-four years of her life in loneliness and isolation.

Papusza's voice was appropriated by Jerzy Ficowski, who edited and published her poems in his magazine for his own literary and political ends; used by the Communists, who saw her as a poster child for the Roma's progress towards 'civilization' and integration; and silenced by her own people, who banished her for betraying the secrets of their culture to representatives of the Polish regime that engineered the destruction of the nomadic aspect of Romani life in the mid-twentieth century. Papusza never really owned the poems that appeared in print, given the extent of Ficowski's interference, which he describes in his book *The Gypsies in Poland* (1989): 'The present author [...] translated them into Polish and published them. He has called them songs, [...] for almost all of them were improvised impromptu to a melody; unfortunately none of the melodies are known, for they were not recorded' (Ficowski, 1989: 113). Because of the manner and context in which Papusza's work and life were framed – she was presented as an exponent of oral 'Gypsy folk literature' whose expressions 'must be documented, and its transitory pieces recorded permanently' (ibid.: 113) – her ethnicity came to eclipse the expression of her individual talent. Good intentions aside, then, McCann's challenge in *Zoli* is to give Papusza a voice without essentializing, manipulating, appropriating, or silencing that voice all over again.

One reason why McCann was drawn to the figure of Papusza was because he felt her story would allow him to make his 'most complicated statement about exile' yet – exile being a theme that had formed his obsession for two decades and a 'particular darkness' he was ready to leave behind with this novel (Hayes, 2006). Such a move into metaphor runs the immediate risk of turning the exile of the already marginalized 'Gypsy' into a trope about modern alienation, and hence a statement about the self rather than the Other. Zoli's case, however, is complicated by the fact that she, like Papusza, is rejected by her own people at the very moment that she herself retracts her involvement with Gadñe culture: in exile, she is forced to embrace hybridity, to find a way of existing between two ways of being, and to question the values and practices of both cultures with an individual and critical eye.

McCann spent four years conducting research for his novel, reading extensively about the culture and way of life of the Roma but also visiting Gypsy settlements in Slovakia, where he decided to set the narrative. His decision to fictionalize the story of Papusza's life came in part from his sense that he did not know enough about the historical figure, but more particularly from his desire to create a more intellectual character, and 'one who eventually finds a less harsh destiny than Papusza did' (Donnelly, 2007). One reason why he moved his narrative from Poland to Slovakia, and why he changed his character's name to Marienka Novotna, affectionately called Zoli by her grandfather (from 'Zoltan', a boy's name – one of many indicators of the character's hybridity), was to guard against usurping Papusza's voice. A vulnerable, betrayed historical subject, Papusza is unlike Rudolph Nureyev, who appears under his own name in *Dancer* because he 'was [...] able to look after himself' (McCaffrey, 2006). As the fictional alter ego of the elusive Papusza, Zoli is, literally, her re-presentation. With this shift, McCann acknowledges the impossibility of presenting an authentic voice, which is always re-presented or enacted as the result of mediation, but he also signals that the challenge of re-writing the dominant discourse that constructs 'the Gypsy' as an eternal other to civilization and modernity consists in 'the methodological effort to negotiate questions of positionality and rhetoricity' (Breger, 2004: 133). Questions like, 'who speaks?' and 'from what position?' are central to the story of Papusza, and McCann therefore makes issues of mediation and positionality crucial elements in the construction of his narrative: as a novel, *Zoli* is as much about the impossibility of authenticity in representation and the hubris of an author who attempts such representation as it is about the character and her story. 'Zoli is a failure', is how McCann puts it in his interview with Michael Hayes.

Martin Stránský, Jerzy Ficowski's alter ego in the novel, equates the Otherness of Zoli's voice with her authenticity, even while he himself manipulates and patronizes that voice: 'he swallowed the portions of abstraction and romanticism that annoyed him with other poets, allowed her what he saw as her mistakes, tamed her line length, structured her work into verses' (McCann, 2006: 110).[1] Zoli's Gypsy 'authenticity' is therefore a non-Gypsy construct, which is subsequently, and paradoxically, utilized by the authorities to promote the 'civilization' of the Roma and hence the destruction of their 'authentic' culture. In other words, the 'authentic' Gypsy can only be celebrated by the dominant culture at the very moment of her eradication. As if to acknowledge that the authentic voice of the Roma can never be represented in a novel, especially one written by an outsider, McCann does not make Zoli speak directly to the reader; in each chapter, instead, he creates a distance – either narrational or temporal – between his character and the events of

---

[1]   All references to *Zoli* will be to this edition and are henceforth indicated by page number only.

her life. He thereby makes it clear that all narratives, including memoirs, are re-presentations: even the 'authentic voice' of personal testimony, in the form of first-person narrated memory, is, as James E. Young puts it, 'necessarily mediated by metaphoric, metonymic displacements, and its actuality cannot be located in an immediate relationship to historical reality' (Young in Breger, 2004: 140).

Zoli comprises eight sections or chapters, imbricated in such a way as to present four different alternating narrative perspectives. Chapters one and six are narrated from a third person omniscient perspective, and focus on the 2003 visit to a Gypsy settlement by a Slovakian journalist, later identified as Dávid Smolenak, in search of information about Zoli Novotna, whose work he had discovered in an old issue of Martin Stránský's journal *Credo*. In his efforts to find the facts of Zoli's story, Smolenak reflects aspects of the author himself, who similarly tries to capture the essence of his Romani character and her culture from an outsider's perspective – an effort that is doomed, on some level, to fail. Smolenak reacts to the contemporary Roma he meets in their Slovakian settlement in much the same way McCann says he did when he visited similar places during his research for the novel: he worries that he will be robbed, then feels shame when he encounters hospitality instead, and is horrified by the 'shitscape' of the camp, only to find that the shabby huts often hide spotless interiors. The banished poet is a forbidden topic, but that does not mean she cannot be talked about:

> They led him this way and that about Zoli, and the more krown notes he laid on the table, the more their stories loosened – *she was born right here, I am her cousin, she wasn't a singer, she was seen last month in Prešov, her caravan was sold to a museum in Brno, she played the guitar, she taught in university, she was killed in the war by the Hlinkas* – and he felt like a man who'd been expertly and lengthily duped. (McCann: 205)

To talk about Zoli in her absence is to create a fiction: the real Zoli is, literally and metaphorically, not there.

Chapters two and seven of the novel are narrated in the first person past tense by Zoli to her daughter Francesca. The voice in the earlier chapter, which covers Zoli's memories of the period between the 1930s and

1949, appears to be oral rather than written – 'I tell this to you directly, there is no other way to say it' (McCann: 15) – and the perspective is that of selective hindsight: 'It is strange now to talk of such things, but these are the moments I remember, [...] this was my childhood, I try to tell it to you as I saw it then, and as I felt it then, when I was not yet shunned, when it was all still free and open to me, and for the most part it was happy' (McCann: 31). Chapter seven is a retrospective, written account in Zoli's voice, dated 2001, also addressed to her daughter, and covering events of the last forty-two years of her life. Zoli tells Francesca that she feels ready to return to writing only now that her husband Enrico, the Alpine smuggler who had helped her cross the mountains from Austria into Northern Italy in 1959, is dead: 'In all those years [of marriage] I never dared put a pen to paper. [...] It reminded me of too much and I could not do it. It seems strange now after all these years [...] , but I feared that if I tried to give written meaning to my life that I would once again lose what I had gained' (McCann: 220–1).

At the end of the chapter Zoli tells her daughter: 'He never much asked me about my past, your father, so I told him willingly, I always thought that he, and you, were the only ones to whom I could trust these words of mine, the dark ink of what they have said' (McCann: 277). 'These words of mine' refers both to the written memories and the poem that immediately follows them in the text, which speaks of the most traumatic loss in Zoli's life: the murder of her family by the Nazis. The poem is entitled, 'Since by the Bones They Broke We Can Tell New Weather: What We Saw under the Hlinkas in the Years 42 and 43', and is dated September 1957.[2] By reading Zoli's thoughts and the poem addressed to her daughter, the reader is made to intrude, however involuntarily, into a private world not intended by Zoli for the eyes and ears of outsiders; through this device, McCann makes both himself and the reader accomplices in

2   Papusza's poem on the same subject is called, 'Bloody Tears: What We Went Through Under the Germans in Volhynia in the Years 43 and 44' (Ficowski, 1989: 117–19). The language of Zoli's poem echoes many phrases of this poem and others by Papusza.

the betrayal of Zoli's trust along with other non-Roma like Stránský and Swann, who exposed her poetry to the Gadñe world.

The third chapter of *Zoli* is a first-person, retrospective account by Stephen Swann, the translator for the magazine *Credo*, covering the period from the 1930s to 1959. Swann recalls his relationship with Zoli, from his introduction to her by Stránský and his growing infatuation with her, through the moment when he refuses to withdraw her poems from the press, motivated at least in part by a desire to control and possess her, a betrayal that contributes directly to Zoli's expulsion from her *kumpanija*. Swann's memories of Zoli are framed by his recollections of his own childhood in Liverpool as the son of exiles, an Irish nurse and a Slovakian dockworker who had changed his name to Swann. His father returned to his native country during World War II to fight with the Partisans and was killed there; his mother also died when her son was still a child. Swann, a product of hybridity and dislocation himself, notes that the mediation of a lived experience through recollection involves an inevitable displacement similar to the shift that occurs in translation between languages and cultures: 'Memory has a heavy backspin, yet it's still impossible to land exactly where we took off' (McCann: 66).

Swann is remembering the events of his and Zoli's past as he is lying in bed in 1959 in his dingy room in Bratislava, his kneecap shattered by a motorcycle accident. Zoli is already gone at this point, and Swann finds it impossible to think that he will 'never see her again, or catch the sound of her, the grain of her voice' (McCann: 65). She is present only as an elusive memory, something Eve Patten, in her review of *Zoli* for the *Irish Times* (2006), saw as a flaw in the novel: 'Why [...] does McCann hand the narrative over to Swann in the crucial episodes where Zoli performs and publishes her work – the episodes where her voice is most required?' (McCann: 12). The point of the technique, however, is precisely to emphasize the extent to which Zoli's voice was appropriated by others during this crucial period: how it was edited and printed by Stránský, put on a platform by the Communists, and ultimately silenced by the Roma. Swann's account is both McCann's refusal to speak for Zoli and an acknowledgement of the impossibility to let her speak unmediated in her own voice.

Like Dávid Smolenak, Stephen Swann stands for a facet of McCann's authorial persona. Swann is introduced to Zoli by Stránský (as McCann was introduced to Papusza via Jerzy Ficowski) and falls in love with her. Stránský tells him that he wants to record Zoli's voice, '[b]ring her to life' (McCann: 83), and that he needs Swann's help to accomplish this. In the National Library in Bratislava, Swann reads everything he can find about the Slovakian Gypsies, just as McCann did in the New York Public Library. On his first visit to Zoli's camp, Swann's response is similar to McCann's when he spent time with the Roma: 'The children sat close to me – astoundingly close – and I thought for a moment they were rifling my pockets, but they weren't, theirs was simply a different form of space' (McCann: 86). Like McCann, who, as an Irishman living in New York, considers himself one of a generation of 'international mongrels' (Carmelio, 2002: 92), Swann is a hybrid figure: 'I had for some years considered myself to be Czechoslovakian but, in retrospect, I was too English for that, too Irish to be fully English, and too Slovakian to be in any way Irish. Translation had always got in the way of definition' (McCann: 91). Unlike McCann, however, Swann cannot accept the transcendent nature of his identity.

Swann is attracted by Zoli's Otherness, as she is by what she considers his strange Englishness; his infatuation with her alterity, however, is a desire to define her and thereby define himself: tellingly, he fixes her picture in a corner of the mirror in his room. Swann relates that he 'wanted nothing more than to bring Zoli to the city, settle her down, have her write, make her mine, but it was impossible' (McCann: 100), an impossibility that is reflected in the unconsummated character of their relationship. Zoli notes Swann's chameleonic nature, in that he 'constantly rubbed his hands over his scalp so that when he was in the printing mill his hair became the color of whatever poster he was printing' (McCann: 169): during the Communist era in Slovakia he 'listened to the workers, developed the same accent, strode out with them under their banners' (McCann: 169), but when he returned to England after 1968, he blended into the bourgeois middle class as the owner of a wine shop. Unlike Zoli, Swann does not have the ability 'to forego a permanent fixed self, which is essential if one is going to understand and appreciate a racial or cultural alterity' (JanMohamed, 1985: 78); rather, his identity takes the form of a series of clearly demarcated, fixed selves. During her wanderings after her expulsion, Zoli observes at one point that borders are exaggerated because otherwise they would cease to exist altogether (McCann: 198), and she ultimately comes to feel pity for Swann because of his need for such clear boundaries. Swann 'did not learn for himself how to be lost' (McCann: 325): he can only experience freedom vicariously through his 'hobby' of attending 'Gypsy' conferences (McCann: 323).

The fourth and eighth chapters of *Zoli* are narrated in the third person present tense and focalized, in free indirect style, through Zoli: the events are presented from her perspective, but not narrated in her voice. The earlier of these two chapters, set in 1959–1960, is the account of Zoli's initial abjection after her expulsion, her lonely wanderings though Slovakia and into Hungary, and eventually her dangerous crossing into Austria. The later episode, which takes place in 2003, focuses on Zoli's visit to her daughter Francesca in Paris, and her reluctant presence at an international conference organized by her daughter, on 'Romani Memory and Imagination' (a fitting title, too, perhaps, for McCann's method of telling Papusza's story through the imagined figure of Zoli). In this final chapter all the book's strands come together, as Zoli encounters Dávid Smolenak, the journalist whose search for information about her among the Slovakian Gypsies is the focus of chapters one and six of *Zoli*, and unexpectedly comes face to face again with Stephen Swann.

The layered and consciously mediated nature of McCann's narrative design for *Zoli* complicates the representation of self and other; it indicates the extent to which Zoli's voice was usurped by others for their own ends while it also draws attention to McCann's own refusal to speak for Zoli by directly adopting her voice. This is the paradox at the heart of the novel: McCann's ambition (discussed in an interview with Laura McCaffrey) to turn around and set free the templates of Papusza's life, to write a story that was true and honest but also positive about a future for the Roma in a way that was not apparent from the historical facts of Papusza's life, could only be fulfilled if he set Zoli free by dissolving the borders around her while also giving her back her own voice, by allowing it to ring out unmediated, and therefore unrecorded. In the closing scene of the book, in her daughter's Parisian apartment, accompanied by Scottish musicians, Zoli sings her own song, in her own voice, a song that exists only in the moment of singing, in the here and now: 'and the room feels as if it is opening, one window, then another, then the walls themselves. The tall musician strikes a high chord and nods at Zoli – she smiles, lifts her head, and begins. She begins' (McCann: 328). The novel ends there. Zoli's authentic voice, 'the secret of it' (McCann: 96), rings out, in a space beyond representation.

Although McCann takes great pains to emphasize, through his main character, that 'nothing is ever arrived at', that 'nothing is ever fully understood' (McCann: 324) in the process of trying to understand another human being, let alone another culture, the fact that the author found himself starting from a 'completely blank slate' when he began to familiarize himself with the culture and history of the Roma may actually have been what enabled him to tackle the subject at all. Had the Roma been more inclined to represent themselves in literature – and the story of Papusza illustrates why they are not – he might have been more reluctant to enter what is potentially a cultural minefield. When asked why, as an Irish writer, he did not write about the Irish Travellers instead of the Central European Roma, McCann – somewhat paradoxically, given his own initial ignorance of Roma traditions – referred to the fact that the Travellers' story 'is in the process of being told by others who are more inside than me, more at the centre, with more access. They will [...] [tell it] better than I could' (Hayes, 2006). This position could be summed up as follows: an outsider may write about the Roma for a predominantly non-Roma audience and 'tell this story that was largely untold' (Hayes, 2006) until an insider comes along who can tell it more accurately. While McCann says he would welcome such an insider's critique of his representation of Romani culture in *Zoli*, such statements, however well-intentioned, indicate how difficult it is to speak about a minority from a hegemonic perspective without coming close to patronizing the very people to whom the author seeks to defer.

Although McCann refers to *Zoli* as 'an Irish novel' because it was written by 'an Irish writer', he did not set any of its scenes in Ireland, perhaps as a tacit acknowledgement of the inevitable gap between himself and his Romani character. At one stage he considered 'bringing Zoli to Dublin, but she refused this option. She just wouldn't get on that ferry!' (Hayes, 2006). Stephen Swann, McCann's partial alter ego in the novel and the only character to have any Irish connections, echoes this sentiment when he reflects that he had 'wanted nothing more than to bring Zoli to the city, [...] but it was impossible' (McCann: 100). Zoli eventually travels to Paris, long the city of her dreams, where her daughter Francesca is a community worker for a marginalized group of immigrants mainly consisting of North Africans and a few hundred Roma. McCann uses the concrete jungle at the outskirts of the city, whether that city be Paris or Bratislava, as an image of a corrupting modernity foisted on the Roma against their will, and actively resisted by them. The tower blocks in the *banlieues* of the French capital where the Roma are housed in 2003 are mirror images of the high rise buildings in Slovakia where Zoli and her family were forcibly moved decades earlier, after legislation was passed that led to the Great Halt of the 1950s: 'Flags were unfurled. Bands played trumpets as Zoli's men and women were guided towards community centers – from now on they'd live in the towerblocks' (McCann: 124–5). Zoli herself has come a long way since then; for her people, however, '[s]o much the world changes, so much it stays the same' (McCann: 308–9).

One of Zoli's final glimpses of her *kumpanija* after being expelled by the elders is in the shadow of those Bratislava towers, among the abandoned and wheel-less caravans:

> In the barren squares of grass, a few of the wagons are already ringed with campfires. [...] One or two dim figures move in and out of the shadows. So, some have abandoned the towers already, taken the floorboards out, come down to the ground, burnt what should have been beneath their feet. A small triumph. Further along the wall, someone has put up a lean-to against the concrete blocks. (McCann: 178)

Half a century on, the Parisian Roma, relegated to delapidated, drugs-infested and graffiti-covered tower blocks on the city's outskirts, also prefer to live in shelters of their own making: 'By the motorway Zoli catches sight of the camp, strung out along a half-finished piece of road. The doors of the caravans are open and four burnt-out vans stand nearby,

their front bonnets open' (McCann: 304). McCann does not depict the
Roma's resistance to their urban environment as a backward denial of
the comforts of 'civilization and modernity', nor as a romantic escape
to a purer, more authentic way of life. He shows a people determined to
express their difference and independence, but also debased and degraded
by being treated as human refuse under the guise of progress.

  While McCann did not bring Zoli to Dublin, and denied that the
recent arrival of substantial numbers of Roma in Ireland had anything
to do with the writing of the novel (Hayes, 2006), to readers familiar
with Dublin the images of the tower blocks in *Zoli* inevitably evoke the
concrete towers of Ballymun. Life has a way of imitating art, or in this
case, supplementing it, because it was in Ballymun, in the summer of
2007, a year after the publication of McCann's novel, that an extended
family of Romanian Gypsies set up camp on the M50 roundabout. They
had arrived in Ireland in search of a better life, but had no work permits
and were not entitled to welfare benefits, nor could they claim asylum.
Having sold all their possessions in Romania to make the trip to Ireland,
and without an incentive to return home, a group of over fifty people,
including many children, lived for almost three months in unsafe and
increasingly squalid conditions on the Ballymun roundabout, until they
eventually agreed to be returned to Romania.

  The details of media reports about the 'Gypsies' on the M50 roundabout would not have come as a surprise to readers of *Zoli*. In a statement
to the media, a spokesman of the Romanian embassy claimed that many of
the Roma had received social assistance at home, had been offered jobs in
a local shoe factory, and had addresses in blocks of flats (O'Brien, 2007).
The Roma argued that they had been living in mud huts and makeshift
houses at a rubbish dump, that they were victims of discrimination and
unemployment (McLaughlin, 2007), and that their life had been much
better under Communist rule (Holland, 2007). In *Zoli*, Dávid Smolenak
hears a similar story from the elders in the 'gray Gypsy settlement' he visits,
with its '[s]hanty houses. Windowless huts' (McCann: 4): '"It was better
under the Communists." [...] "Those were the days"' (McCann: 9). The
Roma in Ballymun received much and sometimes unfavourable attention in the Irish media: 'Callers to radio stations had little sympathy for

the group this week', the *Irish Times* reported (Healy, 2007). In response to such negative opinion, sociologist Ronit Lentin recalled, in an article provocatively titled 'Shades of the Final Solution?', that Romanian Gypsies had been 'targeted by the wartime fascist Romanian government and deported en masse', and argued that attitudes towards the Roma had changed little in the meantime: 'As Ireland joins the global world, it also partakes in human waste disposal, ridding itself of those people deemed not useful to its further economic growth' (Lentin, 2007). What stood out above all during the M50 stand-off was the battle of competing claims about and definitions of the Roma, in which rhetoric often threatened to take the place of facts.[3]

Colum McCann provides a number of crucial instances in *Zoli* where rhetoric about the Roma dissolves into, or is juxtaposed with, stunned silence in the face of their plight. After confronting the abjection of one anonymous family in their Slovakian settlement – the man addicted to huffing paint thinner, the woman unhinged by desperation, the children starving – journalist Dávid Smolenak is robbed of his ability to comment meaningfully on their condition: 'He narrated a brief line into his tape recorder and played it back to himself: it was empty and stupid and he erased it' (McCann: 214). In the novel's final few pages, Zoli and Francesca attend the opening of the academic conference on 'Romani Memory and Imagination', where Zoli feels disconnected from the discourse about her people,

> though every now and then her daughter leans across and whispers the context of the speech in her ear – a sharp sense of our own experience, memory as a funnel, understanding Romani silence, no access to public grievance, the lack of preservation, the implicit memory at the heart of all things. They seem like such large words for small times, and Zoli allows them to wash over her. (McCann: 310)

3   The Roma on the Ballymun roundabout make a cameo appearance in a short story by Roddy Doyle, published in the *New Yorker* in November 2007. The story is about a middle-aged couple in a marital crisis, and the Roma they see walking along a road near Dublin Airport initially serve as a mirror for their own sense of loss and alienation. When they realize the Roma are living on the roundabout, however, their metaphors dissolve into speechlessness in the face of this stark reality.

Earlier that same day, mother and daughter drove by the grim tower blocks and the makeshift shelters of the Roma camp, and took note of the desolation 'in a raw, cold silence' (McCann: 303–4). Through the silences in his novel, before Zoli's voice rings out at the very end and she 'begins' to sound her authentic note, McCann acknowledges that the Roma can only cease to be 'Other' when they are no longer spoken for and defined by outsiders – including himself.

Works Cited

Breger, C. (2004), 'Understanding the "Other"? Communication, History and Narration in Margriet de Moor's *Hertog van Egypte* (1996)', in Saul, N. and Tebbutt, S. (eds), *The Role of the Romanies: Images and Counter-Images of 'Gypsies'/Romanies in European Cultures*, Liverpool University Press, Liverpool, pp. 131–44.

Carmelio, S.V. (2002), 'An Interview with Colum McCann', *Nua: Studies in Contemporary Irish Writing*, 3, (1&2), pp. 89–100.

Donnelly, P. (2007), 'Empathizing with "the other"', *Montreal Gazette*, 20 October, viewed 17 November 2007. <http://www.canada.com/montrealgazette>.

Doyle, R. (2007), 'The Dog', *New Yorker*, 5 November, pp. 78–83.

Ficowski, J. (1989), *The Gypsies in Poland: History and Customs*, E. Healey (trans.), Interpress Publishers, Warsaw.

Hayes, M. (2006), interview with Colum McCann, viewed 17 November 2007. <http://www.colummccann.com/interviews/hayes.htm>.

Healy, A. (2007), 'Human crisis or welfare tourism?' *Irish Times*, 21 July, viewed 17 November 2007. <http://www.ireland.com/newspaper>.

Holland, K. (2007), '"Every day a struggle" in Romania', *Irish Times*, 25 July, viewed 22 May 2008. <http://www.ireland.com/newspaper>.

JanMohamed, A.R. (1985), 'The Economy of Manichean Allegory: The Function of Racial Difference in Colonialist Literature', *Critical Inquiry*, 2, (1), pp. 59–87.
Lentin, R. (2007), 'Shades of the Final Solution?' *Metro Eireann*, 2 Aug., viewed 18 November 2007. <http://www.metroeireann.com>.
McCaffrey, L. (2006), interview with Colum McCann, viewed 17 November 2007. <http://www.colummccann.com/interviews.htm>.
McCann, C. (2006), *Zoli*, Random House, New York.
McLaughlin, D. (2007), 'Romanian mayor is critical of Roma and Irish State', *Irish Times*, 27 July, viewed 17 November 2007. <http://www.ireland.com/newspaper>.
O'Brien, C. (2007), 'Ambassador rejects claims of Roma at M50', *Irish Times*, 24 July, viewed 17 November 2007. <http://www.ireland.com/newspaper>.
Patten, E. (2006), 'The politics of literacy', *Irish Times*, 23 September, Weekend, p. 12.
Welch, D. (2006), 'There Goes Colum McCann, Telling His Bonfire Stories Again', Powells.com, 3 January, viewed 17 November 2007. <http://www.powells.com/authors/mccann.html>.

The Montage of Semblance: Martin McDonagh's Dramaturgy

PADDY LYONS

'A play should be a thrill like a fantastic rollercoaster'

— MARTIN MCDONAGH

1. The montage of semblance

A rollercoaster is an elaborate construct on which, for the time of the ride, there's opportunity to experience change: change in the direction and pace of movement, for example, with slow climbs upwards, hurtling downhill drops, agonisingly twisting spirals; and primary to the buzz of the ride are constant shifts and switches of level. Attend to the temporal dimension of Martin McDonagh's plays and it's apparent the dynamic driving his plays is, too, one of shifting levels, as what's factual and what's fakery swap places, and swap again. Resurrection blasts the line between death and life, for instance, and in these plays is not uncommon. Billy's death, midway through *The Cripple of Inishmaan,* is – so far as the audience is concerned – a dramatic fact: he's seen collapsing in a motel room in America after he coughs up blood, and word back home confirms the trip to Hollywood was fatal. Later in the play, however, dramatic fact is abruptly put in reverse, as Billy is discovered by his Aunt Kate, silhouetted behind a sheet that's been serving as a cinema screen:

KATE:	You're not dead at all, are you, Billy?
BILLY:	I'm not, Aunty Kate.
KATE:	Well that's good. (McDonagh, 1997: 62)

Later still, Billy's death scene will turn out to have been a rehearsal for a screen test, thus explaining the mawkishness of his death speech ('arse-faced lines they had me reading for them'), and making sense of the miracle of his transit from death to life ('a grand little actoreen'). Relatively unexplained multiple resurrections feature in the final scene of McDonagh's recent play, *The Pillowman*. There's a surprise return appearance by the little mute girl who'd been buried alive in the earlier enactment of Katurian's story about the little girl who wanted to be Jesus; but now she's back, smiling, and painted totally bright green, waving gaily to everyone in sight. And then, after Katurian has been hooded and shot, death and life again change places, with this defiantly baroque stage direction:

> *The dead Katurian slowly gets to his feet, takes the hood off to reveal his bloody, bullet-shattered head … and speaks …'.* (McDonagh, 2003: 102)

There's even a reappearance by Michal, Katurian's brain-damaged brother, returning from death to forgive Katurian for the euthanasia he'd administered with a pillow. Fundamental to all these conspicuously showy stage effects is play with and play against illusionism, and this Alain Badiou has described as 'the montage of semblance'.

Badiou first launched the phrase in 1999, in a discussion of techniques common to the early twentieth-century playwrights Brecht and Pirandello; and he expands on it extensively in his recent book *The Century*, positing that

> Distancing – conceived as the way that semblance works out its proper distance from the real – can be taken as an axiom of the century's art …. (Badiou: 49)

He enlarges:

> It is the display – within the play – of the gap between the play and the real. More profoundly, it is a technique that dismantles the intimate and necessary links joining the real to semblance, links resulting from the fact that semblance is the true situating principle of the real, that which localizes and renders visible the brutal effects of the real's contingency. (Badiou: 48)

This use of the term 'the real' borrows from Lacan's account of signification: 'the real' designates all that is outside language, and thus is unspoken, unmapped and untamed; in this sense, 'semblance', because it can
only exist inside signification, is indeed 'the true situating principle of the
real', the real being not what is known, not what is familiar, but rather, all
that is not contained. Whatever is understood is by definition no longer
any part of the real: Billy's seemingly postmortem reappearance gestures
towards the real only so long as it is surprising, troubling, and encountered as a *coup de théâtre*; and it is not so anymore once it's explained
and assimilated into the everyday realities of the Inishmaan islanders.
This strong division between 'the real' and everyday reality activates the
curveballs and turnarounds, as McDonagh swings from semblance to
the real and back again.

On McDonagh's stage everyday reality can be boisterous and extreme.
However, his dismantlings of the montage of semblance proceed through
subtle hints and delicate finely-tuned strokes, as if 'the real' needs little
assistance to assert itself. These shifts and distancings operate over time,
and the daintiness of these modulations becomes evident only across a
sequence of action and dialogue. Let's consider one such run, halfway
through his first play, *The Beauty Queen of Leenane*. Maureen's elderly
mother Mag is beginning her day, by emptying a potty of wee into the
kitchen sink, when a half-naked man appears from her spinster daughter's
bedroom. He is Pato, a local man back on a visit from his labouring job
in England, the man Maureen brought home after a party the previous
night. Mag soon has Pato embarrassed into making breakfast for her, but
their coziness is brief, and is disturbed, as Maureen comes on the scene
in her bra and pants; Maureen sits herself on Pato's lap, and kisses him
at length, lustily:

MAUREEN: Just thanking you for a wonderful night, I am, Pato. Well worth the
wait it was. Well worth the wait.
PATO: *(embarrassed)* Good-oh.
MAG: Discussing me scoulded hand we was before you breezed in with no
clothes!

MAUREEN: Ah, feck your scoulded hand. *(To Pato.)* You'll have to be putting that
thing of yours in me again before too long is past, Pato. I do have a
taste for it now, I do ...
PATO: Maureen ...
*(She kisses him, gets off, and stares at Mag as she passes into the
kitchen).*
MAUREEN: A mighty oul taste. Uh-huh. (McDonagh, 1999: 27–28)

Very obviously, Maureen is theatricalizing to infuriate her mother, striking another uncivil blow in their ongoing domestic war. Not apparent,
though, not as yet, is that Maureen's theatrics are a montage of semblance,
that in fact in bed the previous night Pato was unable to perform sex with
her. As Pato is about to leave, the mood between them shifts into edgi-
ness, briefly, and there's a first tiny hint their night together was perhaps
not altogether wonderful:

MAUREEN: A beauty queen you thought I was last night, or you said I was. When
it's 'Cover your self', now, 'You do sicken me'...
PATO: *(approaching her)* Maureen, no, now, what are you saying that for ... ?
MAUREEN: Maybe that was the reason so.
PATO: *(stops)* The reason what?
MAUREEN: Be off with you so, if I sicken you.
PATO: You don't sicken me.
MAUREEN: *(almost crying)* Be off with you, I said. (McDonagh, 1999: 33)

Mag returns, interrupting Maureen's reproaches, and for the while the
basis for unease is left unexplicit. Not until Pato is writing to Maureen
from England is semblance dismantled for definite; and then Maureen's
coarse assertiveness – 'you'll have to be putting that thing of yours in
me again' – is bounced into a new perspective, and looks like delicacy
in disguise:

PATO: I *did* think you were a beauty queen and I *do* think, and it wasn't
anything to do with that at all or with you at all, I think you thought
it was. All it was, it has happened to me a couple of times before
when I've had a drink taken and was nothing to do with did I want
to. I would have been honoured to be the first one you chose, and
flattered, and the thing that I'm saying, I was honoured then and I
am still honoured, and just because it was not to be that night, does

> it mean it is not to be ever? I don't see why it should, and I don't see
> why you was so angry when you was so nice to me when it happened
> ... because if truth be told I could have looked at you in your bra and
> slip until the cows came home. I could never get my fill of looking at
> you in your bra and slip, and some day, God-willing, I will be looking
> at you in your bra and slip again. (McDonagh, 1999: 35)

There is a graciousness in undertaking exhibitionism to screen the potentially humiliating fact of impotence, and it's matched in the reciprocal tenderness in Pato's stumbling love-letter. But Pato's letter is apprehended, digested and destroyed by Mag, who reads in it Maureen's montage of semblance, and can't resist exposing this, hurtfully:

> You still do have the look of a virgin about you you always have had.
> (McDonagh, 1999: 47)

Mag had claimed there was no new news, no letter, but in this careless sneer Maureen catches the whiff of deceit, and she in turn proceeds to dismantle her mother's theatrics, scalding her with hot cooking oil. The events and gestures are themselves large and lurid, and generate violence; but it's small strokes and deftly placed indicators that forward the gradual alternations between semblance and the real.

2. Not swallowing the story

Alertness to the montage of semblance is widespread among McDonagh's protagonists, as is, too, the distancing such recognition brings. With more than a nod to Borges and to Nabokov – masters in metafiction whose writings McDonagh much admires – *The Pillowman* features as its main protagonist a writer in trouble, Katurian, who's pushed to theorize storytelling. Katurian is under police investigation over the origins and implications of gruesome tales of the deaths of children that he's written, and from this arises conceptualization and analyses of the montage of semblance. During the first act, while his interrogation is underway, Katurian is distressed by screams from an adjacent room, screams he recognizes as coming from his backward brother, Michal. In the second act, however, after Katurian has himself been beaten and tortured, and is flung into a cell with him, Michal tells Katurian he'd in truth not been tortured at all, only persuaded to scream, by a man who 'said I did it real good'. As Katurian grasps that what he'd supposed was his brother howling in pain was a con-trick, a put-up job, and that he'd taken literally what was no more than a montage of semblance, he reflects:

> KATURIAN: Why are we being so stupid? Why are we believing everything they're
>   telling us?
> MICHAL: Why?
> KATURIAN: This is just like storytelling.
> MICHAL: I know.
> KATURIAN: A man comes into a room, says, 'Your mother's dead,' yeah?
> MICHAL: I know my mother's dead.
> KATURIAN: No, I know, but in a story. A man comes in to a room, says to another
>   man, 'Your mother's dead.' What do we know? Do we know that the
>   second man's mother is dead?
> MICHAL: Yes.
> KATURIAN: No, we don't.
> MICHAL: No, we don't.
> KATURIAN: All we know is that a man has come into a room and said to another
>   man, 'Your mother is dead.' That is all we know. First rule of storytell-
>   ing. 'Don't believe everything you read in the papers.'
> MICHAL: I don't read the papers.
> KATURIAN: Good. You'll always be one step ahead of everybody else.
>   (McDonagh, 2003: 39–40)

Katurian's analysis highlights what Badiou described as 'the gap between the play and the real'. What's condemned is literalism, which is equated with disempowerment, whereas the recognition of fictiveness and theatricality is, relatively, a liberation, and it opens and enlarges the space of understanding. Not swallowing the story, but shifting the emphasis, away from the theatrics to which he's been subjected, and over and onto their montage, is – so Katurian explains to Michal – a move towards freedom, 'one step ahead'. His comment has the compelling aspect of a dawning insight, which resonates with the disturbing questions being asked about his own compositions, and chimes with Badiou's more general observation that:

> at stake is the fictionalisation of the very power of fiction, in other words, the fact of regarding the efficacy of semblance as real. (Badiou: 49)

His situation is no safer, no less dangerous, but no longer terminal.

The embattled brothers Coleman and Valene, in *The Lonesome West,* are a further couple, like Katurian and Michal, enmeshed in and invigorated by storytelling and its montage of semblance. Buoyed up with theological lore – that the only sinner doomed to hell is the suicide with no time to confess his sin before he dies – Coleman propounds cheerfully how retelling an event can put its consequences into reverse:

> COLEMAN: It's always the best ones go to hell. Me, probably straight to heaven I'll go, even though I blew the head off poor dad. So long as I go confessing to it anyways. That's the good thing about being Catholic. You can shoot your dad in the head and it doesn't even matter at all. (McDonagh, 1999: 181–2)

After the suicide of their local priest – sadly no longer able to cope with a parish fast becoming 'the murder capital of Europe' – confessing to each other affronts each may have inflicted on the other becomes a 'great oul game' for Coleman and Valene, a game they call 'apologizing'. They elaborate to each other possible foulness each can claim to have committed against the other, with at least as much glee as penitence, each pushing the other to worse and worse admissions. It's a game with high stakes, as Valene makes plain, querying a passing implausibility:

> VALENE: It doesn't hurt me at all when you go making up lies. You don't understand the rules, Coleman. It does have to be true, else it's just plain daft. You can't go claiming credit for snipping the ears off a dog when you didn't lay a finger on that dog's ears ... (ibid.: 189)

The montage of semblance has its rules. This is provocative incitement, an admission that for their mutual cat and mouse tussles to reach the full

thrill of a rollercoaster ride, their accounts of their offences must always
be on the edge of toppling into the danger and violence of the real.

In *The Beauty Queen of Leenane,* Mag and Maureen constitute another
such pair, pressing constantly on the power of fiction. It's her commitment
to imaginative possibilities that sustains Maureen in her enslavement to
her mother Mag, and it's Mag's negations and denials of fiction that spur
and provoke Maureen in her explorations of the fictive:

MAG: ... some people it would be better not to say hello to. The fella up and
              murdered the poor oul woman in Dublin and he didn't even know
              her. The news that story was on, did you hear of it? (*Pause.*) Strangled,
              and didn't even know her. That's a fella it would be better not to talk
              to. That's a fella it would be better to avoid outright ...
MAUREEN: Sure, that sounds exactly the type of fella I would like to meet, and then
              bring him home to meet you, if he likes murdering oul women.
MAG: That's not a nice thing to say, Maureen.
MAUREEN: Is it not, now?
MAG: (*pause*) Sure why would he be coming all this way out from Dublin?
              He'd just be going out of his way.
MAUREEN: For the pleasure of me company he'd come. Killing you, it'd just be a
              bonus for him.
MAG: Killing you I bet he first would be.
MAUREEN: I could live with that so long as I was sure he'd be clobbering you soon
              after. If he clobbered you with a big axe or something and took your
              oul head off and spat in your neck, I wouldn't mind at all, going first.
              Oh no, I'd enjoy it, I would. No more oul Complan to get, and no
              more oul porridge to get, and no more –
MAG: (*interrupting, holding her tea out*) No sugar in this, Maureen, you
              forgot, go and get me some. (McDonagh, 1999: 6–7)

Here fiction and semblance circle around the real of Maureen's desire,
the murderous act she'll herself bring to realization later, though with a
poker rather than a big axe. Mag's faux-naive question – 'why would he
be coming all this way?' – urges Maureen on, much as Michal urges on
the elaboration of Katurian's macabre stories, or as Valene and Coleman
propel 'apologizing' into criminal conversation. Maureen can at one and
the same moment approach the brutal violence of the real while also holding it at bay, as she relishes imagining how her own slaughter at the hands

of 'the fella' will be followed by the beheading of Mag, and by that final vicious spit in her neck; since it's to take place only when she'll be dead, Maureen can take pleasure in it as a fiction; and thanks to 'the fella', it's not an act she pictures herself executing – not yet.

3. Interfaces

These couples are already ensnared in dismantling the montage of semblance and reworking its relation to the real. To draw theatre audiences into the process, McDonagh employs a range of structuring devices, formal explorations into how fiction functions.

The Pillowman is built around quite noticeable alternations between stories played out and stories told, between drama and narrative, enactment versus telling. In the second scenes of both act one and act two of this three-act play, Katurian's stories are enacted while he is narrating. In scene two of act one the theatre audience witnesses the story of 'The Writer and the Writer's Brother', in which Katurian's parents conduct a perverse experiment in child rearing, cosseting one brother (the writer) while subjecting the other brother to vile torture, their plan being to stimulate the imagination of their writer son: this scene concludes with the fourteen-year old writer (Katurian) smothering each parent in turn with a pillow, in his disgust at the atrocities inflicted on his elder brother (Michal). In scene two of act two the story at once narrated and played out is equally horrifying, and is entitled 'The Little Jesus': the audience witnesses how a little girl longs to be the second coming of Jesus Christ, and decks herself out in a false beard and sandals, to go around doing good; like Christ but in a contemporary setting, she's subjected to vile torture, crowned with barbed wire, nailed to a cross while her foster parents watch television, and then buried alive. But otherwise and elsewhere in this haunting play, narration is regularly punctured, and tellers suffer relentless interruption from their listeners whenever stories are told. These constant queries highlight fictiveness, and are incessant, to the point even of foregrounding the montage of semblance inherent in giving a title to a story:

> TUPOLSKI: Well, my story is called ... What's it called? It's called . . . 'The Story of the Little Deaf Boy on the Big Long Railroad Tracks. In China'. *(Pause.) What?*
>
> KATURIAN: What?
>
> TUPOLSKI: Don't you think that's a good title?
>
> KATURIAN: I do think that's a good title, yes.
>
> TUPOLSKI: *(pause)* What do you really think? You have my permission to be entirely truthful, even if it hurts me.
>
> KATURIAN: I think that's probably about the worst title I ever heard. It's got about two commas in it. You can't have two commas in a title. You can't have one comma in a title. It might even have a full stop in it, that title. That title's almost insane.
>
> TUPOLSKI: *(pause)* Maybe it's a title that's just way ahead of its time.
>
> KATURIAN: Maybe it is. Maybe terrible titles *are* way ahead of their time. Maybe that'll be the new thing.
>
> TUPOLSKI: Maybe it will.
>
> KATURIAN: I just think it's a terrible title.
>
> TUPOLSKI: We've established that! I'm taking back my permission to be entirely truthful now and you're lucky you don't get a fucking smack! *(Pause.)* Okay. Where was I? (McDonagh, 2003: 85–6)

Such interruptions recur and recur, again and again opening gaps between the story itself and the act of telling it. The play's ending is interrupted, Katurian interjecting a comment on endings:

> The story was going to finish in a fashionably downbeat mode ... The story *was* going to finish that way, but ... (ibid.: 103)

This is, to cite Katurian's closing line, 'in keeping with the spirit of the thing'; just as the play shuttles between unquestioned enacted stories and stories interrogatively interrupted, the ending too shuttles between alternatives, another formal twist in the non-stop sieving out of fictiveness and the real.

The Pillowman is set in a No Man's Land, where walls dissolve and the dead walk. Its structure is designedly and overtly elaborate. The plays with Irish settings are no less carefully wrought and constructed to engage their audiences in shifting distances, and pacing is the prime means whereby they dismantle smooth-surface illusionism. In the two Aran Island plays, it's accelerations that do the work. Quick spin reversals undermine the montage of semblance in *The Cripple of Inishmaan*, and Verna A. Foster has noted appositely how

> McDonagh overturns every assumption we may make about the play's characters and events and never allows us to rest in any one emotional response for more than a moment. (Foster: 32)

The high speed with which these reversals occur exposes the theatricality of theatre. Patrick Lonergan has commented that *The Lieutenant of Inishmore* 'explores the divergence between representation and reality' (Lonergan: 71); the helter-skelter rush of reversals in its mass slaughter scene illustrates how this is so. Padraic (the lieutenant of the title) is about to shoot his father in the head when he's pinioned by old comrades incensed that he's set up a splinter group, and Padraic's led offstage for execution, proclaiming, 'Something'll turn up, I can feel it!' (McDonagh, 2001: 49). Moments later there's the sound of rifle shots, from Mairead, who's adept in shooting out cows' eyes at long distance; back come the gunmen who'd captured Padraic, but they're bleeding from their eyes (ibid.: 50). As the blinded gunmen shoot wildly in every wrong direction, Padraic and Mairead appear in the doorway, hand in hand (ibid.: 51); Padraic and Mairead begin shooting the gunmen; and *'they seem almost to glide silently around the room, their eyes locked on each other'* (ibid.: 52). The gunmen apparently dead, Padraic and Mairead kiss long and lovingly, and then prepare to kill Padraic's father and Mairead's brother (ibid.: 53). But this killing is interrupted as Christy, one of the supposedly dead gunmen, rises up to make peace before he dies, and Mairead and Padraic instead drag away the dying man for torture with 'a knife, a cheese grate, a razor, an iron' (ibid.: 54). The action is hideous, the pace of the reversals farcically fast and hilarious.

In the three Leenane plays, however, it's through slow-motion effects
that pacing foregrounds fictiveness. Indeed, in his eloquent introduction
to this trilogy, Fintan O'Toole comes close to suggesting these plays operate pictorially, almost through actual stasis:

> The 1950s is laid over the 1990s, giving the play's apparent realism the ghostly,
> dizzying feel of a superimposed photograph. All the elements that make up the
> picture are real, but their combined effect is one that questions the very idea of
> reality. (O'Toole: xi)

But these plays have their own temporal movements, and are not at all
static – far from it: earlier we traced the restraint and gradualness with
which it emerges that Maureen's night with Pato was not the earth-shaker
she'd theatricalised the morning afterwards. In contrast with the accelerations of the Aran Island plays, the Leenane plays frequently employ aching
slowness, and long-drawn-out deferrals play against illusionist closure.
In *The Beauty Queen,* the idiocy of Pato's brother Ray exceeds even that
of Thomas Hardy's peasant messengers, and there's wonderfully excru-
ciating slowness whenever he has a communication to deliver. The core
enigma of *A Skull in Connemara* is whether the death of Mick Dowd's
wife was the result of drunk driving, or whether he'd first butchered her,
and the play again and again strains towards a solution that to the end it
refuses to deliver. Throughout a long, macabre, and very funny graveyard
scene, Mick and his apprentice Mairtin open coffins and exhume bodies
to make more room for the dead, all the while deferring their approach
to Mick's wife's coffin; when eventually Mick does open it, the body
has disappeared. Gradually Mick apprehends the body's been stolen by
Mairtin and his policeman brother in an attempt to frame Mick, and
in the course of long repetitive discussion – of for example a man who
drowned in wee – Mick gets Mairtin so drunk he can easily murder him
in revenge for this montage of semblance. But later, as Mick is writing
out a confession to his murder of Mairtin, Mairtin reappears, blood-
stained but resurrected, and insistent his wounds are merely the result of
a drunken driving accident, not needing medical attention; and instead
of confrontation, side-tracking takes further twists, the attacker and the

victim who's survived straying into extended and highly non-pertinent debate over the social standing of lesbians:

MAIRTIN: Hospitals are for poofs, sure.

MICK: Hospitals aren't for poofs. They let anybody in.

MAIRTIN: For poofs and for lesbos who can't take a middling dig ... 'Lesbos'. Y'know, like Mona McGhee in me school with the beard. (*Pause*) Five times I've asked that bitch out and she still won't go.

MICK: There's nothing the matter with lesbians, Mairtin. They're doing no harm to anybody.

MAIRTIN: They're not, I suppose. And they're great at tennis.

(McDonagh, 1999: 122–3)

Only the Hanlon brothers' plot to frame Mick is dismantled; the matter of whether Mick did murder his wife is never settled. At the end, Mick's alone on stage, holding his wife's skull, perhaps in grief, but equally possibly in remorse. The journey to this moment has been rocky and interrupted; the conclusion remains ambiguous and inconclusive. Likewise, in *The Lonesome West* the long 'apologizing' scene between the warring brothers Valene and Coleman sways again and again, sometimes towards conspiratorial game play, sometimes towards eruption into murderous violence, before returning to stalemate; likewise, as Father Welsh and Girleen converse by the lakeside where local men are prone to committing suicide, the longer their conversation continues, the more uncertain it becomes whether Girleen is heading for success in her project to seduce the priest, or whether he'll at last hurl himself to his death. These cliffhangers can be as alarming for an onstage audience as they are for the theatre audience, such as when Father Welsh finds himself helpless and standing by while Valene holds a gun to Coleman's temple, and Coleman prolongs their conversation with childish insults:

VALENE: Be saying goodbye to the world, you, fecker!

COLEMAN: And fecking Taytos then, the worst crisps in the world ... (*Valene cocks the gun that's up against Coleman's head.*)

WELSH: No, Valene, no!

VALENE: I said say goodbye to the world, ya feck.

COLEMAN: Goodbye to the world, ya feck.

> (*Valene pulls the trigger. There is a hollow click He pulls the trigger
> again ... as Coleman reaches into his pocket and takes out two shotgun
> cartridges.*)
> COLEMAN: Do you think I'm fecking stupid, now? (*To Welsh*) Did you see that,
> Father? My own brother going shooting me in the head.
> (McDonagh, 1999: 158–9)

To a theatre audience, watching these antics in slow-motion is further
reminder it is an audience, spectating on the montage of semblance.

4. Passion for the real

> The real, conceived in its contingent absoluteness, is never real enough not to be
> suspected of semblance. The passion for the real is also, of necessity, suspicion.
> Nothing can attest that the real is the real, nothing but the system of fiction wherein
> it plays the role of the real. (Badiou: 52)

The twentieth century has been remarkable in its dedication to passion
for the real, Badiou tells us, in the domains of politics, mathematics and
sexual love, as well in the arts. Passion for the real, the search for what's
new, not yet coded, and outside signification, sets it apart from and breaks
with the preceding century, when dialectics were in dominance. It's as an
outcome of passion for the real that the montage of semblance is necessarily foregrounded. Because the real is unknown, the means to access it
and to attempt to 'verify' it are of necessity engagements with semblance;
thus in turn semblance and fictiveness are on display and under interrogation. The first exemplary document in which Badiou discerns these
procedures is a poem of 1923 by Osip Mandlestam; but in Irish literature
they are already evident as early as 1910, in W.B. Yeats's poem 'The Mask',
which introduces this direction in Irish literature. This is a poem which
breaks with the nineteenth century in mobilizing theory of the mask to
voice the new century's passion for the real, not least in that the poem

refuses dialectics; and, faithful to its title, is itself a mask, a montage of semblance:

The Mask

'Put off that mask of burning gold
With emerald eyes.'
'O no, my dear, you make so bold
To find if hearts be wild and wise,
And yet not cold.'

'I would but find what there's to find,
Love or deceit.'
'It was the mask engaged your mind,
And after set your heart to beat,
Not what's behind.'

'But lest you are my enemy,
I must enquire.'
'O no, my dear, let all that be;
What matter, so there is but fire
In you, in me?'
　　(Yeats: 144)

Evidently a construct of language and dialogue, the poem locates itself within the fictiveness it celebrates. The mask under debate between the lovers of the poem is patently metaphorical, an opportunity to consider the relative merits of emotional nudity on the one hand, and on the other emotional restraint and disguise; what the lovers in turn interrogate and assert is the importance for sexual love of the montage of semblance. Semblance is regarded with suspicion – 'love or deceit' – and yet it is through the montage of semblance that love has sprung: 'It was the mask engaged your mind / And after set your heart to beat'. The debate as such is not resolved: there is no dialectical progression. Instead, it ends on a beginning, on 'fire', which stands in for the intensity of all that remains unspoken and unaccommodated, for tension that's not and can't be assimilated into the discourse of daily reality. In short, the poem finishes by invoking the real, its tensions and its energy. More precisely,

it closes by opposing a real of mutuality which puts at risk and in danger
the individualities of 'you' and 'me'. We may term the real which Yeats's
poem invokes 'fraternity', and this too is the real which McDonagh's
plays butt up against.

Badiou draws on Lacan to indicate the mutations the twentieth century brought to the key goals of the French Revolution:

> Equality is the Imaginary (since it cannot come about as an objective figure, even
> though it is the ultimate reason for everything), freedom is the Symbolic (since
> it is the presupposed instrument, the fecund negative), and fraternity is the Real
> (that which is sometimes encountered, in the here and now). (Badiou: 102)

Expanding, he conceptualizes 'the real violence of fraternity' in terms
equally pertinent to Yeats's poem and to McDonagh's plays, asking

> what is the content of fraternity, if not the acceptance that the infinite 'we' prevails
> over the finitude of the individual? (Badiou: 102)

Though the means whereby McDonagh foregrounds the montage of
semblance vary from play to play, locating fraternity in this sense on the
side of the real is a constant. It's very evident as a component in the battles between Valene and Coleman, it's implicit in Michal's betrayals of
Katurian, and in Katurian's murder of his brother, and latent too in the
hostility between the Hanlon brothers in *A Skull in Connemara*. But fraternity's violence is not exclusively the domain of brothers, as the struggles
between Maureen and Mag demonstrate. *The Cripple of Inishmaan* is – as
its title suggests – concerned with a mode of community, fraternity, that
sustains itself through exclusionary devices such as scapegoating, most
evidently by branding Billy as 'Cripple Billy', and most ludicrously in the
ongoing tales of the off-stage character Jim Finnegan's loose daughter,
invoked as reprehensible and notorious for every imaginable infringement of the community code, from kissing a bald donkey to poking the
eyes out of worms with a needle. More extreme dimensions of fraternity
underlie *The Lieutenant of Inishmore*, where the threat presented should
an infinite 'we' prevail is countered by a multiplication of splinter groups,
splinter groups that are more vigorous in their hostilities to each other

than to the communities they oppose. In *The Lieutenant* a particularly sinister variant of fraternity is manifested on stage – and significantly this manifestation is wordless – in the episode of *amour fou* between Padraic and Mairead, as they glide around soundless, hand in hand, their eyes locked onto one another, rapt in ecstasy as they slaughter their one-time comrades. For the duration of this rapture, they *are* the real, and it's a relief once they emerge from this Bonnie and Clyde intensity into a relatively unecstactic state:

> PADRAIC: Look at you in that pretty dress, Oh God, now! Half-covered it in blood we have.
> MAIREAD: Ah, what matter? Red goes well with it.
> PADRAIC: You can't go walking the streets of Ulster dripping blood, now.
> MAIREAD: Sure, who would notice, Padraic?
> PADRAIC: Tourists would notice. Be changing it or washing it off now.
> MAIREAD: I'll give it a wee rinse for meself, so. (McDonagh, 2001: 62)

The real of their union was a wordless murderous glide; garment talk restores the everyday and its semblances.

5. Destruction or subtraction?

Is there an outcome to dismantling fiction, other than the violence of the real? Badiou proposes a delicacy in thought which 'opposes minimal difference to maximal destruction', a move that he terms the 'subtractive' option, and in part explanation he quotes from a poem by Malevich:

> Try never to repeat yourself ... Erase, be quiet ...
> so that you may hear the breath of a new day in the desert ... (Badiou: 57)

In McDonagh's plays, such subtractiveness occurs when the fictionalizers stop and listen to their own stories, generating space for themselves to stand back and thus move forwards.

An obvious instance is Maureen. In the second from last scene, as she stands with a poker over the body of her mother, whom she's finally bludgeoned to death, Maureen tells Mag (and thus herself) how she did meet Pato as he was boarding the train, how he kissed her, wrapped his arms around her – 'them blue eyes of his' – and made her promise to join him in Boston once she'd made arrangements not to be encumbered with Mag any longer. Pato's railway-station proposal is Maureen's justification. But in the scene which follows, the final scene of the play, Pato's brother Ray shocks her by telling her 'Be taxicab Pato left', and then

> RAY: ... a lass called, em ... Dolores Hooley, or Healey ... Herself and Pato did get engaged a week ago ...
> MAUREEN: (*shocked*) Engaged to do what?
> RAY: Engaged to get married. What do you usually get engaged for? 'Engaged to do what?' Engaged to eat a bun! (McDonagh, 1999: 56–7)

Maureen sinks in confusion into her late mother's rocking chair, and Ray remarks:

> The exact fecking image of your mother you are, sitting there ... (ibid.: 57)

But this is not the end. As she hears on the radio a song her mother used listen to, Maureen gets up from the chair, picks up a suitcase, dusts it off, and departs, leaving the audience alone with the song on the radio. It's as if she's aware she'd moved from one montage of semblance into yet another, from her fantasy of a railway-station proposal into a replay of her mother – but in these last seconds, dis-identifying from both these stories, she exits from both these repetitions, heading into a space where it's perhaps possible to move on. The real is wordless, not contained.

Equally subtle and as delicately drawn, but more immediately cheering, is the subtraction of herself from the story of herself that slippy Helen arrives at. *The Cripple of Inishmaan* is in many senses a play of dis-identifications – the island community holds itself together by scapegoating, an extreme form of dis-identification; and when the community gathers to watch the film *Man of Aran*, the response is again to dis-identify, and not see itself reflected in the on-screen images. From the first, Helen presents herself as violent and angry.

EILEEN: I heard you did drop all the eggs on the egg-man the other day, Helen, broke the lot of them.

HELEN: I didn't drop them eggs at all. I went pegging them at Father Barratt, got him bang in the gob with fecking four of them.

EILEEN: You went pegging them at Father Barratt?

HELEN: I did. Are you repeating me now, Mrs?

EILEEN: Sure, pegging eggs at a priest, isn't it pure against God?

HELEN: Oh, maybe it is, but if God went touching me arse in choir practice I'd peg eggs at that fecker too.

EILEEN: Father Barratt went touching your ... behind in choir pr ...

HELEN: Not me behind, no. Me *arse*, Mrs. Me *arse*.

EILEEN: I don't believe you at all, Helen McCormick.

HELEN: And what the feck d'you think I care what you believe? (McDonagh, 1997: 12)

Helen is loud in her insistence on the turpitude of priests, so loud it appears she's deaf to her brother Bartley's misfortunes with the clergy:

BARTLEY: Sure, getting clergymen groping your arse doesn't take much skill. It isn't being pretty they go for. It's more being on your own and small.

HELEN: If it's being on your own and small, why so has Cripple Billy never had his arse groped be priests?

BARTLEY: You don't know at all Cripple Billy's never had his arse groped be priests.

HELEN: Have you ever had your arse groped be priests, Cripple Billy?

BILLY: No.

HELEN: Now.

BARTLEY: I suppose they have to draw the line somewhere.

HELEN: And you, you're small and often on your own. Have you ever had your arse groped be priests?

BARTLEY: (*quietly*) Not me arse, no. (ibid.: 14)

Bartley's mishaps are left untold, unseen, real, and he remains the butt of Helen's best jokes, and her frequent pot-shots with the egg-man's eggs. Gradually, though, it becomes apparent Helen is involved with the

egg-man on more than a business basis. Old Mammy observes during
the film show that Helen is over-familiar with the general state of the
egg-man's bed-sheets, and later Helen loses her job because of a quarrel
about which she's unusually reticent:

> BILLY: What did you spit at the egg-man's wife for, Helen?
>
> HELEN: Ah, the egg-man's wife just deserved spitting at. (ibid.: 76)

Change is evident in Helen, who postures far less in these later conversations with Billy, and relishes taking her tales of priest-molestation to a
pitch of parody, and beyond:

> BILLY: Do ya have to be so violent, Helen?
>
> HELEN: I do have to be so violent, or if I'm not to be taken advantage of any-
>   ways I do have to be so violent.
>
> BILLY: Sure, nobody's taken advantage of you since the age of seven, Helen.
>
> HELEN: Six is nearer the mark. I ruptured a curate at six. (ibid.: 76)

Little is stated, much is suggested, but semblance is foregrounded sufficiently to imply an alternative real outside and apart from what is said.
Without abandoning any of her vitality, Helen's new capacity for self-
mockery allows her to act towards Bartley with kindness, and to extend
herself almost amorously towards Billy:

> HELEN: (forcefully) All right so I'll go out walking with ya, but only somewhere
>   no fecker would see us and when it's dark and no kissing or groping,
>   cos I don't want you ruining me fecking reputation.
>
> BILLY: Oh. Okay, Helen.
>
> HELEN: Or anyways not much kissing or groping ... (ibid.: 81)

It's not by brusque demolition of old stories that this new flirtatious Helen
emerges; rather, it occurs obliquely, as her self-mockery distances her –
subtractively – from the repetitions of her old pugnaciousness.

Badiou asks when did the twentieth century begin and end, and suggests
it's with the Russian revolution and the end of World War One that we
first discern the possibility of art based on building and dismantling the

montage of semblance, thereby enabling encounters with the real. Badiou proposes, too, that this century ended sometime in the 1980s. However, Irish writing gives grounds to imagine a different periodicity, and to believe in a beginning staked out by Yeats as early as 1910. McDonagh wrote his six plays in a creative burst in 1994, already well after the end postulated by Badiou, and was redrafting and revising *The Pillowman* in the early days of the twenty-first century. It remains to be seen whether the new century will persist in these approaches to art, and to other fields of human activity, or will follow different paths.

Works Cited

Badiou, Alain (2007), *The Century,* transl. A. Toscano, Polity, Cambridge and Malden.

Foster, Verna A. (2006), '(Up)staging the Staging of Ireland: Martin McDonagh's *The Cripple of Inishmaan*' in *Nua: Studies in Contemporary Irish Writing* Vol. 5, Number 1 / Fall 2006, Missouri, pp. 25–33.

Lonergan, Patrick (2005), 'Too Dangerous to be Done? Martin McDonagh's *Lieutenant of Inishmore*', *Irish Studies Review* 13:1, Dublin, pp. 65–78.

McDonagh, Martin (1999), *Plays 1: The Beauty Queen of Leenane; A Skull in Connemara; The Lonesome West*, Methuen, London.

McDonagh, Martin (1997), *The Cripple of Inishmaan*, Methuen, London.

McDonagh, Martin (2001), *The Lieutenant of Inishmore*, Methuen, London.

McDonagh, Martin (2003), *The Pillowman*, Faber & Faber, London.

O'Toole, Fintan (1999), 'Introduction', in Martin McDonagh, *Plays: 1*, pp. ix–xvii.

Yeats, W.B. (1990), *The Poems,* ed. Daniel Albright, Dent, London.

A Few Shakes of a Bard's Tale:
Some Recent Irish Appropriations of Shakespeare

WILLY MALEY

What Ish My Motivation?

This essay is about relations between Irish writers and Shakespeare, at times anxious and obsessive, giving rise in recent years to more irreverent and oblique responses. If Macmorris and Caliban are the two Shakespeare characters most readily associated with Ireland, then they bring with them different kinds of confusion. Macmorris is the Irish captain in *Henry V* who asks 'What ish my Nation?' (3.3.61), Caliban the colonial servant who cries 'You taught me language, and my profit on't/ Is I know how to curse' (1.2.366–7). Nation and language were for a long time at the root of Irish responses to Shakespeare – Yeats famously declared that 'Ireland had preserved longer than England the rhythmical utterance of the Shakespearean stage' (Yeats, 'An Introduction for My Plays': 407) – but there has arguably been a change in recent years.

I shall focus on four texts – a novella and three plays – all published in the 1990s, in which Irish writers spar with the shadow of Shakespeare. These responses range from explicit adaptations to more edgy appropriations, often scurrilous and scatological. First, though, I'd like to look at the variety and vibrancy of performance culture in the Ireland of Shakespeare's day, a versatility, volubility and capacity for ventriloquism that remains a key feature of Irish culture. Ben Jonson's *The Alchemist* famously starts with a fart, a sort of alchemy in reverse, but that unsubtle smelting, that in-your-face opening stands as the prologue to an entertainment. Nowadays, a fart is an ill wind that blows no good, but in early modern Ireland, the fart is an art in itself, and not just an opening gambit or untimely

intervention. Indeed, breaking wind is the peculiar forte of an itiner-
ant company of – excuse my Erse – *braigetóir* (Irish for 'farters') – who,
together with face-contortionists (muggers in the theatrical sense of the
word), gamblers, harpers, acrobats, tricksters, jesters, jugglers, and hummers – no, not mummers, but hummers – contributed to a vibrant and
loudly trumpeted culture of performance art. Modern Irish drama is the
envy of us all, but it's often portrayed as a colonial legacy, English in origin,
Irish in verbal energy, witness Yeats's celebration of the Elizabethan richness of Synge. In fact, early modern Ireland was a fulcrum of dramatic
activity, steeped in traditions, local and vocal, prior to the Restoration,
challenging (New) English colonial representations of the country as a
cultural vacuum.

Ireland has excited a great deal of interest among Renaissance scholars
over the past three decades, ever since Stephen Greenblatt's decisive intervention on Edmund Spenser and Ireland in *Renaissance Self-Fashioning*
(1980), an essay which drew on important work by Irish historians such
as Brendan Bradshaw, Ciaran Brady, Nicholas Canny, and David Beers
Quinn. A constant complaint from historians of early modern Ireland,
and from those engaged in research on Irish language and literature in the
period, has been that the preoccupation with English literary representations of Ireland and the Irish implies that England had a culture that it
wished to impose on a country without one. Yet Edmund Spenser argued
in his *A View of the Present State of Ireland* (1596) that the Irish had letters
before the English, that the work of Irish poets was worthy of attention
(and translation), and that it was but the other day since England grew
civil. In other words, one of the earliest and most canonical of English
colonists and commentators was prepared to concede that Ireland had a
rich literary culture that predated that of England. Yet the image of the
'wild Irish' promulgated by other observers has persisted.

Alan Fletcher, in *Drama, Performance, and Polity in Pre-Cromwellian
Ireland* (2000), sets out 'to call attention to this rich body of evidence
which hitherto has tended to remain the strict preserve of the Celticist'
(Fletcher, 2000: 4). Fletcher identifies three causes of neglect, 'loss of
sources, insufficient research, and lack of linguistic skill', but there is also
the key question of what counts as drama or theatre. We are back with

the farters once again. For it is Fletcher's contention that it is only by opening up our understanding of performance art in order to embrace Ireland's full array of public spectacle, and appreciating the extent of the Irish gift for oratory – including the oratory of the *braigetóir* – that we can begin to grasp the range and richness of the entertainment on offer. The performing arse is part and parcel of the performing arts.

Fletcher's definition of 'drama' is very broad. It covers performance in the widest sense. Irish buffoons 'who twisted and contorted their faces in public to earn a living' are thus part of the story. Fletcher shows that the three traditions in early modern Ireland – Gaelic Irish, Old English, and New English – between them created a performance culture that was almost unrivalled: 'It is clear that Irish society, from the earliest period to which sources give access, was inhabited by a host of performing artists and entertainers. Early documents witness to a taxonomy of Gaelic performance the like of which is unequalled anywhere in the British Isles' (Fletcher, 2000: 6). This flies in the face – one is tempted to say farts in the face – of received wisdom about the period. According to Fletcher:

> although this accomplishment [i.e. farting] was prized in entertainers throughout these islands during the Middle Ages, it is only from Ireland that substantial early evidence survives for specialists in it. (Fletcher, 2000: 24)

Now, I'm not sure exactly what substantial evidence of farting would entail, and I don't plan to follow through on that one.

Certainly, it's an ill wind that blows no good, and modern Irish writers like Joyce and Beckett got a great deal of mileage out of the fart as an art of expression and interruption. Two familiar examples set the tone. First, in *Ulysses*, James Joyce has Leopold Bloom play the wind instrument:

> I must really. Fff. Now if I did that at a banquet ...
> Bloom viewed a gallant pictured hero in Lionel Marks's window. Robert Emmet's last words. Seven last words. Of Meyerbeer that is.
> —True men like you men.
> —Ay, ay, Ben.
> —Will lift your glass with us.

They lifted.
Tschink. Tschunk.
Tip. An unseeing stripling stood in the door. He saw not bronze. He saw not gold.
Nor Ben nor Bob nor Tom nor Si nor George nor tanks nor Richie nor Pat. Hee
hee hee hee. He did not see.
Seabloom, greaseabloom viewed last words. Softly. *When my country takes her
place among.*
Prrprr.
Must be the bur.
Fff. Oo. Rrpr.
Nations of the earth. No-one behind. She's passed. *Then and not till then.* Tram.
Kran, kran, kran. Good oppor. Coming. Krandlkrankran. I'm sure it's the burgund.
Yes. One, two. *Let my epitaph be.* Karaaaaaaa. *Written. I have.*
Pprrpffrrppfff.
Done.
(Joyce, 1998: 278–9)

In *Molloy*, Beckett has his eponymous hero take the air and figure
out the frequency of flatulence:

And in winter, under my greatcoat, I wrapped myself in swathes of newspaper, and
did not shed them until the earth awoke, for good, in April. *The Times Literary
Supplement* was admirably adapted to this purpose, of a never failing toughness
and impermeability. Even farts made no impression on it. I can't help it, gas escapes
from my fundament on the least pretext, it's hard not to mention it now and then,
however great my distaste. One day I counted them. Three hundred and fifteen
farts in nineteen hours, or an average of over sixteen farts an hour. After all, it's
not excessive. Four farts every fifteen minutes. It's nothing. Not even one fart
every four minutes. It's unbelievable. Damn it, I hardly fart at all, I should never
have mentioned it. Extraordinary how mathematics help you to know yourself.
(Beckett, 1979: 29–30)

Emphatically, the humour and performative prowess of the *braigetóir* is
in safe hands. Now I want to turn briefly, and perhaps fittingly, to a play
whose title suggests a vacuum to be filled: *Much Ado About Nothing*.

Much Ado About Ireland

Ireland used up a lot of paper for a nation famous for its farters. We're familiar with the famous exclamation of James I on seeing the Irish state papers when he came to the throne of England: 'We had more ado with Ireland than all the world besides' (Highley, 1997: 1). But this pervasive presence in the state papers is strangely absent from the London stage. As Michael Neill notes:

> Given the amount of political, military, and intellectual energy it absorbed, and the moneys it consumed, Ireland can seem to constitute ... one of the great and unexplained lacunae in the drama of the period. (Neill, 1994: 11)

Likewise, Andrew Murphy speaks of 'a failure, or unwillingness, on the part of English dramatists to engage with one of the most urgent and important political crises of the close of the sixteenth century: the war in Ireland' (Murphy, 1996: 38). Murphy, like Andrew Hadfield, attributes this silence to censorship arising from ongoing conflict (Hadfield, 1997). Joel Altman cites one contemporary, George Fenner, writing on 30 June 1599, in the midst of the Earl of Essex's unsuccessful Irish expedition: 'it is forbidden, on pain of death, to write or speak of Irish affairs; what is brought by post is known only to the Council; but it is very sure that Tyrone's party has prevailed most' (Altman, 1991: 12). Altman observes that the patron of Shakespeare's company was Sir George Carey, 'whose signature appeared on most of the orders commanding the lords lieutenant to levy soldiers for Ireland' (ibid.: 15).

Alan Fletcher points to an early attempt to stage a Shakespeare play, *Much Ado About Nothing*, that was blocked by the censors. The play – presumably Shakespeare's, though Fletcher observes that it has slipped the notice of most Shakespeareans – was to be staged in Coleraine, County Londonderry, in the summer of 1628, but a song from it – or framing it – so offended the King's Commissioners that the planned performance was pulled. Fletcher speculates as to the possible cause of the play being pulled: '[It is] hard to see how any of the songs in *Much Ado* might have caused ... offence, unless it be Balthasar's song on the faithlessness of men (*Much Ado*, Act II, scene III). But if so, the commissioners must have been touchy indeed. Perhaps more likely they had been the butt of some lampoon' (Fletcher, 2000: 430, note 159). The song in *Much Ado About Nothing* that may have given offence runs:

> Men were deceivers ever,
> One foot in sea, and one on shore
> To one thing constant never...
>   (*Much Ado About Nothing*, 2.3.57–9)

The authorities were eager to suppress many other manifestations of verbal and visual art, including 'all persons calling themselves Schollars'. My own favourite entry, which I'd like to cite in full if I may, is an edict of the Irish parliament dated 1635:

> That all persons calling themselves Schollars, going about begging, all idle persons going about in any Countrey either begging, or using any subtile craft or unlaw-full games or playes, or faigning themselues to have knowledge in Phisiognomie Palmestry, or other like crafty Science, or pretending that they can tell Destinyes, Fortunes, or such other phantasticall imaginations, all persons that be, or utter themselves to be proctors, procurers, patent-gatherers, or Collectors for Gaoles, prisons, or Hospitalls; all Fencers, Beare-wards, Common players of Enter-ludes, & Minstrels wandring abroad, all Juglers, and wandring persons, and Common-labourers, ... all such as wandring, pretend themselves to be Egyptians, or wander in the habite, forme, or attire tire of counterfeit Egyptians, shall be taken, adjudged and deemed Rogues, Vagabonds, and sturdy beggars, and shall sustain such punish-ments, as are appointed by a Statute made in the three and thirtieth yeare of King Henry the eight, chap. 15. in this Kingdome, against Vagabonds, or be otherwise dealt withall, by sending them to the house of Correction in the County where they shall be found, as the Justices of the peace of the said County, or to any one, or more of them, shall be thought fit. (Edict of the Irish parliament, 26 January – 31 March, prorogued to 24 March 1635; cited Fletcher, 2001: 194)

From this it would appear that the English government in Ireland regarded scholars with the same haughty disdain with which they viewed the odif-erous *braigetóir*. Farting is their forte. We have come a long way since then, of course, and there's a wind of change blowing through academe, but perhaps we still have far to go in our understanding and analysis of the role of the arts.

Shakespeare the Irishman

As an Irish Catholic and a republican, William Shakespeare is understandably of interest to Irish writers. What? Is it something I said? (Or did somebody drop one?) Shakespeare is an Irish Catholic Republican if we are to believe Andrew Hadfield, Richard Wilson, and Flannery O'Connor's mother. Not a great deal has been written about Mary Flannery O'Connor's Irishness, though much has been said of her Catholicism, but in an undated letter written in the summer of 1953, Flannery remarks:

> My mamma asked me the other day if I knew Shakespeare was an Irishman. I said no I didn't. She said well it's right there in the Savannah paper; and sure enough some gent from the University of Chicago had made a speech somewhere saying Shakespeare was an Irishman. I said well it's just him that says it, you better not go around saying it and she said listen SHE didn't care whether he was an Irishman or a Chinaman. (O'Connor, 1979: 59)

But an earlier generation of Irish Americans did care, at least James O'Neill, Shakespearean actor and father of Eugene O'Neill did care, as he reportedly became convinced that Shakespeare could not be English but must be Irish. On the other hand, for Frank McGuinness, Shakespeare is neither English nor Irish in any simple sense:

> There is so little to go on when you try to decipher the life of William Shakespeare. But we can say with some certainty that he was not an Irishman. Mind you, I don't know for sure if he was an Englishman either. (Burnett and Wray, 1997: xi)

Shakespeare's national identity is made complex by the fact that he wrote half his plays in Elizabethan England and the rest in Jacobean Britain,

presided over and patronised by a Scottish King. A tempestuous relationship was becalmed by a marriage of convenience. The first fruit of
Anglo-Scottish collaboration was the Ulster Plantation, part of an ongoing process of Anglicization and re-conquest in the south, which brings
me to the first of my Irish writers responding in the 1990s to Shakespeare
(and Spenser).

Robert Welch, *The Kilcolman Notebook* (1994)

Fast forward four hundred years to 1994, and Brandon Publishers of
Dingle, Co. Kerry, publish a novella by Robert Welch, Professor of English
at the University of Ulster, entitled *The Kilcolman Notebook*. The dust-
jacket blurb distils the plot: 'While bringing the manuscript of *The Faerie
Queene* from Kilcolman to London the poet dreams about the relationship between Ireland and Britain, dreams in striking images of a strange
complicity, a mutual exchange between the aggressor and the victim'. The
reader quickly discovers that some of these dreams are far from dry, and
that the notebook should come in a plain brown wrapper. Bob Welch?
Irvine Welsh, more like. There's an intriguing ménage-à-trois with Raleigh,
Spenser and Queen Elizabeth, and there's also some rumpy-pumpy with
Shakespeare. After witnessing 'Raleigh riding the fifty-year old mistress
of the house upon the dining table, dog style' (Welch, 1994: 23), Spenser
sees Shakespeare walking towards him, 'a long phallus in his hand, multi-
colored like a barber's pole, with ribbons of blue and green and red flowing
out of the carved glans at the tip ... I did not like the name Shakespeare'
(ibid.: 24–5). Spenser clearly has poet's envy, as he reflects on Shakespeare's
standing: 'He is London. I am Ireland. No other way. Each by absence
giving the other presence, but he having the best of it' (ibid.: 69).

Frank McGuinness, *Mutabilitie* (1997)

Another encounter between Shakespeare and Spenser – William and
Edmund – is envisaged in Frank McGuinness's *Mutabilitie*, staged in 1997.
The Tempest has become the 'Irish play' since Paul Brown invited us to
'note a general analogy between text and context; specifically, between
Ireland and Prospero's island' (Brown, 1985: 57). Frank McGuinness man-
ages to marry the plot of *The Tempest* with *A View of the Present State
of Ireland*, and though there's none of the scurrility of Irvine – I mean,
Bob – Welch's shenanigans, there is the sense of Shakespeare as a dis-
senting Englishman, Catholic and queer, made homeless by his nation's
breach with Rome. At one point, William says to Edmund enviously:
'I'd like to leave the theatre and get a job in the civil service', to which
Edmund replies, 'When I was last in London, I understood the theatre
was now the civil service'. 'Times have changed', says William, 'The fashion is now subversive' (McGuinness, 1997: 50). And *Mutabilitie* seems
subversive. It offers us a Shakespeare who is a wannabe Irish bard. The
File, an Irish poet, in a passage reminiscent of Stephen Greenblatt's essay,
'Shakespeare and the exorcists' (Greenblatt, 1985), invoking the stage as
a site for séances, asks William: 'Are you not a priest in this new religion
that may attach itself most secretly, most devoutly to the old abandoned
faith? ... You are a Catholic in honest service to a Protestant nation that
shall keep the true faith through your fire, your theatre. It is a holy place
of great, good magic' (McGuinness, 1997: 57). Shakespeare is, like Joyce, a
priest of the imagination, but just in case we get carried away, Richard, an
English captive, chimes in with: 'We'd sell our arses for a plate of bacon'
(McGuinness, 1997: 57). We are back once more with the vendible and
voluble posterity of Ireland.

Marina Carr, *Portia Coughlan* (1996; 1998)

Ghosts, gutsy humour and subversion are the stuff of Marina Carr's *Portia Coughlan*. In an interview, Carr comments: 'The character of Portia Coughlan just came to me. It was the name that came to me, that's all I had, and I thought it would be lovely to write a play about a woman called Portia Coughlan'. Her interviewer, Mike Murphy, asks: '*Is this the influence of your teacher from years gone by and the* Merchant of Venice?' Carr replies:

> I think it is, and of the Belmont River. You know the famous passage in *The Merchant of Venice?* 'In Belmont is a lady richly left, / And she is fair, and, fairer than that word,/ Of wondrous virtues: sometimes from her eyes / I did receive fair speechless messages: / Her name is Portia; nothing undervalu'd / To Cato's daughter, Brutus's Portia: / Nor is the wide world ignorant of her worth, / For the four winds blow in from every coast / Renowned suitors ...'

'In a sense', says Carr, '*Portia Coughlan* is based on that speech because I've always loved it. She lives by the Belmont River. She has suitors. She has everything a woman could desire' (Ní Anluain 2000: 51).

In the play itself, Portia is married but mourning the death of her brother, Gabriel, with whom she seems to have had an incestuous relationship. One of Portia's suitors is Fintan Goolan, frisky and philistine barman of the High Chaparral. One exchange by the Belmont River captures the tensions around myth and misogyny, female fantasy and male desire:

PORTIA: Ever hear tell of how the Belmont River came to be called the Belmont River?

FINTAN: Heard tell alright. Miss Sullivan used to tell us in school. Fuckin' hated English and all that auld poetic shite she used drum into us – wasn't it about some auld river God be the name of Bel and a mad hoor of a witch as was doin' all sorts of evil round here but they fuckin' put her in her place, by Jaysus they did.

PORTIA: She wasn't a mad hoor of a witch! And she wasn't evil! Just different, is all, and the people round here impaled her on a stake and left her to die. And Bel heard her cries and came down the Belmont Valley and taken her away from here and the river was born. And they say Bel taken more than the girl when he swept through the valley. I don't know enough about that, but I think they do say right for this place must surely be the dungeon of the fallen world.

FINTAN: The what?

PORTIA: Gabriel used hear the girl when the river was low; said she sounded like a aria from a cave.

FINTAN: Load of bollix, if ya ask me, them auld stories.

PORTIA: I'm not askin' you.

FINTAN: There's one story as interests me, Portia Coughlan, the story of you with your knickers off. Now that's a story I'd listen to for a while.

PORTIA: Ya fuckin' turnip head, ya! just get off me father's land, Fintan Goolan, because you're a fuckin' clodhopper, just like your people before you and like those you'll spawn after you in a wet ditch on a wet night in a drunken stupor!

FINTAN: You've a lug on ya, Portia Coughlan, that'd turn back a funeral! And you've a tongue on ya that, if I owned ya, I'd mow the big-shot, stuck-up bejaysus out of.

PORTIA: I'm not afraid of ya, so don't waste your time threatenin' me – Think I'll wade home be the river – 'Night.
            And exit Portia.

FINTAN: Fuckin' mickey-dodger!
            And storms off.
            (Carr, 1998b: 35–6)

Here Portia spurns her prospective Blazes Boylan because she likes that 'auld poetic shite' more than Fintan's mickey. Her language is a mixture of the florid and the lurid. She likes to delve under the surface, as she tells her mother:

> I read subtext, Mother, words dropped be accident, phrases covered over, sentences unfinished, and I know the topography of your mind as well as I know every inch and ditch and drain of Belmont Farm, so don't you bluster in here and put a death wish on my sons just because you couldn't save your own. My sons'll be fine for if I do nothin' else I leave them alone and no mark is better than a black one. (Carr, 1998b: 27)

Carr has quoted those lines about Belmont from *The Merchant of Venice* more than once, and she's described Shakespeare as 'the king himself',

without feeling the need to usurp him, though her observations on influence and appropriation are interesting: 'Apollo gave [Shakespeare] so
much that I think he grew jealous and decided never to do that again and
ever since has fed the rest of us on scraps ... And yet Shakespeare too paid
homage. He took from everywhere, but what he did with his plunder!'
(Carr, 1998a: 195–6). That mixture of admiration, acute awareness of an
overweening influence, and the resentment it can give rise to in some
cases, is reflected in the next play I want to look at.

Thomas Kilroy, *Tea and Sex and Shakespeare* (1976; 1998)

Thomas Kilroy's *Tea and Sex and Shakespeare* was first staged in 1976,
revived in 1988, and published by The Gallery Press in 1998. I knew Kilroy
only through his play about Hugh O'Neill, *The O'Neill*, first produced
in 1969, not published till twenty years later, which I think is every bit
as engaging as Brian Friel's much later work, *Making History* (1989), but
I only recently came across *Tea and Sex and Shakespeare*. It's a very lively
piece, more Brian Rix than Brian Friel, a sort of bedroom farce about
writer's block, impotence, and infidelity, anxiety of influence, and fear
of replacement or displacement. The main protagonist, Brien, a writer,
plays by turn Hamlet, Prospero and Othello. At one point, Brien tells the
spectral characters he has summoned to his side: 'You are all figments of
my imagination'. His landlady, Mrs O, who is as real as rain, says: 'The
poor little fella is off again'. Brien persists, 'Mere shapes and airy nothings'.
'Nonsense!', says one of the conjured up characters, 'If you prick us do we
not bleed? If you tickle us do we not laugh? Aha! Shakespeare'. Mrs O is
reassured: '(*Relieved aside*) 'Tis only that Shakespeare. Would you like
something hot, Mr Brien? Maybe the cuppa tea'. Brien is threatened by
this offer: 'Tea? Tea? No tea. Stay out of this, Mrs O. You're terrestrial.
Also, your nympho daughter Deirdre' (Kilroy, 1998: 17).

Since this is a play first produced during the Troubles there is a line running through it as to how helpful Shakespeare can be. Brien has his doubts:

BRIEN: Shakespeare's no help anymore. All those happy endings. Weddings, rediscovered daughters, moles on faces, also other bodily marks of identification, resurrections and sudden reconciliations, fresh-faced princes arriving on horseback. It's a load of manure, Deirdre [...] The daily horror cannot be evaded. No way, no sir. Things are as they are. Besides, Shakespeare's dead. Stratford. April 23rd, 1616. He left a will.

DEIRDRE: Oh, he's not dead! Why do you say such a thing. I'm – I'm going to emigrate.

BRIEN: Farewell content, farewell the tranquil mind.

DEIRDRE: Oh, you mean – thing, you –
           She rushes off down the stairs.

MRS O: It's only them exams, Mr Brien.

BRIEN: Terrible.
           (Kilroy, 1998: 36–7)

And 'them exams' crop up again, as Brien's existential angst and impotent rage extends to Deirdre, Mrs O's daughter, and her schooling. Deirdre shows Brien the exam paper and says: 'It's number three. "Discuss the character of Macbeth."' Brien replies: 'I wouldn't do that, Deirdre, if I were you.' His reading of the play is 'Never trust executive women'. Obsessed by impotence and sexual jealousy, Brien is analysed by one of his creations: 'If you've lost your biro, how can you hope to satisfy her sexually?' It's a hard one for Brien, and it gets harder when the analyst exits and the phone rings:

BRIEN: (*Very tentatively*) Hello? (*Stronger*) Hello? Who? Yes, it's me. Who's speaking, please? (*Pause*) William who? Ha-ha-ha. Go on! (*Pause*) What do you mean who's been fucking around with your plays? Me? (*Pause*) Listen, mate. It's the reverse. Yeah. It's your plays that have been fucking *me* around. Yeah. It's like a theatrical railway station round here. Specially *Othello*. (*Pained pause*) OK. All right. Right, William. Look, calm down. William. OK? OK. (*Pause*) Listen. All right. I promise. Listen. I just want to ask you something. Favour.

What I want to know is, well, how do I end it? You know? Final
curtain. (*Pause*) Throw in a what? A love scene? And then? A what!
A happy ending? (ibid.: 56)

Brien's wife Elmina comes home and asks 'How was your day?, and the
play ends happily enough, albeit with a raised eyebrow, but before the
curtain comes down Brien's case is summed up:

> SYLVESTER: (*Very doctorly*) A clear case of literary impotence. Aggravated by a
> neurosthenic dislike of tea-drinking and an obsessive running up and
> down Shakespearean passages. Symptoms: severely torn pages, also
> evidence of concealed still-born masterpieces as well as other aborted
> odds and ends. I'm afraid there's no known cure.

To which Brien responds: 'He's no doctor, that creep. He's an Italian
waiter. Name of Iago' (ibid.: 67).

Conclusion: Still Harping on Shakespeare

So what have we learned? In *The Kilcolman Notebook*, Shakespeare is the
great metropolitan spear-shaker and sabre-rattler who threatens Spenser's
other Englishness: pastoral, provincial, and planter. In *Mutabilitie*,
Shakespeare is the playwright of the Western World, who comes romanc-
ing and Romanizing into a desolate region riven by colonial and confes-
sional tensions, bringing with him the redemptive power of the stage. In
Portia Coughlan, Shakespeare is both pretext and subtext. Carr doesn't
appropriate Shakespeare. She crowns him then clowns around with him.
The relationship between *Portia Coughlan* and *The Merchant of Venice* is
nothing like that between *Mutabilitie* and *The Tempest* – or between her
own more recent play, *Ariel*, and *The Tempest*. There is also a character
called Ariel in Martin McDonagh's *Pillowman* (2003), and it's a name
that invokes the collaborative colonial figure in Shakespeare's play.

Who's afraid of William Shakespeare? Not the new Irish writers, any more than they are afraid of Joyce (and his happy endings!) Give me Portia Coughlan over Molly Bloom any day of the week. Sure, she does an Ophelia in the end, but she knows her Shakespeare, she loves poetry, and she won't be any man's plaything – to be foxed or – heaven forfend – forgiven. All her mickeys turn out to be Gabriels, or rather, all her Hamlets turn out to be Poloniuses, which is the story of every writer who aspires to Shakespeare. At best they become, like Prospero, a vicious slavemaster disguising their rule with bookish benevolence.

If, to borrow a phrase from the postcolonial paradigm, the three stages of native response to colonial text are adopt, adapt, and adept, then Carr is arguably on the third and final act. She does her own thing with Shakespeare, making of him a springboard rather than a swamp, and there's nothing arty farty about it. Thomas Kilroy takes us back to Joyce in a way, to the male artist struggling with a father figure – and all the misogyny implicit in that struggle. Kilroy gives us in Brien, the Irish writer wrestling with writer's block, a poor man's Prospero with a Caliban complex. Brien is surrounded by spirits and not quite in control of his material, paralyzed and regurgitating what he's learned by quote and rote. Faced with emigration or adaptation Brien tries to adapt, but ends up calling on Oscar Wilde to save him from the worst case of Shakespeareitis since Shaw. It's all cod and caper but it's – to me at least – every bit as valid as Joyce's more self-regarding encounter with Shakespeare. In 1900, at the birth of the Irish National Theatre, a young James Joyce decried 'the Shakespearean clique that dealt the deathblow to the already dying drama' (Joyce, 1959: 39). That Shakespearean clique is now a confident generation, not the Pope's children, fretting in the shadow of the English language, but Bottom's children, letting off fireworks in enclosed spaces, cursing like Caliban, musing like Macmorris.

Works Cited

Altman, J.B. (1991), '"Vile participation": the amplification of violence in
    the theatre of *Henry V*', *Shakespeare Quarterly*, 42, (1), pp. 1–32.
Beckett, S. (1979), *The Beckett Trilogy: Molloy, Malone Dies, The
    Unnamable*, Picador, London.
Brown, P. (1985), '"This thing of darkness I acknowledge mine": *The
    Tempest* and the discourse of colonialism', in Dollimore, J. and Sinfield,
    A. (eds), *Political Shakespeare: Essays in Cultural Materialism*,
    Manchester University Press, Manchester, pp. 48–71.
Burnett, M.T. and Wray, R. (eds) (1997), *Shakespeare and Ireland: History,
    Politics, Culture*, Macmillan, London.
Carr, M. (1998a), 'Dealing with the dead', *Irish University Review*, 28,
    (1), pp. 190–6.
——(1998b) *Portia Coughlan*, rev. ed., The Gallery Press, Loughcrew,
    Oldcastle, County Meath.
——(2002), *Ariel*, The Gallery Press, Loughcrew, Oldcastle, County
    Meath. 2002).
Fletcher, A. J. (2000), *Drama, Performance, and Polity in Pre-Cromwellian
    Ireland*, Cork University Press, Cork.
——(2001), *Drama and the Performing Arts in Pre-Cromwellian Ireland:
    A Repertory of Sources and Documents from the Earliest Times until
    c.1642*, D.S. Brewer, Cambridge.
Friel, B. (1989), *Making History*, Faber & Faber, London: Faber.
Greenblatt, S. (1980), 'To fashion a gentleman: Spenser and the destruc-
    tion of the Bower of Bliss', in *Renaissance Self-Fashioning: From More
    to Shakespeare*, Chicago University Press, Chicago, pp. 157–92.
——(1985), 'Shakespeare and the exorcists', in Parker, P. and Hartman,
    G. (eds), *Shakespeare and the Question of Theory*, Methuen, London,
    pp. 163–87.
Hadfield, A. (1997), '"Hitherto she ne're could fancy him": Shakespeare's
    "British" plays and the exclusion of Ireland', in Burnett, M. T. and
    Wray, R. (eds), *Shakespeare and Ireland: History, Politics, Culture*,
    Macmillan, London, pp. 47–67.

Highley, C. (1997). *Shakespeare, Spenser, and the Crisis in Ireland*, Cambridge University Press, Cambridge.

Joyce, J. (1959), 'Drama and Life', in Ellman, R. and Mason, E. (eds), *The Critical Writings of James Joyce*, Faber & Faber, London, pp. 38–46.

——(1998), *Ulysses*, ed. Jeri Johnson, Oxford University Press, Oxford.

Kilroy, T. (1995), *The O'Neill*, The Gallery Press, Loughcrew, Oldcastle, Co. Meath.

——(1998), *Tea and Sex and Shakespeare*, The Gallery Press, Loughcrew, Oldcastle, County Meath.

McGuinness, F. (1997), *Mutabilitie*, Faber & Faber, London,

Murphy, A. (1996), 'Shakespeare's Irish history', *Literature & History* 5, (1), pp. 38–59.

Neill, M. (1994), 'Broken English and broken Irish: nation, language, and the optic of power in Shakespeare's histories', *Shakespeare Quarterly* 45 (1), pp. 1–32.

Ní Anluain, C. (ed.) (2000), *Reading the Future: Twelve Writers from Ireland in Conversation with Mike Murphy*, The Lilliput Press, Dublin.

O'Connor, F. (1979), The habit of being : letters / Flannery O'Connor; ed. Sally Fitzgerald, Farrar, Straus, Giroux, New York.

Welch, R. (1994), *The Kilcolman Notebook*, Brandon Publishers, Dingle, Co. Kerry.

Wilson, R. (2004), *Secret Shakespeare: Studies in Theatre, Religion and Resistance*, Manchester University Press, Manchester.

Yeats, W.B. (1991) 'An Introduction for My Plays', in Harrington, J.P. (ed.), *Modern Irish Drama: a Norton Critical Edition*, W. W. Norton & Company, London, pp. 406–8.

Northern Irish Poetry in the Twenty-First Century

MATT MCGUIRE

Applying the phrase 'No Country for Old Men' to Northern Irish poetry is a highly suggestive critical enterprise. It presents a number of contexts in which to reconsider one of the most widely theorised corners of the Irish literary terrain. This essay focuses on the generational rather than gender implications of the phrase. This being said, female voices figure prominently in the discussion that follows. Their inclusion is indicative of the fundamental importance of women's writing to the poetic DNA of the contemporary North.

If we were to round up the usual suspects of Northern Irish poetry we might well find ourselves faced with a group of white haired old men. Born in the late 1930s and the early 1940s, Seamus Heaney is now sixty-nine, Michael Longley sixty-eight and Derek Mahon sixty-seven. 'No Country for Old Men' would imply that these are somehow figures of a bygone era – gold watches have been issued, bus passes collected. Fortunately for us, poetry is not your average workplace. Despite their vintage, all three men have continued to produce exciting new work well into the next millennium. Winning the T.S. Eliot Prize in 2006, *District and Circle* showed little sign that Seamus Heaney's star was in any way fading. In a literary climate where novelty and youth increasingly enthral, such seasoned 'pros' offer an important point of stability, a cold eye cast over the promises of our brave new world. 'No Country ...' also implies that these writers, whose careers coincided with rise of the Troubles, are somehow out of place and out of time within the recent reconfigurations of the North. As early as 1994 the critic Francie Cunningham asked: 'now that the ceasefire has been announced, what will happen to all the Northern Ireland writers? Where will they go for all their materials?' (Cunningham, 1994: 24). It is true that for much of the Troubles the

fortunes of Northern Irish poetry seemed to fluctuate in inverse pro-
portion to those of the state. So has the cessation of violence ironically
entailed a moment of crisis for Northern Irish poetry? With the guns
silenced has the well of inspiration finally run dry? It is these questions
that the following chapter will attempt to answer. Posting an obituary
notice for Northern Irish poetry would be, to say the least, somewhat
premature. Cunningham's questions, of course, offer a highly reductive
caricature of Northern Irish writing. They would wrongly suggest that
Northern Irish poetry is merely one long meditation on the nature of
political violence. This kind of misreading will also be addressed in the
discussion that follows.

　　If we cannot dismiss Heaney et al., neither can we ignore the generation game implied by 'No Country for Old Men'. It is worth recalling
that the much famed Belfast Group surfaced at a crucial moment in Irish
history, as civil society in the North dramatically imploded on itself. In
similar fashion, another group of writers has begun to emerge in the
wake of Good Friday Agreement (1997). This might also be regarded
as a period when the island's tectonic plates are once again in a process
of realignment. Born in the 1970s this group includes figures like Alan
Gillis, Nick Laird, Colette Bryce, Sinéad Morrissey and Leontia Flynn.
Together they offer a number of discrete vantage points from which to
view recent attempts to reset the co-ordinates of Irish history. Having
said this, Cunningham teaches us a lesson. There are other narratives,
beyond that of poetry and politics, that demand our attention. This
chapter explores the anxiety of influence, to use Harold Bloom's term,
between this new generation of poets and their much famed literary
forbearers. Instead of crisis, recent years have witnessed Northern Irish
poetry experience a significant renewal. Whilst the following discussion
focuses on aesthetic issues, there are important material aspects to this
story. Opened in 2004 at Queen's University Belfast, the Seamus Heaney
Centre for Poetry conferred a globally unprecedented level of financial
and institutional support for poetry. Employing five poets and a number
of established critics, this £3 million centre has functioned as an incubator
for the writing, performance and appreciation of poetry. With the genre
increasingly playing second fiddle to consumer demands for the novel,

such institutional recognition suggests that the bond between poetry and the North is only set to intensify. At the same time, the Seamus Heaney Centre for Poetry provides a useful metaphor for thinking about some of the crosscurrents in recent Northern Irish writing. Heaney himself might be thought of as both an enabling and disabling figure. No other living poet has enough of a reputation for funders to cough up £3 million for a poetry centre. At the same time, like Robert Burns in nineteenth-century Scotland, Heaney casts a large shadow over subsequent generations. His name is above the door in both a literal and metaphorical way. The various responses of contemporary writers' response to this kind of literary inheritance will be alluded to in the discussion below.

In his acceptance speech for the 1995 Nobel Prize Heaney recalled the wireless radio of his childhood, and being mesmerised by the strange voices emanating from far beyond the family's Derry farmstead. And it was not the BBC English from across the water, but voices from farther afield – Warsaw, Oslo, Stockholm (Heaney, 1997: 449). Technology as liberator: for in this expanded universe was born a poetry that would challenge the received wisdom of 'them and us', a self-conscious writing that looked to argue, first and foremost, with itself. Things have, of course, moved on; from the wireless to the television and onwards (and upwards?) with the digital revolution. The twenty-first century confronts us with a vast array of technologies. The world, it would seem, has both contracted and expanded with the velocity of a second big bang. Space is cyber. Reality virtual. Again the generation game is important. Few would argue that the 'Old Men' of Northern Irish poetry offer the most reliable guides to this rapidly transforming landscape. It is to a younger generation that we turn for insights into many aspects of contemporary experience, both the malaise of modernity and the onrush of the future.

Somebody, Somewhere (2004) is the debut collection by the Belfast poet Alan Gillis. Gillis's work is infused with the inevitable entropy of post-millennial culture. His poetry constitutes an imaginative space where Yeats, Rilke and Celtic myth fuse with Elvis, Guinness and Star Wars. Such imbrications are symptomatic of Gillis's interest in confronting stereotypes about high and low art. His work also seeks to examine the critical orthodoxies that have arisen in response to Irish literature.

The opening poem of the collection, 'The Ulster Way', is something of an artistic manifesto, a statement of intent for much of what follows (Gillis, 2004: 9). It opens:

> This is not about burns or hedges.
> There will be no gorse. You will not
> notice the ceaseless photosynthesis
> or the dead tree's thousand fingers,
> the trunk's inhumanity writhing with texture,
> as you will not be passing into farmland.

The Ulster Way is, literally, the 560 mile scenic walk that stretches along the border of the Northern Irish state. The poem invites us to question the ways in which political notions of place are part of the fabric of everyday culture. Borders have, of course, been central to the political and cultural discourse of the North. The critic Eamonn Hughes comments: 'Northern Ireland as a whole is not so much enclosed by its borders as defined by them: it is a border country.' (Hughes, 1991: 3) At a technical level Gillis's poem is equally resonant. It begins as a poem of recalcitrance and rejection. The repetition of 'not' and 'no' is highly rhetorical, a mixture of pulpit sermon and soap box rant. These words imbue the first verse with a sense of gathering momentum, as if a crowd is being whipped up. The single syllables of the opening lines drive home their message. There is one Northern Irish figure that was the master of such rabble rousing: Ian Paisley. No voice is more iconic or notorious within the history of the North. The image is burned on national psyche: Paisley apocalyptically thundering: 'ULSTER SAYS NO!' The trunks 'writhing' inhumanity is surely the leftovers of a Paisleyite sermon on the sexual debauchery of our times. Perhaps this is the real Ulster Way? To define oneself by what one is against. Or, like Paisley himself, is the Ulster Way to fuse religion and politics to a point where the two can no longer be separated. In mimicking this voice the poem deliberately undermines such Paisleyite politics. Gillis employs a strategy familiar within Northern Irish poetry. He appropriates the language of politics and, by submitting it to the rigours of poetic form, turns it back on itself. We are reminded of Heaney's longing to open up and contest the ideological certainties of the North:

'whatever is given / Can always be reimagined, however four-square, / Plank-thick, hull stupid and out of its time / It happens to be' (quoted in Hughes, 1991: 24).

If there *is* an affiliation with Heaney, we might also sense the need to escape the shadow of such a large literary forbearer. 'The Ulster Way' rejects the kind of natural landscape that Heaney enshrined as *the* imaginative space of Northern Irish poetry. Gillis attempts to forge a distance between his own work and this tradition of rustic mediation. The bold declarative rhythm of the opening lines is broken by the 'ceaseless photosynthesis' that the poem ironically tells us we will not notice. The five syllabled 'photosynthesis' slows us down, focusing our attention. The repetition of 's' sounds momentarily enact the cyclical process the image describes. In the very process of dismissal, Gillis demonstrates his own ability to use both nature and sound as sources of sublime metaphor. He is, of course, not alone in castigating this predilection for scenic diversion within Northern Irish art. In a famous scene from *Eureka Street* (1996) Robert McLiam Wilson parodies this image of the rustic bard of the North. Shaughe Ghinthoss (a pun on 'shag and toss') is described as 'a vaguely anti-English Catholic from Tyrone': 'He read about hedges, the lanes and the bogs. He covered rural topography in detail. It felt like a geography field trip' (McLiam Wilson, 1996: 176). This turning away from the land is, of course, part of a wider narrative of change within twentieth-century Irish society. By the year 2000 less that 3% of the country's GDP would be generated by farming.[1] In the Northern Irish context, however, this antinomy to the rural landscape signals a deeper dissatisfaction. For years images of land have been used to imbue the ideologies of nationalism and unionism with a sense of organic inevitability. The critic Aaron Kelly terms this the 'rusticative imperative' within the predominant modes of theorising the North (in Gillis and Kelly, 2005: 84). Images of a green and pleasant land figure prominently within nationalist iconography. Similarly, during the annual 12 July marches,

---

1   Source: Irish Agriculture and Food Development Authority. http://www.teagasc. ie/agrifood/index.htm (accessed: 2/06/08).

Orange parades leave Belfast to congregate in 'the Field' on the outskirts
of the city. Both Republicanism and Unionism deploy such symbolism in
attempts to confer a sense of historical legitimacy upon their respective
political claims. In dismissing the naturalistic tendencies of Northern
Irish poetry, Gillis asks us to recognize the elliptical nature of imaginative spaces. If the Ulster Way invokes a path, a 'way' of travelling, it also
suggests a 'way' of seeing. It is the familiar perspectives, the received narratives of the North that Gillis is interested in deconstructing. The poem
demands we revisit and rethink accepted mythologies; that we begin over,
unencumbered by the weight of a familiar, yet exhausted, rhetoric – 'All
this is in your head. If you walk / don't walk away [...] There are other
paths to follow. / Everything is about you. Now listen' (Gillis, 2004: 9).
In a final reckoning perhaps this is the real Ulster Way – challenging, con-
testing and contending; activities that seem increasingly worthwhile in an
evolving Northern Ireland. *Somebody, Somewhere* can be read as a series
of answers to the questions posed by 'The Ulster Way'. It takes Northern
Irish poetry into a *terra incognita*. Its locus is an urban, technologised
landscape. Its presiding theme, the decommissioning of experience that
pervades twenty-first-century life.

   If the incantatory rejections of 'The Ulster Way' invoke the work of
Heaney, they also contain echoes of another Northern Irish poet, Louis
MacNeice. MacNeice's poem 'Wolves' also foregrounds the failings of
poetry. It begins: 'I do not want to be reflective any more / Envying and
despising unreflective things' (MacNeice, 2005: 17). MacNeice attempts
to distance itself from the mediated nature of poetic utterance. It is active
resolution rather than passive meditation that he favours:

> The tide comes in and goes out again, I do not want
> To be always stressing either its flux or its permanence,
> I do not want to be a tragic or philosophic chorus
> But to keep my eye only on the near future
> And after that let the sea flow over us.

Gillis's own doctoral thesis focused on Irish poetry of the 1930s and
included detailed readings of several MacNeice poems. As a literary
precursor to a new Northern Ireland, MacNeice is a highly compelling

figure. Whereas Heaney often aligns himself with the politics of nationalism ('my passport's green'), MacNeice cuts across a number of the more
established ways of thinking about Irish literature. He poetry sought to
demythologise the very concept of the nation: 'Ireland is hooey, Ireland is
a gallery of fake tapestries' (MacNeice, 2005: 52). Moreover, his own place
within Irish literary history is also constructively problematic. Writing
from the 1930s to the 1950s MacNeice interrupts certain post-colonial
paradigms of Irish culture. Such analysis, made famous by Field Day,
reads Irish poetry as intimately bound up with questions of nationalism
and as such enters a hiatus between 1922 and 1969. MacNeice remains
outside any such convenient cultural narratives. Gillis writes: 'neglected
by English literature in the shadow of W. H. Auden and seemingly failing
the litmus text of Irishness for the national canon, [MacNeice] proffers a
telling antinomy in the conventional problematics of Irish literary criticism' (in Gilles and Kelly, 2001: xvii). He represents a fault line, existing
in the cracks of both English and Irish literary history. For Edna Longley
it is MacNeice's resistance to established critical paradigms that make him
such a meaningful figure in the context of post-Agreement politics.[2]

The MacNeicean influence on Gillis's work is apparent in a poem
like 'Progress'. Here it is questions of time that preoccupy Gillis's poetic
imagination. How do we relate to the past? How might we begin to journey into the future? In a Northern Irish context, of course, such questions
are highly pertinent. In his early poem 'Mayfly' MacNeice writes:

> Let us make our time elastic and
> Inconsequently dance above the dazzling wave. (MacNeice, 2005: 5)

'Progress' takes a similar view of time; not as a fixed or constant force,
but as something pliable and open to manipulation. Through stopping
time and running it backwards Gillis explores what it might mean for
Northern Ireland to be awaken from the nightmare of history.

---

2   Edna Longley, 'Going with MacNeice's Flow', http://www.qub.ac.uk/schools/
     SeamusHeaneyCentreforPoetry/LMN/GoingwithMacNeicesFlow/ (accessed
     2/06/08).

They say that for years Belfast was backwards
And it's great now to see some progress.
So I guess we can look forward to taking boxes
from the earth. I guess that ambulances
will leave the dying back amidst the rubble
to be explosively healed. Given time,
one hundred thousand particles of glass
will create impossible patterns in the air
before coalescing into the clarity
of a window. Through which, a reassembled head
will look out and admire the shy young man
taking his bomb from the building and driving home. (Gillis, 2004: 5)

'Progress' takes on the meaningless rhetoric, the lazy thinking that has accompanied much theorising of the North in the post Agreement era. The poem reconfigures notions of 'them and us'. It avoids the exhausted logic of sectarianism and instead draws its divide between those that lived through the conflict and those that didn't. The opening couplet sets up the outsiders' view, 'They say', and their casual use of abstract ideas like 'backward' and 'progress'. This is the language of the professional historian. It is dispassionate and authoritative. The remainder of the poem sets out to undercut such convenient and cosy rhetoric. It achieves this through the insider's perspective, indicated by the colloquial 'So I guess' at the start of the third line. The insider wrests control of time from the authority of the outsider and puts it to work to undermine such glib notions of progress. The imaginary reversal of time takes the form of a montage. The successive images, through their fantastic impossibility, make clear the ridiculous nature of trying to undo the past. On the ground the big ideas of history are difficult to ascertain. The poem presents progress in a highly oblique fashion. What has gone before can never be undone. MacNeice's comments on the 1930s might also be applied to the integrity of Gillis's vision: 'This is an impure age, so it follows that much of its poetry, if it is honest – and poetry must be honest even before it is beautiful – must be impure' (quoted in Muldoon, 2007: 17).

Another young poet who acknowledges the influence of MacNeice on his work is Nick Laird. Born in Tyrone in 1975 Laird attended the

University of Cambridge where he wrote his first year thesis on the Northern Irish poet. Laird's own poetry resonates with the MacNeicean desire to challenge received narratives and openly critique the place of his birth. The intolerance of intolerance suggests a point of connection between both poets. The title of Laird's debut collection, *To a Fault* (2005), plays on the classic form of the ode, as in Ode to a Fault. It is the cracks in the narrative, the 'fault' lines within our personal and political experience of the world that Laird is particularly interested in. Laird's poem 'Remaindermen' examines the psychological hangover of the Troubles. It examines those who would stay behind and stay comfortable in the familiarity of old hatreds.

> There are others who know what it is
> to lose, to hold ideas of north
> so singularly brutal that the world
> might be ice-bound for good.
>
> Someone has almost transcribed
> the last fifty years of our speech,
> and has not once had the chance
> to employ the word *sorry*
>
> or press the shift to make the mark
> that indicates the putting of a question. (Laird, 2005: 9)

Reacting against this type of entrenchment is one source of the readiness with which Laird embraces notions of fluidity and flux. Imprisoned in the deep freeze of history, Laird's 'Remaindermen' echoes Yeats and 'Easter 1916' with its hearts enchanted to a stone. Agreements have been signed, history has moved on, but for some reconciliation reeks of surrender. From his hospital bed a recently knee-capped victim looks out a window as two cranes slowly turn over Belfast. As the rebuilding of the city begins the cranes offer a silent benediction on the lives of those below.

Looking over what has been discussed so far one might be mistaken for thinking that these poets are content to wallow in the past, hugging their little destiny. This is decidedly not the case. If their poetry takes on the issue of Northern Irish history, it might equally be characterised by a desire to distance itself from this subject altogether. The clichéd image of the Troubles poet, extracting the lyrical moment from the unfolding chaos, is something this new generation has also had to negotiate. In doing so their work examines twenty-first-century experience in a variety of forms. In Gillis's poems Bob the Builder is a dickhead, Czech waitresses are checked out, and childhood is revisited – 'when lying on our bellies was brilliant'. (Gillis, 2004: 10, 55, 60) One of the most playful of these poems features in Gillis's second collection, *Hawks and Doves* (2007), and is entitled 'The Lad'. The poem contains a remarkable 123 ways for a male to describe his penis.

> my hazel wand, my straw-haired vagabond,
> my Pirate of Penzance, my lilac love lance,
> my ramrod, my wad, my schlong, my tube, my tonk,
> my Jimmy, my Johnny, my tarse, my verge my honk,
> my bishop, my pawn, my rook, my king, my knight,
> my Gonzo, my Kermie, my Bert, my Ernie, (Gillis, 2007: 41)

Gillis takes the most clichéd of stand-up gags, the knob joke, and subjects it to the rigours of poetic form. The search for rhythm and rhyme generates a barrage of metaphors. There is a sense in which this too could be read by way of the MacNeicean idea of 'the drunkenness of things being various' (MacNeice, 2005: 18). There is another influence at work here, namely the American poet Wallace Stevens. The poem 'Thirteen Ways of Looking at a Blackbird' in particular springs to mind. In the act of revisiting Stevens's multiple perspectives Gillis is ludic, irreverent, tongue in check. Furthermore, he shows that poetic influence and the choice of subject matter can never be limited to matters of geographical proximity.

'The Lad' places male sexuality centre stage, albeit in a highly contrived and ironic fashion. In contrast, recent Northern Irish poetry might be defined by the confidence with which female poets have begun to take their share of the limelight. Derry-born Colette Bryce is one such case in point. The title poem from her second collection, *The Full Indian Rope Trick* (2004), is about escaping the claustrophobia of small town life. In Derry's Guildhall Square amidst a crowd of shoppers a miraculous vanishing act becomes a metaphor for poet's own departure from the city of her birth.

> There were walls, bells, passers-by;
> then a rope, thrown, caught by the sky
> and me, young, up and away,
> goodbye.
>
> Goodbye, goodbye.
> Thin air. First try.
> A crown hushed, squinting eyes
> at a full sun. There
> on the stones
> the slack weight of a rope
>
> coiled in a crate, a braid
> eighteen summers long,
> and me –
> I'm long gone,
> my one-off trick
> unique, unequalled since. (Bryce, 2004: 3)

'Up and away' is of course a pastiche of Superman, its appropriation giving the poet's own disappearance a sense of other worldly heroism. Leaving is not an act of betrayal as Bryce casts herself as one of the good guys. The music in 'Goodbye, goodbye. / Thin air. First try' suggests that the poet's own facility for language is the magic spell that makes this vanishing act possible. In the creative opportunities of poetry lie an escape, both literally and imaginatively, from the conservative expectations of the outside world. If such narratives of escape were particularly relevant in the context of the Troubles, in the twenty-first century they speak to a much more general experience of place. Global capitalism and the free flow of labour has seen many people take up residence far from home. Bryce argues that such dislocations are not an automatic cue for mourning. Home is an oblique idea; a place left behind and yet continually longed for.

The global perambulations of modern life also inform the work of Sinéad Morrissey. Born in Portadown in 1972, Morrissey lived in Japan and New Zealand before eventually returning to Belfast. A kaleidoscopic experience of culture underpins her poetry. Poems like 'Goldfish' playfully inhabit the terrain of Zen riddle, the voice of the poem 'coming to rest in the place where closing eyes is to see' (Morrissey, 2002: 41). Morrissey's own sense of belonging is similarly characterised by contradiction and the experience of being away. In the poem 'In Belfast' she can only manage a conditional acceptance of place: 'I am / as much at home here as I will ever be' (ibid.: 8). Place is held at arms length, and yet it is held nevertheless. Whilst Morrissey does explore the familiar terrain of Northern Irish poetry, the 'dent and fracture' of history, her work is equally as interested in broader questions. She examines and champions the peculiar insight provided by the poet: 'All see round childhood's corner. / Or through puberty's anger / Jealousy's pressure, sex's swagger, mercy's hunger' (ibid.: 17). In '& Forgive us Our Trespasses' she approaches that most familiar of poetic subjects, love. Taking its title from the 'Our Father' the poem asks for forgiveness for human sins:

> Of which the first is love. The sad, unrepeatable fact
> that the loves we shouldn't foster burrow faster and linger longer
> than sanctioned kinds can. Loves that thrive on absence, on lack
> of return, or worse, on harm, are unkillable, Father.
> They do not die in us. And you know how we've tried.
> Loves nursed, inexplicably, on thoughts of sex,
> a return to touched places, a backwards glance, a sigh –
> they come back like the tide. (Morrissey, 2002: 21)

Morrissey carefully recalibrates our expectations of love. The origins of her poem, as a rewritten prayer, invokes one of the most iconic (and clichéd?) idealisations of love, Corinthians 1:13: 'Love is always patient. Love is always kind. Love is never envious or arrogant with pride ... '[3] If Morrissey is at pains to put religion in the dock, her target is also poetry itself. Her ironic use of the sonnet, that most paradigmatic form of love poem, contains an implicit accusation. Poetry is charged with perjury.

---

3   1 Corinthians 13. http://www.biblegateway.com/passage/?search=1+Corinthian
     s+13 (accessed 2/06/08).

It only offers false testimony regarding the true nature of love. In contrast to the exaggerations of traditional poetry, for Morrissey love is Jungian *anima*, undirected and uncontrollable. Again the music of the poem contributes to its effect. As 'the loves we shouldn't foster burrow faster and linger longer', the assonance of 'er' sounds enact the recurring nature of these runaway emotions. Burrowing also anticipates Morrissey's use of the ocean as metaphor for our subconscious desires. In casting its critical gaze on poetry itself '& Forgive Us Our Trespasses' can be seen to resonate with both Gillis and MacNeice. Again, MacNeice's preference for honesty over beauty is particularly apposite.

Contemporary Northern Irish poetry enjoys an oblique yet playful relationship with notions of poetic tradition. A poem from Leontia Flynn's debut collection, *These Days* (2004), helps illustrate this concluding point. 'When I was Sixteen I met Seamus Heaney' offers an irreverent take on the Bloomian anxieties over influence.

> When I was sixteen I met Seamus Heaney
> outside a gallery in Dublin. I was with a friend
> who knew her way round better than I did.
> She was carrying Flann O'Brien's *The Poor Mouth*.
>
> As I have it Heaney winked when he signed her copy
> of *The Poor Mouth*. He said: That's a great book.
> I ground my teeth: she hadn't even *read* it.
> It was summer: UV-haze, bitumen fumes, etc.
>
> I had read *The Poor Mouth* – but who was Seamus
> 　　Heaney?
> I believe he signed my bus ticket, which I later lost. (Flynn, 2004: 19)

Flynn's poem borrows from a well known series of Irish literary anecdotes: the young Joyce turning up on Yeats's doorsteps, poems in hand; the youthful Beckett transcribing *Finnegans Wake* and hearing the famous knock at the door. Such stories illustrate the untidy and often haphazard nature of literary inheritance. In the poem Flynn refuses to genuflect at the altar of Irish literature, unaware that she is in the presence of high priest Heaney. Her friend on the other hand, despite her duplicity

(she hadn't even read the book), behaves with due deference. In a highly
clichéd image, the great Irish poet signs her copy of a great Irish novel. In
contrast Flynn is highly irreverent. She doesn't even recognise Heaney.
Moreover, all he can sign for her is her bus ticket, which she must have
lost anyway. The presence of *The Poor Mouth* is highly significant, imbu-
ing the poem with a certain satirical undertone. The leap from Flann to
Flynn is, after all, merely a jump of a single letter. The poet openly teases
us regarding our love for cosy notions of literary inheritance. Did Heaney
pass on to her the torch of poetic inspiration? No. At best he passed her a
signed bus ticket, which she would in fact only lose. Ironically, of course,
this kind of comic irreverence situates Flynn firmly within a long tradition of Irish literary iconoclasm. If there is story of continuity in recent
Northern Irish poetry then Flynn's poem, with its comic near miss, offers
a highly appropriate metaphor. After all, the journey from past to present
is more chaotic, messy and unpredictable than most of us are in the habit
of recognising.

Works Cited

Bryce, C. (2004), *The Full Indian Rope Trick*, Picador, London.
Cunningham, F. (1994), 'Writing in the Rag and Bone Shop of the
     Troubles', *The Sunday Business Post*, 11 Sept, p. 24.
Gillis, A. and Kelly, A. (eds) (2001), *Critical Ireland: New Essays on
     Literature and Culture*, Four Courts, Dublin.
Gillis, A. (2004), *Somebody, Somewhere*, The Gallery Press, Oldcastle,
     Co. Meath.
—— (2007), *Hawks and Doves* The Gallery Press, Oldcastle, Co.
     Meath.
Heaney, S. (1991), *Seeing Things*, Faber and Faber, London.
—— (1997), *Opened Ground: Poems 1966–1996*, Faber and Faber,
     London.

Hughes, H. (ed.), (1991), *Culture and Politics in Northern Ireland 1960–1990*, Open University Press, Milton Keynes.

Flynn, L. (2004), *These Days*, Jonathan Cape, London.

Kelly, A. (2005), *The Thriller and Northern Ireland Since 1969: Utterly Resigned Terror*, Ashgate, Hampshire.

Laird, N. (2005), *To a Fault*, Faber and Faber, London.

MacNeice, L. (2005), *Poems Selected by Michael Longley*, Faber and Faber, London.

McLiam Wilson, R. (1996), *Eureka Street*, Picador, London.

Morrissey, S. (2002), *Between Here and There*, Carcanet, Manchester.

Muldoon, P. (ed.), (2007), *Contemporary Irish Poetry*, 2nd edition, Faber and Faber, London.

Art and the Artist in Deirdre Madden's Fiction

BRITTA OLINDER

The visual world as perceived through the eyes of the writer is very important in Deirdre Madden's fiction. Not only landscapes, the differences
between them in different parts of Europe, and the varying apprecia-
tions of them by her characters, but also houses, inside and out, people's
looks and clothing, along with their visual assessment of each other, play
a prominent role in her novels. If this answers the wider definition of
the concept of *ut pictura poesis*, understood as the ability of the writer to
make her reader see the object as painted, what I am going to focus on
here is rather the narrower one of *ekphrasis* or Madden's translation of
paintings into words, with the extension of what she says about painters,
their aims and struggles to achieve them.

It is particularly in three of her novels that art is central, *Remembering
Light and Stone* (1992), *Nothing is Black* (1994) and *Authenticity* (2002).
The first of these is set mainly in Italy. The main character and first person
narrator, Aisling, had come south to escape violence and death which is
what she associates with the north. She settles in a hill village, appreciating the opportunities to go to Rome, to Siena and Florence to experience
painting and architecture as often as she can afford it. She also declares:
'I used to drive over to Assisi to see S.Chiara and the Basilica of S.
Francesco ... I was always struck by their beauty, and at every visit I got
something new from them' (Madden, 1992: 16). Art becomes a catalyst for
her reflections on life and the world, food for her spiritual development.
We may observe that it is mainly Medieval and early Renaissance art she
focuses on, but there are also reflections on contemporary painting.

Nothing is Black concerns Claire, a painter preparing for an exhibition, trying out new materials, new forms, and seeking to combine form
and feeling. She has agreed to have her cousin stay with her for a couple

of weeks in a remote part of the coast of Donegal that she has made her home. Occasionally she goes back in memory to Italy or other places on the continent.

In *Authenticity* the established painter Roderic and twenty-year younger Julia, who is taking her first steps as an artist, are trying out a close and warm relationship combined with freedom and independence. At an earlier stage Roderic lived and had a family in Italy, but compared with the many artistic treasures described in *Remembering Light and Stone* there is only one of that kind here. The description of the experience those many years ago of this altarpiece, suddenly flooded with light and warmed by his love for the expert on art restoration showing it to him, is quite stunning. Otherwise, however, as far as art is concerned the novel is more focused on the struggles of contemporary artists.

There are thus two sides to art: the maker and the viewer. The latter, at the receiving end, is represented in *Remembering Light and Stone* but only occasionally in the two other novels, where the artist's aims, efforts and problems come to the fore. This is actually indicated by their titles which could be said to represent the material and spirit of their art. 'Nothing is black' is the conclusion, after consideration of the qualities of other colours, of an epigraph from Frida Kahlo, while authenticity or artistic integrity is a key issue, particularly in the novel of that title, and at the same time something that spills over from art to life.

An important aspect in visual art is seeing as an activity *per se*, a sharpened consciousness, first on the artist's part as when Roderic is teaching his young daughter drawing: '...it's about how you see things. You need to learn how to look properly at what's before you, but really look, with a fresh eye and no preconceptions' (Madden, 2002: 314). But also for the viewer it is important – even if not very common – to really see the work of art and allow it to reach your imagination: 'You must respond to art with your nerves and your heart ... you should *feel* something. If not, then there's something amiss' (Madden, 1994: 60). Roderic clarifies this by referring to his different ways of seeing the Dublin Custom House in his childhood: as a print on the wall at home, a photograph that gave the wrong impression and the Custom House itself: 'Every time I saw it, it looked different, depending on the light and weather'

(Madden, 2002: 289). What is important is 'the idea of seeing things, and that what we take for reality isn't fixed, isn't static' (Madden, 2002: 290). Similarly Claire, the artist in *Nothing is Black,* takes her daily exercise in painting by making a quick watercolour of the landscape she sees from her studio. 'The view from the window never bored her. It was different every day, and she liked the act of concentration it required to look at it every morning and paint it as though she were seeing it for the first time ever' (Madden, 1994: 19).

The effect of something seen and, not least, of visual art might, thus, vary a great deal from time to time and from one spectator to another, 'while the paintings did not alter, the way in which they were viewed was now completely different' as Aisling explains before going on:

> One fresco in particular made me think of this. It showed two life-size figures, the man on the left was writhing, his mouth wide open and he was vomiting a large, black-winged devil. Before him stood a flat, blank-faced friar in a brown habit, his right hand raised. It was he who was casting out the devil from the man, to join the dark, spiky-winged swarm at the top-right-hand corner of the picture. This fresco had shocked me the first time I saw it, and even after having seen it so many times, it could still unsettle me. I used to be amazed at how often I would see people standing in front of it, laughing. I didn't laugh. I took evil seriously. (Madden, 1992: 25)

Looking around at other visitors on another occasion, this time in an art gallery Aisling observes her companion, 'rapt before the paintings', but also a couple, the woman looking puzzled and somewhat anxious and the man with a rather expressionless face. Trying to see with their eyes she wonders 'what on earth they saw in all these gilt Madonnas, stern saints and stiffly holy angels' (Madden, 1992: 131). Later she stands herself in front of a painted scene, showing 'The Washing of the Feet'. 'I looked deep into it, and I tried to see it as it was when it was made. I was trying now not to re-create in my mind the form of the original, but to see the meaning of it, to enter as fully as possible into its original spirit' (Madden, 1992: 135). She certainly makes an effort to reach the essence of it but realizes that she cannot make it since the theology and iconography is no longer relevant for her. All these magnificent old images seem to be 'painted on doors to the past that were shut and locked' (Madden, 1992: 136). She feels the weight of the past.

Really looking at art you enter other worlds. Even if Aisling in *Remembering Light and Stone* can argue rationally about the frescoes in the main church of what she calls 'her' village as nothing out of the ordinary, especially when compared to what Giotto, Cimabue or Lorenzetti had achieved, and she recognizes that her fondness for the paintings of the Maestro di S. Giorgio is actually based on familiarity, there is particularly one she likes 'of S. Giorgio himself as protector of the village, holding a thing like a covered platter with the lid half lifted, and under it you can see S. Giorgio [the village], completely recognizable with its walls and its church and the bell-tower. I like the crafty old faces of the velvet-hatted burgers kneeling at his feet' (Madden, 1992: 11). Those paintings in medieval churches also seem to come threateningly to life when 'the raw power of Christianity could speak to me from the anguished face of a painted angel' and she hears 'a tormented angel scream down through the centuries to me' (Madden, 1992: 9).

Here we can also consider Julia in *Authenticity* and her childhood interest in pictures, first on postcards and old calendars. She had a keen sense of details and was fascinated by a picture as a world that she felt drawn into. She wanted to be able 'to break its spell. Then she would be able to see into that lost world'. She imagined what might happen there when the figures come to life and start moving. Then her father gave her a book of colour reproductions of old masters and looking at the pictures she entered 'those other worlds' and found the things in the pictures 'realer than real things'. She even imagined the painter of a still life and 'how he would have stared at the things to get to their essence' and then translate that essence of things on to the canvas. She entered so completely into the world of the painter 'that she can feel how stiff his fingers are and his eyes strained' (Madden, 2002: 30) when he has finished. Her father did not understand this in her and asked her: 'What do you mean by real anyway?' (Madden, 2002: 31).

This childhood memory can be compared with a situation many years later with Roderic gazing at a postcard representation of a still life with all its minute details. Astounded he says: 'That was how they saw the world. And now we can't trust our own eyes, can't believe that what we see before us is what it is: a table, a bottle, a dish. Why is it, do you think, that people like still life paintings so much nowadays? Is it for the quality of attention that is in them?' (Madden, 2002: 140). The grown-up Julia does not think so. A still life, she says 'is full of repose. That, above all, is so hard to find in the world as it is now. That's what people respond to, that's what they seek' (140). In connection with still-life painting Claire in *Nothing is Black* points out the difference between words and pictures; the former lacking in subtlety, as when you write about apples, this does not tell you much about other things, whereas 'when you looked at a Cezanne painting of a bowl of fruit, it expressed knowledge of other things – mortality, tenderness, beauty – in a way that was only possible without words' (Madden, 1994: 60).

This leads to the issue of the function of art. Aisling and her friend Ted in *Remembering Light and Stone* discuss what is decorative or beautiful or even sublime. The definition of the last term is elusive but what they end up with is a sense of wholeness, something that is gone now in what Ted thinks of as our crazy modern age. He concludes that what people in different eras and cultures have in common, even if expressed in different ways, is love and death, fears and desires. This is further developed in *Nothing is Black* as Claire remembers an artist friend arguing:

> People in Europe now aren't interested in art because it has to do with death. It teaches you how to die, and people don't want to know about that. In that way art is religious. There was always, until this century, a distinction between things which were true art, connected with religion, and things which had a social function, which were decorative or for entertainment. Now we have only two divisions: money and entertainment. What matters is making money, and then you rest from that by being entertained with what people like to think of as art. (Madden, 1994: 8–9)

In *Authenticity*, referring to his experience of a *Sister Art*, his father's passionate love for music, Roderic speaks lyrically about 'this other thing, this sublime music, this ... this parallel, radiant world' and goes on to say that 'as well as this functional, bread-and-butter world in which we all must live, there was also this ... fabulous reality, I suppose you could call it, that is art' (Madden, 2002: 288).

So how long will art last? As to the physical material, Aisling in *Remembering Light and Stone* looks at the frescoes in the Sistine chapel thinking:

> No matter how magnificent they are, paintings are made of paint, wood, canvas, clay, and no matter how well they are preserved or restored decay is built into them. (Madden, 1992: 8)

> On the other hand, looking at the frescoes in 'her' Italian village she was struck, as always, by how immutable they were. There was San Giorgio himself, holding the village on its covered dish, as he had done now for over five hundred years, through so many wars and revolutions ... Huge social chages had taken place since the frescoes were painted, including changes in the religious sensibilities of people, so that while the paintings did not alter, the way in which they were viewed was now completely different. (Madden, 1992: 25)

With so much of the art described to be found in churches the relation between art and religion becomes a recurring motif. In *Authenticity* some characters talk first about 'the concept of religious art in a secular age, then of spirituality in art' (Madden, 2002: 241) and in another context we find the observation: 'Art had taken the place of revealed religion for so many people nowadays; loss of faith was taken for granted' (Madden, 2002: 115). In *Remembering Light and Stone* Aisling is mystified by her friend loving early religious art so much but then he declares explicitly: 'Religion interests me in terms of its relation to a given society, and of course above all in its connections with art' (Madden, 1992: 134). As to Claire in *Nothing is Black* she remembers her visit to the churches of Ravenna where she realized that her beliefs had changed; faith had withdrawn, just as the sea had abandoned the city. And yet it was in Ravenna that she had begun to appreciate for the first time the spiritual dimension of art. The arrogance of it, for Theodora and Justinian to have their portraits put up like that in a church, above the high altar beside representations of Christ and the saints. For all that, the images of the dead faces touched her more than she could understand. Is this the only possible immortality? Nothing more than this? The decadence of it, the richness of the gold, and the shimmering colours. The Imperial portraits were a strange combination of vulnerability and brute power. She remembered going outside afterwards into the curious lightness of the air, and how frail and lovely the world had looked. For days afterwards she could not stop thinking about the mosaics, was haunted by them, not wanting to believe how much of existence was embodied in those stern faces (Madden, 1994: 18).

Something that comes back in all three novels is the conviction that paintings must be seen in their intended, original context and that reproductions, however good cannot give a satisfactory idea of the artist's achievement. In *Remembering Light and Stone* it is discussed in connection with a visit to Siena to see Duccio's *Maestà*, not above the main altar in the cathedral, where it belonged but in the cathedral museum and even so some of its parts had gone to the States. We see Aisling trying to imagine it back again as a whole and trying to imagine 'the effect of candlelight on all that gold, and how the eyes of the angels would look' (Madden, 1992: 135). There are other aspects of seeing art in its context. In *Nothing is Black* Claire thinks of how absurd it is to use slides 'to teach art appreciation, not least because it gave the impression that all paintings were the same size. The sense of scale is lost' (Madden, 1994: 44). She also explains to her cousin leafing through a book about the mosaics of Ravenna why reproductions never can do full justice to paintings, especially so in the case of mosaics. It is a question of the colours not being accurate, of the effect of light and space, of the mosaics being integral parts of the architecture and she sums up: 'The scale, the light, the texture, even the atmosphere: it's all so different when you're actually there' (Madden, 1994: 17). This may remind us of Roderic's comments on the Custom House, discussed earlier in this piece.

The expectations people may have and how that affects their experience is yet another element in the appreciation of art. Claire's cousin remembers seeing the *Mona Lisa* in Paris and being sorely disappointed, feeling sure that she shares that disappointment with most people. Claire then tries to explain that the paintings you see in a gallery 'were never meant to be displayed or viewed in such a way' (Madden, 1994: 17). At the same time she recalls how disappointed she herself had been by the town itself on her first visit to Ravenna. The old historic cities like Ravenna, Corinth, Carthage, Rome 'could never adequately fulfil the expectations one had of them' (Madden, 1994: 17). But that disillusionment did not taint everything for her and she continues:

> Only when she went to the churches did she find what she had looked for, found more than she had expected. Nothing could have prepared her for the impact made by that strange combination of dimness and vibrant colour, the coolness of the buildings and the vivid, shimmering images they contained. The frieze of women on a gold field: she remembered the sense of motion conveyed by their pointing feet, each figure different, each an individual with her shawl and almond eyes. She remembered the looped curtains of the Emperor's Palace, the curved boats on a sea of tessellated glass ... (Madden, 1994: 18)

If vibrant colours, vivid shimmering images, motion and variation are the qualities emphasized here, we can look at the failings Aisling points out in the frescoes she claims to like in her village church, painted by

> our poor Maestro di S.Giogio': He does not use the space available to the full, his sense of perspective and composition leaves something to be desired and there is often something sentimental about his paintings. This forms the background to the artistic qualities appreciated in all three novels: skill or technical accomplish-ment; vision or ideas; energy, in adjectival form as strong, assertive. Further it is necessary to get to the essence of things, the 'essence of the subject. Of the material used. (Madden, 1994: 45)

Control of colours or a combination of freedom and control is important. In one case a painting is admired not only for 'the beauty and energy of it' but also for 'the tension ... between the rich pigment and the decisive intelligence of the form' (Madden, 2002: 261). The same picture is also described like this: 'The fields of green and blue paint complemented each other like voices singing in harmony, each depending on the other for its full resonance and power, the formal restraint serving only to accentuate a wild beauty that it barely contained' (Madden, 2002: 259).

This has brought us to contemporary art, seen in the three novels in different ways. Aisling of *Remembering Light and Stone* cannot under-stand why her friend 'had no time for modern or contemporary art' (Madden, 1992: 130). His view is that contemporary painting 'won't last. It's incoherent' (Madden, 1992: 131). She on her side 'could see how necessary the forms of twentieth-century art were, and how they had had to come into existence to express the way people thought now, how they lived, how they saw things: in short to express how the world was now' (Madden, 1992: 130). Claire in *Nothing is Black* seems to go on from there:

> You need new materials to express new realities, just as you need new forms. How to combine the material, the form and the consciousness, that was what it was about. That was why she knew better than to give serious attention to figurative watercolours of landscapes. She was interested in the idea of combining forms and materials which seemed inexorably opposed to each other. (Madden, 1994: 45)

We turn then to look at the works of the three most prominent modern painters in the novels, Claire in *Nothing is Black*, Roderic and Julia in *Authenticity*. Roderic's paintings are first seen through his brother's eyes. Dennis does not like or understand abstract art but gets quite attached to the pictures his brother offers him. When one of them is included in a retrospective exhibition, however, he feels pleased to discover that the painting 'created its own well of calm in the hubub of the room. Its cool, magisterial stillness astounded him' (Madden, 2002: 40). On a visit to Roderic's studio he finds that 'the startling energy of the paintings that surrounded him, strong rigorous works executed in pale colours, contrasted uneasily with the silent lassitude of the man who had made them' (Madden, 2002: 325). Later we hear that Roderic 'had spent most of his waking hours in a conscious and active struggle to translate the vision in his mind on to paper and canvas' (Madden, 2002: 342). When, therefore, a fellow patient in hospital shows him the result of his endeavours in his art class, he cannot help but feeling 'what a disaster it would have been for him had he ever allowed his art to have this function: to become self-expressive and to serve him rather than he serving his art'. Even if he had not been able to paint much in the period before getting to hospital and not at all while there 'he had at least been true to it [his art] until the end. He thought of his painting as though it were a flame, a fragile lit thing that he had guarded with his life, all his life' (Madden, 2002: 344). The relation between art and life is further explored: 'Although much of his inner life – his losses, grief and self-doubt – made its way into his work, it did so in such a manner as to be translated into something distanced and controlled, something formal and impersonal' (Madden, 2002: 344). The last painting by Roderic described in the novel 'used his familiar range of colours – grey and cream, pale blue and pink – in a series of interlocked rectangles that gave the effect of a *mise en abime*' (Madden, 2002: 366).

Claire is at an earlier stage in her career as an artist than Roderic. Every morning she paints her landscape but after a while changes over to draw a still life of an apple instead. Her real work, however, is something different, 'she wasn't happy with her work and wanted to push through on to a new level' (Madden, 1994: 46). Lying awake during the night she tries to focus her thoughts: 'Painting. Think of her work, yes, think of that. She was glad she was a painter, she'd rather be that than anything else, no matter that it brought her frequently, painfully, against her own limitations. Sometimes people said painting had come to the end of its natural life' (Madden, 1994: 59). For a while Claire tries something new, 'based on a series of anatomical drawings she had made years earlier' but then suddenly when she is out walking she realizes that the drawings 'were a blind alley' (Madden, 1994: 138) and changing back to painting again she hopes to be able to combine form and feeling. 'Now she painted bones and muscles as though they were not just beautiful abstractions, but also parts of a strong and vulnerable body' (Madden, 1994: 139).

Julia is the youngest of them. She is just out of art college, working in mixed media. In a group exhibition her contribution, 'Found Objects for a New Millennium' is a series of wooden boxes with one glass side through which all kinds of small things can be seen, evoking 'a mysterious, elegiac atmosphere, each [box] presenting a small, sealed, rather beautiful but utterly inaccessible world' (Madden, 2002: 98). After the exhibition she is trying out new developments, experimenting with scents, asking people what their associations are. Roderic sees her as working away at her own view of the world, 'determined to be absolutely true to your own vision' (Madden, 2002: 230).

What is striking is the absolute dedication of the artists. The first epigraph of *Authenticity* by Eugène Delacroix emphasizes this: 'The practice of an art demands a man's whole self. Self-dedication is a duty for those who are genuinely in love with their art'. This corresponds with what Claire remembers a dead artist friend once saying:

> what I love about [art] is just that: the energy of things. I like the paradox of it. Strength and frailty ... People confuse immortality with the indestructible, but it's not the same thing at all. Take, say, Vermeer's *Portrait of a Young Woman in a Turban*. What that painting means is beyond words, beyond time. And yet, in purely material terms, it's a layer of paint a couple of millimetres thick on a piece of canvas ... it's so much more that it's beyond comprehension, it's almost eerie. That's the magic of it, the only magic I could ever believe in. To take things and make something charged with that sort of knowledge and energy. It's worth devoting your life to that. (Madden, 1994: 139–40)

There is a long history of writers commenting on painting or turning visual images inte words. This essay – in the meaning of attempt – tries to map the landscapes of the visual arts in three of Deirdre Madden's novels. There is more material there to be studied and room to go more deeply into it. I have not defined more precisely her relation to the tradition of *ekphrasis* or *ut pitura poesis*, nor has there been space enough to consider more closely how the *Sister Arts*, in this case literature and painting are made to cooperate in the search for an interpretation of the existence of humanity as a whole or the meaning of life for the individual. What I hope has emerged is that the celebration of spirit and art in Yeats's 'Sailing to Byzantium' is taking place in these three novels as well, which indeed include word pictures of the glories of Byzantine mosaics.

Works Cited

Madden, Deirdre (2002), *Authenticity*, Faber and Faber, London.
—— (1994), *Nothing is Black*, Faber and Faber, London.
—— (1992), *Remembering Light and Stone*, Faber and Faber, London.

Interview with Glenn Patterson

CAROLINE MAGENNIS

CAROLINE MAGENNIS: Within your fiction and your journalistic writing collected in *Lapsed Protestant* you represent non-traditional Northern Irish men. Do you feel this resistance is represented in the aesthetic presentation of both yourself and the characters you portray?

GLENN PATTERSON: I suppose it goes across all cultures, that messing around with the boundaries of sexuality, particularly in one's teens. I don't know if it's coded into you, the idea of provocation. I was a very nervous teenager; I think there was always that tension between standing out and wanting to separate yourself from the caste. There was a particular danger of being outside the group in Northern Ireland in Belfast in the 1970s. It was a very real danger for many people that if you didn't fit in there was the prospect that you would fit in very badly. I wouldn't like to speculate on how many people fell foul of paramilitaries over the years for no other reason that they looked funny. And yet despite the anxiety that need to stand out, to forge an individual identity is strong. So, you start to do things, you tie your tie a different way, you wear your trousers tighter, you do things that signal you are an individual. At a certain point I became more interested in not belonging than belonging, or at least choosing who I aligned myself with people. The Glenda incident[1] was an interesting time for me because I had spent most of my late teens trying to distinguish myself from the people in had grown up with, the place I had grown up in. I didn't want to belong to that, I had to try and make myself different, not to be mistaken for *them*. But, all of that was done with the expectation I was moving away. Then suddenly in the early

---

1   *Lapsed Protestant*, 30.

'90s I found myself here again and that was troubling, having become
this person thinking differently and making pronouncements, writing
fiction that, in my own head at least, said something critical, if not about
the individuals, then about the fixed formulas.

CM: In Northern Ireland these performances have particular resonances.
In *Lapsed Protestant* you can trace your own ideological development
from your aesthetic presentation; from Orange Order sash to football
shirt to make-up and tight trousers.

GP: I often joke about how superficial I am, but I do actually think that all
these things are very important, that they are signals, that you do project
something when you put something on. Not everyone does it consciously,
but you dress in a particular way, you say something about your society,
large or small. Now, I wasn't a first wave punk and to see drainpipes was
shocking. Everyone wore flares, the bigger the better. I remember people
being chased for wearing tight trousers and their hair being short. I was
fascinated, confused by punk, London punk; when I saw people with
swastikas, I didn't know what was going on with it, I took these things
literally, I was just confused, scared by it. But there was also a degree of fascinated horror, so that when the Manchester bands came along, it wasn't
spiky hair, bands like The Buzzcocks, there was some other DIY thing
going on, and I could fit in with that a little bit better, I could recognise
that. I heard Mick Jones from the Clash on the Radio a week or so ago
talking about how, in the 1970s in London if you went to Hammersmith,
it was 'Ted' country. Things were much more demarcated then, not just
in Northern Ireland. There is more fluidity now, a co-existence of styles.
The journalist Henry McDonald writes about Johnny Adair, remembers
him and the Shankill crowd going to punk gigs. In a lot of instances, it
was entirely superficial, but for a lot of other people, what first expressed
itself in fashion terms was also the start of a more profound shift. Just
being introduced to other people, other ideas, was important.

CM: Sexuality can be used as a tactic of subversion/resistance to mainstream political discourses. In *The International* why was your protagonist a sexual dissident and does this have political resonances?

GP: I think with any new character you are always asking yourself just who this person is. You are listening as write and this person has a voice that you eventually hear. There may have prompts with Danny, but that's it. Around the time that I had started *The International*, I had been writing a play, a monologue, called *Monday Night Little Ireland North of England* and the actor who acted it was gay, in his fifties and had told me something about going to a bar, about the gay scene in the late 1950s. I suppose that might have been in my head when I came to write about the period immediately after. I'm not saying there was no conscious decision on my part, especially given my interest in identity. I have this very firm belief that none of us are anything, we are not aware of ourselves in terms of gender and sexuality, we are not aware of ourselves in race terms, in ethnic terms, religious terms. Of course, you can look at me and say you're a white heterosexual male, it's easy for you to talk like that. But I think that we are – there is this core of us that's, that's me, that's you, without labels. I don't feel like it's fixed, I don't feel our identities are fixed, and I think that most identities are limiting positions. In *The International*, Danny is simply who he is, you know, he doesn't really even call himself gay; he was alive to anything that went on. It was as simple as that and as he says he'd grown up believing all sex was furtive and dirty, so there was no difference. I deliberately didn't make an issue of it because I didn't want it to be an identity. I wanted to undermine fixed, essential notions of identity. It was just something as simple as I thought I hadn't read anything like that before. I am aware that there are other bits and pieces right through the fiction, like the scene in the toilet in *Black Night at Big Thunder Mountain*. It's 'speeded' up, but there's something there. There's also in *Number 5* a 'homo-fascinated' thing going on

CM: There seems to be a atmosphere almost of pre-troubles erotic hedonism about *The International*.

GP: On the one hand, the narrator is someone for whom the city hasn't closed down yet. The murder of Peter Ward in Malvern Street, in a way, was the first definite signal that you were no longer free to move about Belfast. Historically, there were always periodic troubles but the real fractures in the city were expressed in the peace lines we see today, and the first indication of this was Ward's murder, he was just in the wrong place, a Catholic barman drinking after hours. The point at which the novel is set is in the aftermath of this, but just before the Civil Rights Association meeting, which is about to take us into the next phase. The murder has happened, something has been signalled, but the narrative hasn't really started, the prologue is there. I had my Danny in there representing that go-anywhere moment. I think there is also another thing, rather than sexuality, which is 'camp'. I am interested in 'camp'; there is a sort of positioning of yourself, a stepping outside. A positioning of yourself in a place where you can commentate.

CM: Unlike the vast majority of Northern Irish novels, yours contain a positive view of maternity.

GP: Well, with *That Which Was* I had become a parent myself at that stage, and there are obvious autobiographical resonances, it was a particularly good experience. And then I've come from a stable family life. There is also a sense of trying not to write what has gone before. I think of *Burning Your Own*, lots of it is predictable with the relationship between the mother and the father. There are places in that book where the relations are more complex and interesting than I intended. I thought of it quite schematically, the slightly abusive father, as well as the father in *Fat Lad*. They are more predictable in some ways. In *Number 5*, there are quite a variety of relationships, quite a few children born. I'm at a loss to account for the lack of it in other Northern Irish novels.

CM: Sexuality and love are treated in your fiction with an optimism rarely seen elsewhere. Why do you think this is?

GP: I remember with *Fat Lad* talking to Robert [McLiam Wilson] about this. I thought, as with violence, so with sex, when you come to write about it you have to write it straight. Not to view it with any mystery. I thought the sex in *Fat Lad* was fairly crap, but no more crap than sex generally is. You know, it was somewhat fumbly. I was asking myself 'what is it?' 'what do you do?' 'what is it *like*?' I think Robert does the same in *Eureka Street*. Of course, it's writing, it's wrought, but the art is to make it seem matter of fact: You do this; you put that there. It's slightly ludicrous but I don't think the individuals I describe are more ludicrous than any other individuals doing it are. The miracle of that for me is that the participants make of this something that is much more eloquent than the breakdown of the actions. There is a passage in *Fat Lad*, which is a deliberately wrought thing, between Drew and Anna. It was what was involved when they came together, all their personal histories. It was a different kind of heightened writing about sex. It was slightly parodic, but the comedy wasn't directed at them. In *Lapsed Protestant* there's a sexual spin given to the 'Act of Union'. In a very naïve way I find love enabling and liberating. To go back to Jake and Kate,[2] what they actually prove is that, when it comes to it, you cannot legislate for what happens when you look at someone and love them. What goes on there goes right underneath all concepts of identities. That is why so many people find themselves in compromising positions; they make pronouncements about what other people should do. It is a fundamental belief of mine, part of the growing away from the tribe. For me, it's not just a personal belief; it's an article of faith, an absolute truth. Anyone asks me why did you move here, why did you do this or that in your life, it was for love, or running away from being in love with somebody. In *The Third Party*, there's an instance where the protagonist is walking through the Hiroshima A-Bomb museum, and keeps on catching a woman's eye, who he presumes is newly married. They keep looking at each other and he

2   Jack and Kate are Patterson's grandparents, whose mixed marriage and involvement in events in the early twentieth century are the subject of his non-fiction book *Once Upon a Hill: Love in Troubled Times* (2008).

thinks that this woman's look represents a potentially life-changing decision and he doesn't act, and that's part of the reason that he is where is he is when the novel opens. In that look, her husband isn't there, nothing else is there. I am drawn to that moment – could you, would you? – that moment of decision. Although sometimes all that is on offer is plain old sex. The first time I was in the States I was at a party, someone said to me and a girl I was talking to, 'Are you guys fucking?' It was years before I found myself putting that in a novel, in *Number 5*. It's in contrast to the first people who lived in the house for whom all sex was illicit. When *The International* came out I did a reading of it in the Crown and there were a lot of people there, my dad, my mum, their friends. I read the bit about Ingrid deciding to sleep with as many boys of her acquaintance as she could one summer and one of the men who had been there said to me that he wished it had been like that. I frankly disbelieve this, society tries to control that, but that's how we are.

CM: Your novels are not traditionally seen as 'troubles fiction'. Why do you think this is?

GP: If I think about it, in my head, they are all concerned with the ramifications of violence, rather than engaged in acts of violence themselves. I am interested in how people in societies where violence like that occurs conduct their lives. My direct experience of violence was very limited. It's always there, but doesn't impinge upon the narrative directly. The murder of the Hungarian guy in *Number 5*, I have a very clear memory of being out playing and hearing a murder, the gunshot, the car, the ambulance, those sounds, it was only afterwards that I began to put it all together. People have said to me they're not really about the troubles, but that's fine, that's just the way they come across. But to me they were always when I was writing them. *Slaughterhouse 5* was very important to Robert and me, the idea that when someone dies that's a story ended. I think that, if I thought about my work and Robert's, no-one gets shot off their horse from the back of a stage-coach. It means something when someone dies. It means more when someone dies if they had a life before it. A novel is an invitation to imagine, and the impact should be felt, the purpose is to remind the reader that this is what happens anytime someone dies. The person you just read about is no longer alive and able to have fumbly sex.

Works Cited

McLiam Wilson, R. (1996), *Eureka Street*, Picador, London.

Patterson, Glenn (1995), *Black Night at Big Thunder Mountain*, Chatto & Windus, London.

—— (1988), *Burning Your Own*, Chatto & Windus, London.

—— (1992), *Fat Lad*, Chatto & Windus, London.

—— (2006), *Lapsed Protestant: Collected Pieces*, New Island Books, Ireland.

—— (2003), *Number Five*, Hamish Hamilton, London.

—— (2008), *Once Upon a Hill: Love in Troubled Times*, Bloomsbury, London.

—— (2004), *That Which Was*, Hamish Hamilton, London.

—— (1999), *The International*, Anchor, London.

—— (2007), *The Third Party*, Blackstaff, Belfast.

'A River Runs Through It': Irish History in Contemporary Fiction, Dermot Bolger and Roddy Doyle

DAMIEN SHORTT

> Eventually, all things merge into one, and a river runs through it. The river was cut by the world's great flood and runs over from the basement of time. On some of the rocks are timeless raindrops. Under the rocks are the words, and some of the words are theirs. I am haunted by waters.
>
> — NORMAN MACLEAN, *A River Runs Through It* (1976)

> Sometimes, if you stand on the bottom rail of a bridge and lean over to watch the river slipping slowly away beneath you, you will suddenly know everything there is to be known.
>
> —A.A. MILNE, *Winnie-the-Pooh* (1929)

Dermot Bolger and Roddy Doyle are two of Ireland's most popular contemporary authors, and share strikingly similar backgrounds: they were both born in Dublin (Doyle in 1958 and Bolger in 1959) and grew up within 10 miles of each other on the 'Northside' of the city. Their work is predominantly peopled with working-class Dubliners, and usually presents discussions of social issues in a contemporary setting. However, there are two texts that thematically stand out from the rest: Doyle's *A Star Called Henry* (2000) and Bolger's *The Family on Paradise Pier* (2005). In these, both authors turn their attention to the subject of Irish history, and present a blend of fact and fiction that appears to encourage the reader to question the veracity and reliability of supposedly official/accepted accounts of history. This essay will explore how both authors represent

Ireland in the early decades of the twentieth century in these texts, and will suggest that their conceptualisation of history is one in which the present determines the past.

Rivers are mentioned in the title of this essay because they conveniently serve several metaphorical functions for both Doyle and Bolger, and also for the purposes of this critique of their work. The notion of water, and the symbolic value it holds, is of crucial importance in *A Star Called Henry*, and rivers and water also hold important meanings in works by Bolger, such as: *Night Shift* (1989), *The Woman's Daughter* (2003a), *The Journey Home* (2003b), and also *The Family on Paradise Pier*. In addition to this symbolic facet of the texts, it will also be interesting to explore how both authors utilise the novel form in conducting a critique of history and its narration. In a sense, the epigraphic quotations at the head of this essay succinctly encapsulate the ideological and philosophical thread of this discussion: it appears that both Bolger and Doyle present a version of Irishness that is haunted by the linear flow of time and of the repercussions of this flow on notions of history and tradition; additionally, by metaphorically bridging time and history (standing above and/or outside of it) both novelists endeavour to come to a deeper understanding of things like origins, identity and teleology. This analysis seems important since both authors grew up in an Ireland that may be reasonably described as a society that was strongly influenced in its cultural tastes by tradition, nationalism and conservatism.

Bolger has likened the writing of a novel as similar to being 'thrown into a raging river and not being able to swim, and you grab hold of any piece of driftwood that floats by, so you're not necessarily aware of where the journey is going to bring you at a certain time' (Shortt, 2006: 465). What he appears to be saying is that the fictional world of the novel, and, more importantly, its history and its future, is undefined and uncharted until the novelist has written it. Unlike the historian who claims to look backwards in time and see his narrative already plotted out in chronological fashion, the novelist begins *in media res* and, as the work progresses, he can simultaneously see both the history and future of his characters and events unfold before him. The novelist's awareness of the apparent temporal paradox (that things which seem absolute constants are actually

in flux, that history is as unpredictable as the future and both are dependent upon the present) links him to some of the most ancient philosophy
in the Western tradition.

It was Heraclitus who first stated 'that change is universal and con-
tinual', and it was he who first compared time to a river when he said:
'You cannot step twice into the same rivers; for fresh waters are ever flowing in upon you' (Heraclitus, cited in Laguna, 1921: 242). Laguna argues
that we accept this claim 'not because it is proved but because it appeals
to us, and it appeals to us because it lies in the direction of our expanding knowledge' (ibid.: 242–3). In other words, that which appeared to
be constant only did so because our view of it was relatively superficial,
whereas when knowledge expands and our view becomes more focused
then the flux and change become noticeable: 'The hills, the sky, the stars
seem stable. But so does the river, if one looks at it from a distance' (ibid.:
243). The suitability of the river as a metaphor for the operation and
interaction of time, history and humanity ('from Homer's Scamander to
Joyce's Liffey', as Blanche Cannon puts it (Cannon, 1969: 181)), perhaps
makes it the site where the novelist, the historian, the traditionalist, and
the nationalist collide.

In the same way, and perhaps in a linked way, in which rivers have
long functioned as powerful symbols in literature, they (and other geographical features) have also served as sites of repository for collective
memories, which Anthony Smith feels 'since the time of Ernest Renan [...]
have always been recognized as a vital element in the construction of the
nation and the self understanding of its nationalism'. Smith argues that
'what is less often appreciated is that, to become national, shared memories
must attach themselves to specific places and definite territories' and that
'the process by which certain kinds of shared memories are attached to
particular territories' results in landscapes becoming ethnically charged
(ethnoscapes), and homelands becoming historicised; Smith terms this
process the 'territorialization of memory' (Smith, 1996: 453–4). Yet, when
we recall Heraclitus, place is just as susceptible to change and flux as
anything else, and perhaps when civilisations try to territorialize their
collective memories and traditions by mapping their historical narratives
onto the surrounding environment, they are inadvertently undermining

those very traditions. It is this, it seems, that Bolger and Doyle seek to explore and discuss in their anomalous historical narratives.

This bringing together of history and fiction appears to pose problems for both historians and novelists alike. In discussing Doyle's work Roy Foster suggests that 'historical novels run a risk of lurching into costume drama, especially when they employ "real people"' (Foster, 1999), perhaps because the genre has become so commonplace in contemporary broadcast media. On the other hand, historians tend to commonly project themselves as quasi-scientists, whose social function, as Longxi Zhang argues, is 'to rescue historical knowledge as *epistème* from whatever transitory *doxa* or opinions that came to pass at the time' (Zhang, 2004: 389). In other words, it seems that if the historian is to retain professional credibility then he must focus upon extracting pure knowledge (if such a thing can exist) from the contemporary cultural contingency of recorded events. Despite this, it seems the historian has never been able to completely extract himself from the necessity of narrative, since even Herodotus, the lauded father of history, was forced to extrapolate and 'make sense of the seemingly random pile of data and discover some kind of "inner truth"' when he claimed the Trojans were destroyed because they had committed such wrongdoings (ibid.: 394).

Zhang appears correct, then, when he claims that history can never really escape the associations it has with its French etymological parent-word 'histoire' which connotes both 'history as what happened in the past and as a story about what happened', and which 'seems to contain the tension from the very beginning between truth and imagination, objective account and subjective projection, reality and fiction' (Zhang, 2004: 388). Thus, in the intellectual and cultural milieu within which Bolger and Doyle write, where certainty and tradition are questioned, 'the rigid opposition between history and fiction collapses, and we become more appreciative of the power of representation in narrative fiction', which is a domain where the novelist supplants the historian, since the novelist has no reticence in imaginatively filling in the gaps in knowledge that the historian finds so problematic (ibid.: 391).

This obviously has significant repercussions on the idea of the nation, whose function, Prasenjit Duara argues, is to enable the nation-state and the nationalists 'to stake their claim to sovereign authority, in part, as custodians of this [spiritual] authenticity' that posits the nation as a 'continuous subject' against linear conceptualisations of history that are the 'falling of events into the "river of time"' (Duara, 1998: 287). Thus, the novelist who re-imagines the past is, metaphorically, threading dangerously close to the conceptual space where the nation is born. According to Duara, if the idea of the nation is to mean anything, and if it is to survive, then the founding myths and narratives that form its core must 'be unaffected by the passage of time' (ibid.: 289). In other words, for traditionalists and nationalists, if the nation's history is shown to be capricious or malleable, then its future becomes uncertain, since it is only a society's 'conception of the past [that] enables it to propel the nation into a desired future direction' (ibid.: 289).

Thus it seems that when novelists like Bolger and Doyle turn their attentions to the nation's past then they bring side by side two intellectual disciplines, poetry and history, that have been practically irreconcilable since the time of Aristotle. Sean Gaston states that Aristotle defined the poet's task as being 'to describe not the thing that happened, but a kind of thing that might happen', whilst the function of history is concerned with 'the thing that has been' (Gaston, 2007: 324): hence, when the historian writes, he writes about the past, and when the poet writes, he writes about possible futures; but when the poet writes about history then things get complex. Gaston is predominantly concerned with working through how Jacques Derrida theorised the possibility of a history of literature, but his conclusions seem just as relevant in a discussion of how Doyle and Bolger set about writing (or re-writing) the literature of Irish history. Ultimately, Gaston concludes that the conceptual gap that Derrida identifies 'between a history of literature and a literature of history, is always with-drawing, retreating and repeating and exceeding itself, remarking a gap that is at once irreducible and ungraspable' (ibid.: 328). These river-like qualities of literary history and historical literature run throughout several of Bolger's works, and feature pivotally in one of Doyle's.

In Bolger's first novel, *Night Shift*, Irish history and tradition are embodied in the character of Dan, an old Galway man who works in the same factory as the teenage protagonist, Donal. Initially, Dan seems pure and honourable to Donal; however, he is seriously injured following a practical joke that goes horribly wrong. He asks Donal to go to his bed-sit and destroy a collection of photographs which he is afraid anyone else will find. The books that Donal finds in the bed-sit firmly position Dan as being representative of what might reasonably be called traditional Irishness (Catholicism and Nationalism): 'The Singer and Other Plays, a Legion of Mary handbook for 1953, Morality and the Younger Catholic Teenager by a Fr. Thomas O'Brien S.J., and The Easter Rising 1916–1966, A Souvenir Record of the Celebrations' (Bolger, 1989: 124).

Nevertheless, Donal finds the photographs in a suitcase under the bed and discovers that they are pornographic pictures. As he leafs through them he is shocked that the women portrayed in the photographs get progressively younger and the circumstances in which they are pictured become evermore extreme and sexually perverted (Bolger, 1989: 126). Bolger perhaps suggests here that the older generation, embodying and perpetuating tradition, Catholicism and nationalism in Ireland, have to some degree been guilty of fetishising youth whilst simultaneously bemoaning the failings of the younger generation. This paradox, it seems, is what Bolger seems to identify as having caused Ireland's social and cultural inertia in the 1980s: the idolisation and fetishising of the youthfulness of Ireland's revolutionaries was used as a yardstick up to which Donal and his generation could never measure.

Following the discovery of the photographs, Donal leaves the bed-sit and walks through the centre of Dublin in a daze. Bolger presents a hellish portrayal of the centre of Dublin, with glaring advertisements, fast-food shops, drug addicts and glue-sniffers all combining to disgust Donal (Bolger, 1989: 127–130), who finds himself 'being carried down the brightly lit river of O'Connell Street' (ibid.: 127) until he is eventually left standing over the Liffey on O'Connell Bridge (ibid.: 128). Here, almost at the conclusion of the novel, the reader sees Donal standing at the confluence of two symbolic rivers: the 'lit river of O'Connell Street', and the river Liffey. These two rivers may be interpreted as symbolising a disjuncture between young and old that Bolger identifies as existing in Irish culture and society at that time. Donal stands on the bridge just off O'Connell Street and just above the Liffey; having 'paused for directions' (ibid.: 128) he is unsure where he should go from this point; he is a Dubliner lost in his own city. This portrayal of the city centre is echoed again in Bolger's play *The Lament for Arthur Cleary* (2005) when the eponymous hero states:

> It's all smaller, different when you return. Look at it ... O'Connell Street. Just like some honky-tonk provincial plaza. Everywhere closed except the burger huts, all the buses gone, everyone milling around drunk, taking to the glittering lights like aborigines to whiskey. (Bolger, 2005: 21)

Like Donal, Arthur sees the Irish as existing at some position between the past and the future. In the tasteless, kitsch transformation of the street into a soulless thoroughfare, Arthur feels the Irish have struggled to come to terms with their own past. The classical, symmetrical facades of O'Connell Street are strikingly at odds with the shops housed within. Through Donal and Arthur's descriptions of the city centre, Bolger presents Ireland as a society unable to create a space where the past and present can coexist without one making the other appear wholly alien.

The notion of place as historical palimpsest is also evoked in *The Woman's Daughter* which begins with two epigraphs highlighting Finglas's (the north Dublin suburb where Bolger was born and reared) association with water and rivers, and utilising a prominent literary metaphor of the river as definitive of place and symbolic of local knowledge and identity. Originally the river was the lifeblood of the community, but in more modern times it becomes a hindrance causing problems for the expansion of the suburb until it is eventually channelled underground, resurfacing only at a couple of points (Bolger, 2003a: 215). Eventually, old Turlough, the bard-like custodian of its history, is the only one who can trace the river's route. The river is ambiguous in its symbolic literary connotations; on one hand it evokes changelessness in that even though it may not be seen it is still present beneath the surface. Paradoxically, in a Heraclitean sense, this ever-presence of the river also evokes the notions of constant change. Thus, for Bolger, it appears that the history attached to a place is similarly ambiguous. History is simultaneously a constant, always providing the undercurrent for the present; yet it is always in flux, dependant upon the position of the viewer or from which point one chooses to enter the river of time.

Like history, the Finglas River in *The Woman's Daughter* carries along the flotsam and jetsam of everyday life until eventually it becomes so polluted it actually catches fire: 'Once in winter this stream used to flood, now it goes on fire on choked summer evenings, full of oil and shit, a tiny current pulsing through the build-up of rubbish' (Bolger, 2003a: 236). The pollution of the river perhaps implies that the constant working, reworking, inscriptions and re-inscriptions of history make the community's mythologies so uncertain as to make them sites of combustible conflict rather than harmonising shared narratives. Ultimately, Turlough is burned to death in his small cabin by a large group of drunken teenagers. His death appears ritualistic or sacrificial, and perhaps signifies the passing of curatorship of the community's history from one generation to the next, since Turlough has groomed a young local boy, Johnny, to carry the community's collective memory. Significantly, given Turlough's death, Johnny is free to do what he will with his historical knowledge; he is free to interpret it, to remould it, to understand it in different ways and to pass it along in whichever fashion he chooses. The past, Bolger appears to be saying, is the property of the young, for it is they who will transmit the community's history to future generations.

This disjuncture between the past and the future reoccurs in another of Bolger's early novels, *The Journey Home*, where the notion of subterranean water reoccurs in a slightly different form when he seems to use it to point to the irrelevance of the past for many young people in contemporary Ireland:

A water main had burst near the old monument across from the shopping centre in the village. The water soared up from a hole in the road and splashed down onto the tar macadam. Two girls with a ghetto-blaster had climbed into the enclosed green triangle around the mock Celtic cross that had been paid for by the Plunkett brothers in honour of their grandfather. Graffiti was smeared across its patriotic inscription. Reggae music blared as children twisted and jived, running in and out of the high spray. I paused to watch ... They were an autonomous world, a new nation with no connection to the housewives passing or the men coming home from the factories. (Bolger, 2003b: 302)

Here, as in *The Woman's Daughter*, subterranean water comes to the surface, but this time it is not a river – it is a burst water-main, water that has been cleaned of the impurities of river water. And the young people dance in it, not listening to Irish music, but listening to Reggae. They dance around a patriotic 'mock Celtic cross' that has been paid for by local corrupt businessmen and politicians, and the patriotic inscription has been smeared with graffiti. These are not the comely young maidens dancing at the crossroads as envisaged by de Valera in his St Patrick's Day speech of 1943. This is Bolger's version of modern Ireland where he perhaps believes that Ireland must be imagined as a more European constituency where the city and suburb have supplanted the rural as the dominant signifiers of Ireland and Irishness, and where the dual carriage-way and roundabout are as indigenous as the pastoral landscapes of turf and boreens (Bolger, 1986: 10).

The autonomy ascribed to these youths in *Night Shift*, *The Woman's Daughter*, *The Lament for Arthur Cleary*, and *The Journey Home*, their ignorance, or disregard, of Ireland's history and what some could perceive as the desecration and undermining of traditional and national culture, imbues them with a *joie de vivre* demonstrated through a freedom from association with place or time – since they seem not to care about either. In a similar tone of critiquing nationalist and traditionalist shibboleths, Roddy Doyle also frequently represents contemporary Irish culture as being at odds with its past. In texts such as *The Barrytown Trilogy*, *Paddy Clark Ha Ha Ha*, and *The Woman who Walked into Doors*, Doyle depicts an Ireland that seems a world removed from tourist board adverts of traditional music, Aran sweaters and turf fires.

However, it is arguably in *A Star Called Henry* that Doyle most obviously presents a critique of history, nationalism and tradition in Ireland and, as in Bolger's work, rivers form an important part of that critique. In *The Commitments* Doyle famously articulates how the Liffey divides Dublin: 'The Irish are the niggers of Europe, lads [...] an' Dubliners are the niggers of Ireland [...] an' the northside Dubliners are the niggers o' Dublin' (Doyle, 1998: 13). However, in this instance, the Liffey only serves to separate those who live on its working-class northern banks from those who live on its more salubrious southern side. In *A Star Called Henry* it is the less well known, predominantly subterranean rivers like the Swan, the Poddle, the Bradoge, the Cemetery Drain and the Hangman's Stream that serve the most important symbolic functions.

When the five-year-old Henry Smart, who will later play a pivotal role in both the Easter 1916 Rising and the subsequent War of Independence, tells the king of England to 'Fuck off with your hat' during the royal visit of 1907, a large group of 'the King's loyal Irish subjects' round on him. In the ensuing melee Henry and his younger brother are rescued by their father. Several officers of the Dublin Metropolitan Police give chase, but the Smarts make their escape because of their intimate knowledge of Dublin, and drop into the subterranean Swan river, which they access through a hole they find behind some bushes in a back-garden (Doyle, 2000: 51–6). This escape is mirrored later in the novel when, following the surrender of the revolutionaries at the General Post Office (GPO) in 1916 Henry Smart escapes from his British captors down a manhole and into the Camac river – which eventually deposits him into the Liffey and safety (ibid.: 138–41).

The Smarts, in all their poverty, degradation and crime, are perhaps Doyle's re-envisaging of Dublin's and Ireland's past. Their encyclopaedic knowledge of the city presents them as the true custodians of Irish history in this novel. If the Liffey is the public symbol of tradition and history, then the Smarts know what goes into making the Liffey; they know all the sewage and waste waters that are kept hidden from public view and buried beneath Dublin's streets. If the rivers do, in fact, function as symbols of collective memory and intentional forgetfulness, then perhaps when Doyle has the father say 'I'll tell yis something for nothing boys [...] Wherever you find water you'll find people queuing up to piss in it' (Doyle, 2000: 57) he suggests that history can never flow in absolute purity, and that awareness of this is key to understanding the past, present and future.

Through Henry Smart, as curator of history (since it is he who narrates) Doyle critiques and revises what is perhaps the most sacrosanct of all Irish historical narratives: the story of what takes place within the GPO in Dublin during the Easter 1916 rebellion. The teenage Henry Smart is at this point a trusted aide to James Connolly, leader of the Irish Citizen's

Army, and soon finds himself at ideological odds with members of the Irish Volunteers, led by Padraig Pearse. When the Irish rebels take over the GPO, and various other strategic positions around the city, many Dubliners take the opportunity granted by the ensuing confusion to loot the large stores along Sackville Street (now O'Connell Street).

Pearse's Volunteers want to shoot the looters because their robbery reflects poorly upon the morality of their insurrection, Smart intends to shoot Pearse in retaliation:

> I got ready to shoot Commandant Pearse [...] For the duration of those five, crawling seconds Britain stopped being the enemy. Pearse saw my rifle and saw my eyes and my intentions in them, and he turned slightly, giving me his profile, hiding his squint; he was ready for an elegant death. (Doyle, 2000: 115)

He perceives the Volunteers' hatred of the looters as yet another manifestation of the hypocrisy of traditional nationalism, in its Irish context, as professing to speak for the poor and disenfranchised while simultaneously discriminating against them. In this instance Smart hates Pearse's Volunteers, describing them as 'the poets and the farm boys, the fuckin' shopkeepers. They detested the slummers – the accents and the dirt, the Dublinness of them' (ibid.: 103). He especially hates them because he finds himself in a situation where his survival is dependent upon their survival. In the deathly calm following their seizure of the GPO, and as the British forces slowly creep into position to surround them, he is amazed to see the Volunteers begin to pray:

> [...] behind me, my colleagues and comrades, my fellow revolutionaries, were on their knees – and they'd be on them and off them all day – with their eyes clamped shut, their heads bowed and their cowering backs to the barricades. What sort of a country were we going to create? If we were attacked now we were fucked. (Doyle, 2000: 112)

Their refusal to eat meat on a Friday, their fear of ejection from the GPO if Pearse overhears them swearing, and their refusal to steal from their British oppressors when they find tills full of money because they are 'Christian Brothers' boys, here to die for Ireland, dying to please [their] betters' (ibid.: 88, 89, 130) leave Smart in little doubt that, should the rebellion prove successful, life for the working-class Dubliner would change little.

Thus, Doyle's reinterpretation of this originary moment in the history of the Irish State seems geared towards a critique of the confluence of religion and politics in the formation of Irish identity as traditionally understood, and which he perhaps sees as having been inimical to a socially just state. Therefore, in seeking to posit the possibility of a more just state, both Doyle and Bolger appear to reject supposedly official history, and they reject the ability of a single group to act, as Prasenjit Duara suggests above, as the nation's custodians of authenticity. In *Night Shift, The Woman's Daughter, The Journey Home*, and *A Star Called Henry*, the authors utilise the symbolic potency of water and rivers to suggest the Heraclitean qualities of history – where no two people can interpret the same historical events in exactly the same way. In a sense, they appear to foreground what Zhang argues is the impossibility of the separation of history from story, of reality from fiction (Zhang, 2004: 388). Indeed, it is through the discussion of story, and its existential reliance upon narrative that this critique can move towards its conclusion.

Recalling the Derridean discussion by Sean Gaston above, where he identifies the gap between historical literature and literary history, it can be seen that it is in the act of narration where the origin of historical unreliability must necessarily lie. It is through this act of narration, and in their foregrounding of it, that Doyle and Bolger self-consciously betray the contingency and unreliability of their version of history. They both utilise this stylistic peculiarity of story-telling in order to deconstruct Ireland's national and traditional mythologies. It is possible to see similarities in both authors' conceptualisations of time and history in their narrative choices in *The Family on Paradise Pier* and *A Star Called Henry*.

The Family on Paradise Pier is Bolger's only full-length historical novel. In it, he presents the story of the Goold-Verschoyles – a family of Anglo-Irish Protestants from Donegal – covering the first half the twentieth century. During this time the Goold-Verschoyles experience, and have involvement in World War I, the Easter Rising, the Russian Revolution, Ireland's Wars of Independence and Civil War, the Spanish

Civil War and World War II. Through all of this tumult the story of Eva
Goold-Verschoyle is the narrative thread that Bolger follows. She is not
involved in any of these world-changing events and hers is a story of quiet
dignity and intellectual and spiritual integrity. In the author's epilogue
he states that he is aware that 'fiction can never tell the full truth' but
that perhaps it is better suited to telling 'altered but equally important
truths' (Bolger, 2005: 548).

He argues that 'our lives are invariably viewed through the prism of
whatever version of reality we construct from selected memories so that
our pasts begin to consist not of what has happened, but what we remember happening' (Bolger, 2005: 548). Memory, then, is what Bolger sees as
the foundation upon which history stands, and the inherent unreliability
(and prejudice) of memory is obviously implied to be detrimental to the
notion of a true history. It is possible to counter-argue by claiming that
documentary evidence is the means by which civilisation transcends the
fallibility of memory, but Bolger's novel (especially the narrative style of
its opening) contest the reliability of the written word by highlighting the
gap between writing and experience – a gap which Zhang claims worries
the historian but intrigues the novelist (Zhang, 2004: 391).

Paradise Pier begins with a series of eight interlocking vignettes
depicting the Goold-Verschoyle family, and their neighbours, in different places of the world, but at the same instant of time. The reader later
learns that the action described in these vignettes occurs chronologically
towards the end of the novel's narrative, evoking how understanding
only comes from the perspective of the future when the events can be
contextualised. The initial style of writing is non-emotive reportage. By
beginning in this manner Bolger prepares the reader for what follows; he
seeks to demonstrate that when history is viewed as abstract and objective it appears distant and lifeless, incapable of eliciting emotion. The
remainder of the novel seeks to establish an empathetic attachment with
the various members of the family and thereby suggesting that history is
relevant only when it is able to elicit emotion.

The vignettes are set during World War II, and depict Brendan
Goold-Verschoyle aboard a train bound for a Soviet Gulag following his
betrayal during the Spanish Civil War; simultaneously, his older brother,

Art, is imprisoned in the Curragh military camp as part of the neutral
Irish Government's internment of political radicals during World War II
(Art is there because of his vociferous Communist politics); elsewhere
their parents, once so active in their local community, sit in a small apartment in Oxford and dream of their idyllic ancestral home in Donegal
which they abandoned when political opinion swung against their class;
Mr Ffrench, a former neighbour and onetime Communist radical, has
died and the reader learns in another vignette how his wife regrets the
fact that all along the locals considered them harmless eccentrics rather
than the dangerous revolutionaries they desired to be; and finally, Eva
is presented in her garden in Mayo surrounded by her playing children,
far removed in her edenic idyll from the war raging in Europe (Bolger,
2005: 1–19).

These vignettes serve to help Bolger create the parallel and condensed
fictional universes that allow the reader a fleeting experience of omni-
science and omnipresence. In twenty pages the reader knows everything
about the Goold-Verschoyles' lives in one moment of time, and can understand their parallels, differences and ironies. The overtly constructed
nature of this section, however, should also communicate that this is not
how readers normally experience life, that their knowledge about the
lives of others is limited only to their direct sensory input. Bolger thus
explores the role that grand-narratives may have in creating meaning and
understanding since it is always necessarily a retrospective creation and
fabrication – as demonstrated by the deliberate and obviously constructed
nature of the vignettes.

Perhaps in *The Family on Paradise Pier* Bolger is implying that any
attempt at grand-narrative is as much a fabrication as his attempt in this
novel; his point may be to underline the impossibility of ever being able to
assemble the multitudinous narratives of a community into one coherent
monologic history. Consequently, grand narratives, and the ideologies
that arise out of them, can never aspire to the level of episteme, or true
and pure knowledge, but must always be seen as doxa, the contingent
beliefs of a particular community at a particular moment in time. Bolger
thus appears to show the reader that history does not happen in neat
temporal sequences. The jarring shifts in narrative focus in this opening

sequence of vignettes show that only someone looking backwards in time can impose a narrative order. From this novel, therefore, it seems history belongs to the present.

Bolger's deliberate foregrounding of the unreliability of narrative is mirrored in Doyle's narrator Henry Smart. *A Star Called Henry* is part of an intended trilogy called The Last Roundup and, in it and its sequel *Oh Play That Thing* (the final part of the trilogy is, as yet, unpublished), Henry Smart narrates his own story and that of other people about whose lives he could not possibly know. His story, and consequently Doyle's reworking of Irish history, is self-evidently unreliable. In addition to this, the idea that Smart moves from narrating the moment of his own birth through his time as a Dublin street urchin, his friendships with James Connolly, Louis Armstrong and John Ford, seems to be purposely ridiculous.

It is through this use of narrative and unreliable narrators that both Doyle and Bolger endeavour to reveal the inherent subjectivity of history and its contingency upon the position of the observer. Through the often unbelievable Henry Smart, Doyle highlights what could have been, whilst Bolger goes so far as to admit in his epilogue that he has manipulated time and characters to suit his narrative (Bolger, 2005: 548). In their utilisation of rivers as symbols, it is possible to see that both authors are less concerned with debates over the possibility of historical accuracy than they are with the humanisation and personalisation of history. It appears that for Bolger and Doyle history is untraceable, and perhaps irrelevant, in its sequences and causality. They appear to see the events of the past merging into one, and that it is the task of the author to extract the most relevant elements for analysis. If history is like a river, then literary history, such as *A Star Called Henry* and *The Family on Paradise Pier*, allows the reader to stand outside of the cultural contingencies and doxa, and to explore the possibilities of narrating the self through the self-narration of the past. Ultimately, what this type of literature celebrates is the dependence of the past upon the present for interpretation; it challenges the cultural and political tyranny of the dead, and replaces it with the uncertainty of the future. In the texts discussed here, Bolger and Doyle reject the traditional custodians of the community's past – the historians, traditionalists and

conservatives – and demonstrate the possibilities of invention and rein-
vention through their celebration of the unreliability of narrative.

Works Cited

Bolger, D. (1986), 'Introduction', in Bolger, D. (ed.), *The Bright Wave*/ An
    Tonn Geal: *Poetry in Irish Now*, Raven Arts Press, Dublin.
—— (1989), *Night Shift*, Penguin, London.
—— (2000), *The Lament for Arthur Cleary*, collected in *Plays: 1*, Methuen,
    London.
—— (2003a), *The Woman's Daughter*, Flamingo, London.
—— (2003b), *The Journey Home*, Flamingo, London.
—— (2005), *The Family on Paradise Pier*, Fourth Estate, London.
Cannon, B. (1969), 'The Haunted Stream: Rivers and Fountains in
    Milton's Poems', *The Bulletin of the Rocky Mountain Modern Language
    Association*, 23, (4), pp. 181–8.
Duara, P. (1998), 'The Regime of Authenticity: Timelessness, Gender,
    and National History in Modern China', *History and Theory*, 37, (3),
    pp. 287–308.
Doyle, R. (1994), *Paddy Clarke Ha Ha Ha*, Minerva, London.
—— (1998a), *The Barrytown Trilogy*, Vintage, London.
—— (1998b), *The Woman Who Walked into Doors*, Vintage, London.
—— (2000), *A Star Called Henry*, Vintage, London.
—— (2005), *Oh, Play That Thing*, Vintage, London.
Foster, R. (1999), 'Roddy and the Ragged Trousered Revolutionary'
    in *Guardian Unlimited Books*, available at: http://books.guardian
    .co.uk/reviews/generalfiction/0,,97001,00.html (accessed on
    11/06/08).
Gaston, S. (2007), 'Derrida and the History of Literature', *Textual Practice*,
    21, (2), pp. 313–34.

Laguna, T. de (1921), 'The Importance of Heraclitus', *The Philosophical Review*, 30, (3), pp. 238–54.

MacLean, N. (1976), *A River Runs Through it*, University of Chicago Press, Chicago.

Milne, A.A. (1991), *Winnie-the-Pooh*, Mammoth, London.

Shortt, D. (2006), 'An Interview with Dermot Bolger', *Irish Studies Review*, 14, (4), pp. 465–74.

Smithy, A.D. (1996), 'Culture, Community and Territory: The Politics of Ethnicity and Nationalism', *International Affairs*, 72, (3), pp. 445–58.

Zhang, L. (2004), 'History and Fictionality: Insights and Limitations of a Literary Perspective', *Rethinking History*, 8, (3), pp. 387–402.

PART TWO

New Readings

Flann O'Brien in the Devil Era: Building Hell in Heaven's Despite

JOHN COYLE

'Everything comes in circles: even Professor Moriarty'

—ARTHUR CONAN DOYLE, *The Valley of Fear*

The Third Policeman, a novel by Flann O'Brien, was submitted for publication in January 1940, rejected on both sides of the Atlantic, forgotten, disavowed by the author to the extent that he faked its disappearance (motor tour, Donegal, looseleaved manuscript blown from car boot) and finally resuscitated and published, posthumously, in 1967. It is, in matter and manner as well as publishing history, altogether a very posthumous work, dealing as it does with the fate of a man boobytrapped into an eternity of suffering and want which is inexorable, however civil, convivial and congenial its inhabitants. The dark games which Flann O'Brien plays with time's ironies and incongruities survive his death, and sustain a puzzling afterlife for the novel. One question resulting from the publishing history might be whether it is a worse thing to be read as a 1960s novel written in the 1930s, or as a 1930s novel read from the 1960s on. Is it ahead of its time, as many have claimed, or simply belated? Certainly the accumulation of critical accounts of the work since 1967 might have been expected to have paid more attention to the changing terms, revisions and counter-revisions of critical debate within both the Irish and the international academies, despite what Anne Clune calls a 'veritable explosion of full-length studies' (Clune & Hurson, 1997: xii).

In between the two decades there was another afterlife, that of Myles the newspaper columnist, who returns several times, and too often dismissively, to the subject of Joyce. For all that Brian O'Nolan, abetted by his many heteronyms, appeared to follow Joyce into an exile from the mainstream, and although O'Brien is mentioned often as the neglected third in a triumvirate with Joyce and Beckett, he is also the one who stayed at home, and who resisted the appropriation of their work by an International Modernism which was largely a creation of the American academy. The collection *A Bash in the Tunnel,* co-edited by O'Nolan shortly before his death, was indeed the first book by Irish writers about Joyce as a specifically Irish writer, for John Ryan in his introduction 'quintessentially an Irishman to the extent that Wilde, Shaw or Yeats could never be' (Ryan, 1970: 10). You would not look to Ryan for subtlety.

The rediscovery of Flann O'Brien in the 1960s as posthumous postmodernist *avant la lettre* managed to co-opt him into a version of internationalized Irishry, all puckish charm and meretricious whimsy, with the rough edges and barbs of local context diligently rubbed away. The Canadian critic Hugh Kenner was usually an exception to this, noticing as he did the darker and despairing overtones within the mimicries of Myles, but even his ear deserts him when he comes to attempt a pastiche of Mylesian cadences (Kenner, 1997: 61–72). More recently, even a writer as fine as John Updike can't, it seems, resist the lure of the blarney, the craic, the theme pub loquacity, when he wants to demonstrate his familiarity with what he thinks his author is about.

> Begob, and the truth would not be played false were a frank man to say that Flann O'Brien, born Brian O'Nolan in Strabane, Ulster, in 1911, and known as Myles na gCopaleen to the readers of his long-standing column 'Cruiskeen Lawn' in the Irish Times, when acting as a novelist proffered a mixed bag of blessings and their opposite. (Updike, 2008)

Elsewhere in the same review Updike asserts that 'some of his books have the twilight shimmer of a Celtic fairy tale.' It can be imagined what Myles na Gopaleen would have made out of that.

If it's a shame that Flann O'Brien should remain representative of a kind of Hibernian caprice, a metonym for a particular shape of Irishness, it is because his best fiction presents versions of a peculiarly Irish dystopia. On the other hand, O'Nolan is not entirely blameless for this reputation, since anyone who published a magazine called *Blather* in the mid-1930s ought to have been aware of comic language as an accretion as well as a confutation of the myth, as boast as well as self-deprecation. If *At Swim-Two-Birds* was hailed as being postmodern before its time, how much more was *Blather* prematurely complicit in the other side of postmodernism, with its jokily affectless agnosis about Hitler (compare Jack Gladney, Don DeLillo's Professor of Hitler Studies in *White Noise*), which is symptomatic of a refusal to accord any weight to political discourse. Blather emphasises its own vast importance at the same time as it announces that it is 'just a poor amateur affair, not worth the paper it besmirches' (Jackson, 1988: 97).

In *The Third Policeman*, however, blarney and blather are no laughing matter, having become necessary techniques for survival when, finding himself in Hell but thinking himself still on earth, the narrator realizes the value of his eloquence as a protection against the terrors of silence.

> I found I spoke lightly enough. While speaking inwardly or outwardly or thinking of what to say I felt brave and normal enough. But every time a silence came the horror of my situation descended on me like a heavy blanket flung upon my head, enveloping and smothering me and making me afraid of death. (O'Brien, 2007: 242)

Or, it might be suggested, a fate worse than death. Here, as everywhere else in O'Nolan/O'Brien's works, it is language which acts as palliative and protection against unspeakable torments, or the torment of the unspeakable; and it is language, in the guise of the de Selby Codex and various commentaries, which has tempted the protagonist into murder in the first place, and which distracts him throughout the story; so that there is no demonstration of the marvels of the Policemen's barracks which is not accompanied by some protracted, and wordy, explanation, such as:

> the beauty of reading de Selby is that it leads one inescapably to the happy conclusion that one is not, of all nincompoops, the greatest. (O'Brien, 2007: 302)

The word 'inventiveness', a standard element of the critic's vocabulary, takes on a special sense and weight with this novel. Description as creation is everywhere apparent in the text, and never more than when our noman speculates on how he will deploy the prize of his quest, his four ounces of Omnium. He first speculates on how it might be used paradisiacally:

> Sitting at home with my box of omnium I could do anything, see anything and know anything with no limit to my powers save that of my own imagination. Perhaps I could even use it to extend my imagination. (O'Brien, 2007: 394)

But he then moves to dwell on more infernal applications, as punishments are devised for the policemen MacCruiskeen and Pluck:

> Each of the cabinets could be altered to contain, not bicycles and whiskey and matches, but putrescent offals, insupportable smells, unbeholdable corruptions containing tangles of gleaming slimy vipers each of them deadly and foul of breath, millions of diseased and decayed monsters clawing the inside latches of the ovens to open them and escape, rats with horns walking upside down along the ceiling pipes trailing their leprous tails on the policemen's heads, readings of incalculable perilousness mounting hourly upon the – (O'Brien, 2007: 396)

This Boschian fantasy is curtailed by the bathos of P.C. Fox's interruption, commenting on the efficacy of Omnium as a means for boiling an egg just right.

Omnium, which MacCruiskeen has previously described as 'the essential inherent interior essence which is hidden inside the root of the kernel of everything' (O'Brien, 2007: 110), represents, in a work which otherwise eschews the self-referential high jinks of the first novel, a clear enough metaphor for verbal imagination, it being itself the very stuff of fictive invention. It is that of which everything in the novel is made, and everything which can be imagined in the novel is made. In this it is of course like the words which comprise the novel, and like language. And as with language in *At Swim-Two-Birds* and the newspaper columns, any attempt to deploy it in the service of the complicated, the lofty and sublime is doomed to be undercut and hijacked by bathetic interjections in the persons of Jem Casey (The Poet of the Pick), and that figment so dear to De Valera's heart, The Plain People of Ireland.

Someone as cagey as Brian O'Nolan was about blasphemy would be unlikely to indulge in rebellion, even against a Catholic Church as sentimental as it was censorious in the 1930s. But there is in his work evidence of a marked reluctance to be impressed by theocracy, even an inverted one. There is no Satan in this hell. Brian O'Nolan was taught by the Christian Brothers in Synge Street, then by the Holy Ghost Fathers in Blackrock College, yet aside from the early adoption of the persona of brother Barnabas, there is very little discussion of religion in his writing. One can either put this down to the default secularism of urban intellectuals, or, perhaps to the canny self-censorship advocated in his essay on Joyce 'A Bash in the Tunnel'.

> A man once said to me that he hated blasphemy, but on purely rational grounds. If there is no God, he said, the thing is stupid and unnecessary. If there is, it's dangerous. (O'Nolan, in Ryan, 1970: 15)

O'Brien's wider argument is that all blasphemers must be believers, and for all his agnosis in this regard, he is happy to entertain the possibility of hell, in his play *Faustus Kelly* as well as in *The Third Policeman*. The signature bathos is present again in the title of the play, and bathos protracted into eternity is one of the conditions of hell, the other being, in a profoundly moralistic way of which both Dante and Sartre would approve, that the punishment fits the crime. The protagonist of *The Third Policeman* is a robber and a murderer who spends most of the novel ignorant of his fate. We are told some bare details of his life in between the confession with which the novel starts and the meat of his adventures in the underworld. His own parents disappear from this earth as suddenly and inexplicably as he himself has disappeared. He has no name. If names are not adhered to, if it is possible or advisable to adopt any one of a number of names or indeed to admit to none at all, then this is not because names do not matter, but because they matter very much indeed: they are a necessary evil for the outlaw, the refugee or the stateless person, since not to be free in the Free State is to be in a pretty state altogether. Prosthetics are important in the novel: our hero has a wooden leg and is rescued by a gang of wooden-legged bandits. The Atomic theory with its insinuations continues this theme, and the relation of the after-death world, with its strange and inorganic instrumentalism, bears a prosthetic relation to real life, as an unfeeling affectless extension bearing only a superficial resemblance to the real thing. It is therefore especially unfortunate for our understanding of O'Brien that his work should so often have been regarded as merely a jokey appendage to the corpora of Joyce and Beckett.

Flann O'Brien, along with Beckett, James Stephens and Anita Loos, was one of the very few younger writers to be praised by Joyce, and to write, as it were, in his shadow. The underworld of O'Brien's devising is one where inventive power is archival and encyclopaedic on a Joycean scale. If the example of *Ulysses'* 'Cyclops' chapter presides over the patter, hyperbole and barroom scholastics of *At Swim-Two-Birds*, then with *The Third Policeman* it is 'Ithaca' whose exhaustive catechism governs the prose, with its projection of scientific objectivity to absurd lengths, and its abandonment of human scale in favour of a chill regard *sub specie aeternatis*. Imagine Bouvard and Pécuchet put in uniform and left in charge of a particle accelerator and you have MacCruiskeen and Pluck. In its dream-like states and cycles of eternal recurrence *The Third Policeman* is also, of course, echoic of *Finnegans Wake*, and Joyce's epic, contemporaneous with Flann O'Brien's, helps us along with a useful pun, which characterizes the years of De Valera as the 'devil era'.

> Life, it is true, will be a blank without you because avicuum's not there at all, to nomore cares from nomad knows, ere Molochy wars bring the devil era, a slip of the time between a date and a ghostmark, rived by darby's chilldays embers, spatched fun Juhn that dandyforth, from the night we are and feel and fade with to the yesterselves we tread to turnupon. (Joyce, 1975: 473)

O'Brien's hell is remarkably similar to that of Beckett, and especially that of his most famous play, *Waiting for Godot*. The title of both teases its audience and protagonists with a character, Godot or Fox, who is the matter of rumour, speculation and suspense. The setting meanwhile is one of rural anonymity, a place by a road, detached somehow from history and modernity. What order there is is upheld by the threat of violence and even torture, yet these are encountered with a seeming nonchalance which is puzzling to the reader or audience. Crucially, hell is a place where one encounters one damned thing after another, where the present situation repeats itself for eternity, and where there is nothing to be done in a world governed by *ricorso* and regression, as in Vladimir's song at the beginning of Act Two.

> A dog came in the kitchen
> And stole a crust of bread
> Then cook up with a ladle
> And beat him till he was dead
>
> Then all the dogs came running
> And dug the dog a tomb
>
> (*He stops, broods, resumes.*)
>
> Then all the dogs came running
> And dug the dog a tomb
> And wrote upon the tombstone
> For the eyes of dogs to come:
>
> A dog came in the kitchen ...
> (Beckett, 2000: 48–9)

In what is still one of the best single accounts of O'Brien's work and its place in both Irish and international traditions, Lorna Sage points out how Flann O'Brien figured Ireland as a place of stillness and rest. She outlines compellingly how the succession of standstills invoked by De Selby's extension of Zeno's paradox into the postulation of a series of resting-places comes to describe a state, and a historical condition, of paralysis:

> The argument that motion is a series of 'rests' fits in beautifully with O'Brien's vision of Irish inertia. You don't need, if you think about it, to move at all. Indeed you don't move. De Selby, we're told, makes an epic journey from Bath to Folkestone by shutting himself up in a room with lots of picture postcards of the countryside in between 'together with an elaborate arrangement of clocks and barometric instruments for regulating the gaslight.'

> Apart from retailing such extraordinary experiments, *The Third Policeman*
> affords a great deal of evidence of the effects of Zeno's paradox on one's view of
> the world: actions are fragmented into parts until they arrive at near-stasis: the
> flow of time breaks apart into droplets, each of which contains within it further
> tiny bubbles; narrative is a series of stills. The materials of life are all there, but the
> dynamism has gone. (Sage, in Dunn, 1975: 202–3)

Torture and torment are previously announced in *At Swim-Two-Birds*, and
there is more than a hint of the scientific and mechanical in the exhaustive accounts of violence which bespatter its pages. For Brian O'Nolan
the civil servant, torture is something to be civilly engaged in as well as
endured, with 'honeyed words in torment.' William Gass praises Flann
for his perfect pitch, saying that he 'could capture and copy any tone,
even before he'd heard it' (Gass, 1998: 5). R.W. Maslen points out how
the language involved always adheres to civility, even when promising
unspeakable pain (Maslen, 2006: 86). The mimic detachment of Flann's
prose is that of the exam candidate or civil servant, where adoption of the
correct register is a matter of survival rather than commitment.

> Leaden-hard forked arteries ran speedily about his scalp, his eye-beads bled and
> the corrugations of boils and piteous tumuli which appeared upon the large of his
> back gave it the appearance of a valuable studded shield and could be ascertained
> on counting to be sixty-four in number. He suffered a contraction of the intestines
> and a general re-arrangement of his interior to this result, that a meat repast in the
> process of digestion was ejected on the bed, on the coverlet, to speak precisely. In
> addition to his person, his room was also the subject of mutations unexplained by
> any purely physical hypothesis and not to be accounted for by mechanical devices
> relating to the manipulation of guy-ropes, pulley-blocks, or mechanical collapsible
> wallsteads of German manufacture, nor did the movements of the room conform
> to any known laws relating to the behaviour of projectiles as ascertained by a study
> of gravitation enforced by calculations based on the postulata of the science of
> ballistics. (O'Brien, 2007: 174)

The infernal calculations of the hellfire sermon in *A Portrait of the Artist
as a Young Man* are not a poke in the eye away from this (or from those
of another O'Brien in Orwell's *Nineteen Eighty-Four*. 'If you want a picture of the future, imagine a boot stamping on a human face – for ever')
(Orwell, 1989: 280).

Ever to suffer, never to enjoy; ever to be damned, never to be saved; ever, never; ever, never. O what a dreadful punishment! An eternity of endless agony, of endless bodily and spiritual torment, without one ray of hope, without one moment of cessation, of agony limitless in extent, limitless in intensity, of torment infinitely lasting, infinitely varied, of torture that sustains eternally that which it eternally devours, of anguish that everlastingly preys upon the spirit while it racks the flesh, an eternity, every instant of which is an eternity, and that eternity an eternity of woe. Such is the terrible punishment decreed for those who die in mortal sin by an almighty and a just God. (Joyce, 1992: 143–4)

But if Joyce's hell-sermon was lavish in abstractions, O'Brien's hell is rich in explanatory matter, more everyday, and more attached to the physics of bodies and objects.

Is it about a bicycle?[1]

Well, quite a lot of it is, and certainly the conversation between Sergeant Pluck and Mr Gilhaney is about nothing else. Noman is sceptically resistant to this obsession at first, as he is incredulous about the Atomic theory and its rumoured consequences (hybrid bike-centaurs, lady schoolteachers impregnated by osmosis), but by the novel's climax he has been converted, a conversion celebrated in prose of astonishing lyric exactness.

> How can I convey the perfection of my comfort on the bicycle, the completeness of my union with her, the sweet responses she gave me at every particle of her frame? I felt that I had known her for any years and that she had known me and that we understood each other utterly. She moved beneath me with agile sympathy in a swift, airy stride, finding smooth ways among the stony tracks, swaying and bending skillfully to match my changing attitudes, even accommodating her left pedal patiently to the awkward working of my wooden leg. I sighed and settled forward on her handlebars, counting with a happy heart the trees which stood remotely on the dark roadside, each telling me that I was further and further from the Sergeant. (O'Brien, 2007: 380)

1   O'Brien, 2007: 267, 321.

To praise this is to run the risk of bathos, of course: we are after all talking about a man's erotic communion with a bicycle, but the agile sympathy of style here, as throughout *The Third Policeman*, is a marvel. Seldom have the damned been graced with so much felicity, as when even a crack in the ceiling opens a lane to the land of the dead. Again, and again as with Beckett, fluency functions only as a mournful last resort.

In *The Third Policeman* the recurrently characteristic juxtaposition in play is that between the sophistication and elegance of atomic theory and variously scholastic ruminations and calculations on the one hand, and on the other the earthy, peasant, agrarian setting and language, with the bicycle the one available interface between the pre- and post-industrial, as it is between the organic and inorganic. The most famous example of this is the elaboration of de Selby's atomic theory, and its Berkleyan ramifications:

> The gross and net result of it is that people who spend most of their natural lives riding iron bicycles over the rocky roadsteads of this parish get their personalities mixed up with the personalities of their bicycle as a result of the interchanging of the atoms of each of them and you would be surprised at the number of people in these parts who nearly are half people and half bicycles. (O'Brien, 2007: 302)

The model of interaction here, linguistically as well as physically, is that of *Insinuation*. Insinuation was a category of classical rhetoric; it is also the cozy face of infiltration, and stands in opposition to conflict or violence, which is what happens when a bar of iron is walloped by a good coal hammer, or when Mathers's jaw is smashed in with a spade.

For Dante, as for Milton, Hell is measurable. So many cubits are accorded so many times a man's dead length, so that the reader, and sinner, can root the calculations as relative to his own experience. The law of fear, however, as further developed by the Jesuits and others in succeeding centuries, insists on the amplification and intensification of suffering. With all things being relative, and quantifiable as such, the arrival of quantum theory ups the ante: a theory of relativity making of previously comforting calculations a matter of Pascalian terror and panic. Amidst the bleakness of an attempted theocracy, Flann deliberately and consistently refigures

Ireland as Hell. If the Green Isle was getting greener, Myles na gCopaleen suggests, it was largely through a process of ulceration.

In a book which is overfull of explanations, one or two things have still to be explained. The first problem is that of narration. Where the hell is our narrator, and when, and why? And how is a first person narrator possible in a world of ultimate relativity? Then there is the question of identical recurrence, urged by the repetition of the first encounter with Pluck, mostly *verbatim*, at the conclusion to the novel. The general idea, sanctioned by the author himself in a letter to William Saroyan, is that he is doomed to repeat the same experience for eternity. Yet exact repetition cannot be possible, since the second time round he is accompanied by his former accomplice who has been shocked into death by the apparition of noman. Will this not change the experience of hell the second time around?

Eternity in *The Third Policeman* is figured not just in terms of the recurrence of the doomed protagonist's fate, but also by spatial invocations of infinite regress, of *mise-en-abyme* projected in to the realm of the sub-atomic. This is manifested in various ways throughout the novel: in the Russian-doll chests fashioned by MacCruiskeen, the last four of which are so miniaturized as to be invisible, just like the point of the spear so sharpened as to prick the hand from half a foot away, and in the eyes of Mathers' ghost.

> Looking at them I got the feeling that they were not genuine eyes at all but mechanical dummies animated by electricity or the like, with a tiny pinhole in the centre of the 'pupil' through which the real eye gazed out secretively and with great coldness. (O'Brien, 2007: 239)

There are other intimations of infinity, and in other directions – like, for example the magnifying glass which magnifies objects to such a degree as to become indiscriminate, and therefore invisible. The human imagination is stretched on the rack of itself with such calculations of hell's intensities.

In 1932 Aldous Huxley argued that the findings of quantum mechanics can only lead to civil disorder:

The news of the disintegration of the atom brings into focus one special aspect of the great problem posed by the existence of an incessantly growing corpus of scientific knowledge. It is this: What should society do with such embodiments of developing thought as are calculated, temporarily at any rate, to derange its organisation and imperil its stability? ... One of the chief factors making for the paralysing uncertainties of the present time is an altogether too efficient science. (Huxley, 1932; in Bradshaw, 1994: 123–6)

Huxley's solution here is to put a kind of moratorium on learning. There can be too much knowledge, too much efficiency, too much curiosity about the nature of matter to be conducive to the healthy operations of an industrial democracy. *The Third Policeman*, like a time capsule or black box recovered in the Atomic Age, looks back to a world still governed by ideals of the scholastic, the agrarian, and medieval visions of heaven and hell, through the paralyzing uncertainties of its present time. We have all heard more than enough over the years about the paralysis of Joyce's Dublin at the turn of the Twentieth Century: it would be a lot more fruitful, and truthful, to think of the Thirties of Kavanagh and MacNeice and Beckett and Flann O'Brien in such terms, and to take more seriously the titles of Anthony Cronin's two memoirs of Ireland in that era, and of O'Brien: *Dead as Doornails* (originally: *Dead as Doornails Under Dev*) and *No Laughing Matter*.

Works Cited

Beckett, Samuel (2000), *Waiting for Godot*, Faber and Faber, London.
Clune, A. and Hurson, T. (1997), *Conjuring Complexities: Essays on Flann O'Brien*, Institute of Irish Studies, Belfast.
Huxley, A. (1932), 'Notes on the Way', *Time and Tide*, xiii, 14 May 1932, 542–4; reprinted in David Bradshaw, *The Hidden Huxley*, London, Faber and Faber, 1994; pp. 123–6.

Gass, William H. (1998), 'Introduction' to Flann O'Brien, *At Swim-Two-Birds,* John F. Byrne Irish Literature Series, Dalkey Archive Press, Chicago.

Jackson, J.W. (1988), *Myles Before Myles,* Paladin, London.

Joyce, James (1992), *A Portrait of the Artist as a Young Man*, Penguin, Harmondsworth.

——(1975), *Finnegans Wake*, Bodley Head, London.

Kenner, Hugh (1997), 'The Fourth Policeman' in Clune and Hurson, *Conjuring Complexities*; pp. 61–72.

Maslen, R.W. (2006), 'Flann O'Brien's Bombshells: *At Swim-Two-Birds* and *The Third Policeman*,' *New Hibernia Review/Iris Éireannach Nua,* (10:4); pp. 84–104.

O'Brien, Flann, (2007), *The Complete Novels,* ed. Keith Donoghue, Everyman's Library, London.

Orwell, George (1989), *Nineteen Eighty-Four*, Penguin, London.

Ryan, J. (ed.) (1970), *A Bash in the Tunnel: James Joyce by the Irish,* Clifton Books, Brighton.

Sage, L. (1975), 'Flann O'Brien' in *Two Decades of Irish Writing: a Critical Survey,* edited by Douglas Dunn, Carcanet, Cheadle; pp. 197–206.

Updike, John (2008), 'Back-chat, funny cracks: the novels of Flann O'Brien,' *The New Yorker,* 11 February 2008.

Joyce's City of Remembering

BARRY LEWIS

> The daughters of memory, whom William Blake chased from his door,
> received regular employment from Joyce, although he speaks of them
> disrespectfully ... He was never a creator *ex nihilo*; he recomposed what
> he remembered, and he remembered most of what he had seen or had
> heard other people remember
>
> —RICHARD ELLMANN

I

When James Joyce was in Trieste in the early years of the last century,
he often entertained friends and visitors from Dublin. On these occa-
sions he loved to test his powers of recall. He would ask about local Irish
characters or list all the shops in O'Connell Street. As Ellmann notes,
Joyce took great pride in remembering things accurately: 'When a shop
had changed hands he was a little disgruntled, as if a picture had been
removed from his museum' (Ellmann, 1982: 579).

Dublin was seemingly preserved in Joyce's mind in a static visual
form. This leads directly to my theme, which is concerned with considering the Dublin of *Ulysses* as if it were a memory theatre. Famously,
Joyce once remarked to Frank Budgen that if Dublin were to disappear,
it could be rebuilt (at least in its 1904 incarnation) from his description
of it in the novel. The various schemas that Joyce distributed amongst his
friends as tools for understanding his epic novel can be seen as memory
aids towards a possible reconstruction and the text is illuminated by an
understanding of memory systems. The schemas are, I will suggest, the

blueprints by which the symbolic architecture of Joyce's text can be rebuilt by the attentive and retentive reader.

To explore this further, I will firstly discuss the development of mnemonic systems in general before looking in detail at the famous Renaissance memory theatre of Giulio Camillo. This will provide us with a model by which we can begin to explore the mnemotechnic aspects of Joyce's *Ulysses*. Several parallels between Joyce's schema for the novel and Camillo's theatre will be noted, before focusing upon an essential difference. I will then examine some passages from *Ulysses* to demonstrate how the stream-of-consciousness narrative technique is also informed by mnemonic principles.[1] The aim throughout will be to further comprehension of Joyce's memory of the city of Dublin and of Joyce's Dublin as a city of memory.

II

The idea that the Dublin of *Ulysses* is a memory theatre has been asserted, with subtlety and sophistication, by John S. Rickard. In his monograph, Rickard (1999) establishes the degree to which *Ulysses* is preoccupied with memory in all of its manifestations. His chapters deal with memory and identity; memory and the past; involuntary memory; textual memory; and intertextual memory.

Memories weave together the disparate episodes of *Ulysses*. Also, the central challenges faced by Dedalus and Bloom are each related to painful memories of the death of loved ones. Dedalus tries to come to terms with the recent loss of his mother; whilst Bloom still struggles with the untimely demise of his baby son, Rudy, almost eleven years ago. At different times of the day, the two main characters are haunted by their pasts

---

1   *Ulysses* was originally published in 1922. The edition I will refer to is a reprint of the text that was corrected and reset in 1961.

and the residual guilt they feel about these pivotal events. Catharsis is approached in the 'Circe' episode, when the ghosts of Mrs Dedalus and Rudy return as hallucinations, like the ghost of Hamlet's father in the Shakespeare play that features so prominently in Joyce's novel.

Rickard not only outlines the value of remembering to Dedalus and Bloom, but also argues persuasively that *Ulysses* is itself a 'mnemotechnic', a textual repository of the unconscious that works through the insistent recall of certain 'trigger words'. Throughout the eighteen chapters, various words and ideas are triggered again and again, either by the circumstances of external environment or the internal associations of private thought processes. Think of the weight given to the term 'metempsychosis' by Bloom, or the lines of the riddle about the fox burying its grandmother that recur frequently in the thinking of Dedalus. Such trigger words and phrases serve to remind the central characters of their traumatic memories, despite their efforts to avoid coming to terms with them. Rickard's perspective is broadly Freudian in orientation, with its emphasis upon trauma, associative ideas, repression and parapraxis. He is keen, though, to point out that his reading does not necessarily entail a psychoanalytical interpretation. Rather, psychoanalysis furnishes some of the terms and concepts by which to describe the figurative 'memory theatre' of *Ulysses*.

With Rickard's study in mind, I would like to elaborate upon how the Dublin of Joyce's *Ulysses* can be conceived as a form of memory theatre. There are several issues to be broached. By what mechanisms does the city function as a space for remembrance and recall? How can Joyce's schemas be seen as memory aids? In what ways does the stream-of-consciousness technique embody mnemonic principles?

III

Ulysses is organised by a number of journeys undertaken by Dedalus and Bloom as they navigate the streets of Dublin and its environs on a single day in 1904. During the course of their travels, they run errands, bump into acquaintances, drink in the local public houses and generally muse upon what they see, think and feel.[2]

However, this is not the only method by which the novel is structured. This temporal combination of events is matched by the spatial journeys that take place in each episode. These journeys are physical, but also perceptual or epistemological, and guide us through an encyclopedic range of subject matter. As Dedalus and Bloom wander through the day, preoccupied with their own individual memories and desires, their flows of consciousness eddy and swirl, follow many tributaries, and often lead to stagnant pools.

The physical travels of the characters across Dublin beget the virtual journeys through the museum or theatre of human knowledge. The activity of wandering through a physical space to recall or review ideas or information is at the heart of the art of memory and the concept of the memory theatre. But what exactly is a memory theatre? A memory theatre is a mental structure (which may or may not be actualised in concrete form) for recalling information and ideas in a systematic manner, using the mnemonic principles of associating key images with fixed locations through visualisation and repetition. These principles were devised in classical times, but the art of memory flourished again in the medieval and Renaissance periods.

The main surviving source from classical times for our knowledge of the *ars memoria*, the Latin name for the art of memory, is the *Ad Herennium*. This was composed in the first century B.C. and, for a long time, was thought to be by Cicero as it shares much in common with his

---

2   Joyce took great care to ensure that the geographical details in *Ulysses* were accurate. See Gunn, I., Hart, C. and Beck, H. (2004).

De Inventione. Both works are systematic accounts of rhetoric and draw upon earlier Greek texts. Memory is treated as a rhetorical tool in the *Ad Herennium.* It distinguishes between two types of memory, the natural and the artificial. The former is that kind of memory that is imprinted without effort upon the mind as a natural consequence of thought and experience. By contrast, the second kind of memory is artificial, in that things are remembered through training or the conscious application of a technique to enhance recall. The so-called 'Roman Room' method is a good example of this. It uses locations in a familiar room as reference points. By placing key images of the items to be remembered at fixed loci, memory is artificially strengthened. The information to be recalled can be associated with objects around the room, such as chairs and tables, or images placed on the walls, floor or ceiling. Frequent visualisation of the room and recitation of the things within it are recommended to strengthen recall. It was most likely some version of this method that Joyce employed when listing the shops in O'Connell Street or regurgitating other impressive roll-calls of Dublin for the benefit of his visitors in Trieste. Alternately, Joyce may have possessed – like Mozart – an eidetic memory, popularly known as a 'photographic memory'. Either way, the images of the city were apparently fixed in his mind's eye for easy access.

To the Greeks and Romans, living in a predominantly oral or pre-print culture, memorisation was a vital part of rhetoric. It was one of the five essential elements for forming a persuasive argument (the others were invention, arrangement, style and delivery). In an oral culture, most speeches were delivered without written notes; artificial memory was necessary to help retain the structure and content of the argument. The strength of the connection between memory and oratory is gauged from the fact that we derive our word 'topic' from 'topos', meaning 'place'. Even today, our essays and debates are often structured by tags such as 'in the first place', 'in the second place' and so on. Such phrases are reminders of how mnemotechnic (i.e. techniques of memory) informs our discourses.

At the fulcrum of the mnemonic process is the metaphor of 'inner writing'. Just as the Ancients wrote by impressing signs upon a waxed tablet, artificial memory works by stamping a mental image upon a pre-designated imagined place. The significance of this to Joyce is obvious. When Stephen Dedalus declares that 'Signatures of all things I am here to read' (Joyce, 1990: 37), he alludes to a way of apprehending reality that has resonance with the classical mnemotechnic. Perception becomes a matter of recognising and interpreting visual images. In addition, Joyce was unusually aware of the significance of rhetoric in the formation of speech and thought. We need only browse through the 'Aeolus' chapter, which is practically a manual of rhetorical figures and tropes, to see the extent of his knowledge and interest in the subject.

The classical techniques of memory were revived in the Middle Ages, as Frances A. Yates (1966) charts at length in the seminal study *The Art of Memory*. The principles of associating images with fixed loci and rein-forcing them in memory through repetitive visualisation were promoted by the Church. They helped clergy and congregation alike to memorise passages from the Bible, recall the Christian virtues and the Seven Deadly Sins, and keep in view the rewards and punishments awaiting the dead in Heaven and Hell. Mnemonics made it easier to deliver sermons on these matters.[3] Yates even posits that mnemotechnical imagery had a profound influence upon ecclesiastical architecture. Almost every nook and cranny of a cathedral functions as a memory aid for the faithful.

During the Renaissance, the art of memory took a detour in a most surprising direction and was linked with magical pursuits. The Jesuits (formed in the fifteenth century) and other religious orders contin-ued to emphasise memory and catechism in their doctrinal training. Mnemonics were becoming disentangled from the Church, however. They were increasingly used as means by which to master the rising flood of knowledge created by humanist advances in science, geography and other worldly affairs. There was a dark side to this, too. Some occult advocates of mnemotechnic principles believed these techniques to be the portals

3   In the light of this, it would be interesting to look at Father Arnall's sermon about the torments of Hell in chapter three of Joyce's *A Portrait of the Artist as a Young Man* (1916).

to special magic powers. The acquisition of a prodigious memory could lead to God-like insights into man, the world and the universe. This is not the place to dwell upon this: again, Frances Yates provides an exhaustive account of these historical developments.

By the sixteenth century, the time was ripe for the introduction of the memory theatre. This concept had always been implicit in the classical and medieval arts of memory. Indeed, the idea of a theatre of memory – a location with many fixed places that can be used for mnemonic associations – simply enlarges the 'Roman Room' method by placing images in a larger space and thereby introducing the possibility of movement into the equation. Quintilian puts it like this: 'What I have spoken of as being done in a house can also be done in public buildings, or on a long journey'.[4] Whether it is in a room, a building or on a journey, the placement of images in a physical space in order to recall or review ideas or information is at the heart of the concept of a mnemotechnic. The most notorious memory theatre of all was devised by Giulio Delminio Camillo, and it caused a sensation in the Europe of the 1500s.

IV

Camillo was an obscure and obese Italian scholar with a speech impediment and a tremendous ambition. He wanted nothing less than to unite the classical mnemotechnic with 'an encyclopedic arrangement of all the existing knowledge of his time in such a manner that it could be set to memory through a system of magical emblematic images' (Radcliff-Umstead, 1972: 47). He apparently built an actual structure that served as a mnemonic repository for vast amounts of information by using images

---

4   Quintilian's *Institutio Oratorio* from the first century A.D. is one of the three prime Latin sources for classical memory techniques (alongside *Ad Herennium* and Cicero's *De Oratore*).

fixed to loci in a space similar to that of a classical auditorium. The scale of his building is unclear, although it must have been bigger than a model as it was large enough for two people to enter it at the same time. Viglius Zuichemus, who was shown the theatre by Camillo himself, described it as such in a letter of 1532.

Camillo first presented this construction in Venice in the early 1530s and was then invited for an audience with King Francis I of France in Paris. The monarch was impressed and bound Camillo to secrecy about his creation. The oath was broken when Camillo dictated a comprehensive outline of the theatre to Girolamo Muzio in the last year of his life (i.e. in 1544). This was later published as *L'Idea del Theatro dell'eccellen. M. Giulio Camillo* in 1550. From this publication we can deduce that the shape of the memory theatre was that of the Vitruvian theatre. In other words, it exhibited a harmony of form based upon proportions derived from basic geometric forms such as the square and the circle. The most famous example of such an arrangement is Leonardo da Vinci's famous drawing of the so-called 'Vitruvian Man'.

How does Camillo's theatre observe the Vitruvian symmetries? The theatre was proportioned according to a similar logic of simple shape and symmetry. It was semicircular in arrangement and rose in seven rows or tiers, with each of these tiers divided by seven gangways. In the centre of the auditorium is a space occupied by the Seven Pillars of Solomon's House of Wisdom. It is here that the user of the memory system would stand, looking out at the seven tiers of seats and gangways (thus reversing the usual direction of gaze in a theatre). The bottommost tier consists of seven doors governed by the seven planets (with the Earth excluded): the Moon, Mercury, Venus, the Sun, Mars, Jupiter and Saturn.[5] The Sun

---

5   The number seven has magical properties, connected with the Renaissance belief that there were seven planetary bodies and therefore seven spheres of celestial influence. It is for this reason that Camillo organises his memory theatre according to the seven known planets. Joyce was aware that 'Seven is dear to the mystic mind' (Joyce, 1990; 160). His third schema is organised according to seven distinct modes. Bloom lives at 7 Eccles Street; he reads two pages of seven books every night; a seventh gravedigger stands beside him at Dignam's funeral, and so on.

door is slightly different in that this prime image is located in a special place on the second tier. Every door is stamped with the image of the deity or agent connected with a specific planet and these images recur on the same vertical axis of each tier. So the Moon is represented by Diana; Mercury by Mercury; Venus by Narcissus; the Sun by Apollo; Mars by Vulcan; Jupiter by Juno; and Saturn by Cybele.

Each horizontal row, with the exception of the first tier which is occupied by the planets, has a governing symbol that is also derived from classical myth. Here, in ascending order, is the sequence of images on the remaining levels:

Row 2: The Banquet
Row 3: The Cave
Row 4: The Gorgon Sisters
Row 5: Pasiphae and the Bull
Row 6: The Sandals of Mercury
Row 7: Prometheus

These rows of related images are each connected with a special theme that shows the relation between the microcosm and the macrocosm. The Planets are primary symbols; the Banquet stands for the elements; the Cave, the properties of things; the Gorgons, the intellect and soul; Pasiphae and the Bull denote behaviour and morals; the Sandals of Mercury, natural processes and the emotions; and Prometheus symbolises the arts, sciences, crafts and other divisions of knowledge.

The whole memory theatre can be collapsed into a two-dimensional Cartesian coordinate grid. In mathematical terms, any point on the horizontal or 'x' axis is known as an abscissa, whilst a point on the vertical or 'y' axis is called the ordinate. By assigning numerical values to these 'x' and 'y' coordinates, we can refer precisely to any point on the grid by a bracketed notation of two numbers: for instance, (1,6) denotes the intersection of the first column and the sixth row. Pinpointing this location on the Camillo grid, we can see that it demarcates the 'square' or place that is formed by the intersection of the Moon or Diana column with the topmost tier of the Promethean rows. This contains the images of the Elephant; Hercules; Iris and Mercury; the Three Pallases; Mercury and the Cock; and Prometheus with his torch of stolen fire. Every one of these items has a precise referent i.e. the unit of information that is to be recalled. The Elephant represents religion and its myths, rites and ceremonies. Hercules, shooting a three-pointed arrow, represents the sciences, eloquence in prose and libraries. Iris and Mercury represent embassies and letter-writing. The Three Pallases represent drawing, architecture, painting, perspective and culture. Mercury and the Cock represent trade and commerce. Prometheus with a torch represents the arts and artifice in general.[6]

The rationale for Camillo's choice and ordering of images is too complex to go into for our purposes. Suffice to say, in the syncretic spirit of the times he draws freely upon a diversity of sources such as the Old Testament, the Jewish Kabbala, St John's Gospel, astrology, Platonism and the arcana of Hermes Trismegistus. The overall organising principle is the story of Creation: not as recounted in Genesis, but the version presented in Ficino's Latin translation of the *Corpus Hermeticum*, a collection of Hellenic magical texts from the second and third centuries A.D. The point of Camillo's somewhat bizarre hodgepodge of sources was to form a system that would enable the individual to memorise a vast array of information and knowledge. Each location within his memory theatre acts as a 'place-holder' or locus for what is to be remembered. By combining figures from classical literature and myth with images from the astrological properties of planets, Camillo's mnemotechnic comprises a set of easily remembered coordinates.

V

Camillo's mnemotechnic is fascinating in its own right, but how does it relate to Joyce? It is my contention that Camillo's memory theatre provides a useful model for examining Joyce's Dublin as its own unique memory space. As is well known, the composition of *Ulysses* was executed

6   For a more detailed analysis, see Robinson (2004).

with reference to an underlying system of correspondences for each chapter. One group consists of parallels to Homer's *Odyssey* and another group correlates with a variety of features with which Joyce structures each chapter. These correspondences were drawn up in table form by Joyce and used as the blueprint for the novel.

There were, in fact, three different versions of the schema which Joyce distributed to friends after being pressed many times to explain his complex and confusing narrative. The first schema dates from a letter of 3 September 1920, sent to John Quinn, a New York lawyer who supported Joyce's work financially and in other ways. This version makes clear the parallels between the novel's chapters and episodes from Homer. It also divides *Ulysses* into three sections: the first three chapters form the 'Telemachiad'; the middle chapters the 'Odyssey'; and the final three chapters, the 'Nostos' (i.e. homecoming). Later that month, on 21 September, Joyce forwarded an expanded version of the schema to Carlo Linati, an Italian critic and friend. This version, written in Italian, provides the Homeric titles and expands on the correspondences relevant to each chapter. It is laid out in tabular form. The vertical axis shows the sequence of chapters in *Ulysses*, each named after a Homeric person, place or event. The horizontal axis contains eight further columns, each of which denotes an element that determines the content of a chapter. In the original hand-written Linati manuscript, the order of the columns is as follows: time, colour, persons, technic, science or art, sense, organ and symbol.[7]

The Gorman-Gilbert schema is a simplified and modified version of Linati's. This third version was originally produced for a lecture on the (then unpublished) novel by Valery Larbaud, a French writer, scheduled for 7 December 1921. It was given to Jacques Benoît-Méchin, who was translating the 'Penelope' chapter into French. It then circulated secretly amongst several of Joyce's friends. These included the American Sylvia Beach, whose Paris bookstore Shakespeare and Company became the first publisher of *Ulysses* in 1922, and Herbert Gorman, an American reporter who wrote the first Joyce biography. It eventually wound up in the possession of British critic Stuart Gilbert, the first editor of Joyce's

7   The full schematic table can be seen in Ellmann (1972).

168 BARRY LEWIS

letters, who used the schema as part of his exegesis in his early influential
study (Gilbert, 1930). This Gorman-Gilbert schema is close to Linati's,
but it adds details of the place in which each chapter is set and contains
a different set of symbols.

If we consider Camillo's memory theatre and Joyce's schema in
tandem, some fruitful parallels emerge. In the first place, it is striking that
both Camillo and Joyce use images from classical literature and mythology
to govern each row of their systems. In Camillo, this function is fulfilled
by various classical gods, heroes and images, such as Prometheus, Pasiphae
and The Cave. With Joyce, too, each horizontal row (representing the
chapters) is presided over by a classical person, place or event, culled from
Homer's *Odyssey*. There are three types: people/animals (Telemachus,
Nestor, Proteus, Calypso, the Lotus Eaters, Aeolus, the Lestrygonians,
Scylla and Charybdis, Sirens, Cyclops, Nausicaa, the Oxen of the Sun,
Circe, Eumaeus and Penelope); places (Hades and Ithaca); and events
(Wandering Rocks). The employment of such *imagines agentes* (imagi-
nary agents) in mnemonic systems is widespread, as recall is strength-
ened by links with images that are more concrete than abstract. Joyce
was fully alive to the potency of such associations. As he wrote in his
Linati letter:

> Each adventure (that is, every hour, every organ, every art being interconnected
> and interrelated in the structural scheme of the whole) should not only condition
> but even create its own technique. Each adventure is so to say one person, although
> it is composed of persons–as Aquinas relates of the heavenly hosts. (quoted in
> Ellmann, 1982: 521)

There is a second broad parallel between Camillo's memory theatre and Joyce's schema in that the vertical axes consist of columns of
correspondences that determine the ordering of their material. With
Camillo, it is the planets that provide a spectrum of influences (e.g. fiery
Mars and judgemental Saturn).[8] These characteristics are echoed in the

---

8   Strictly speaking, the Moon and the Sun are not planets, but are 'luminaries' within
     astrology.

very names of the planets, which refer to Greek and Roman deities and heroes. Joyce's vertical determinants are drawn from aspects of literature, rather than astronomy or astrology. For each chapter they represent its physical setting (place and time); its imagery and symbolism (art, colour and symbol); its relation to a part of the body (organ); and its narrative mode (technic). Such a strong interrelation of elements is conducive to recall and operates in much the same manner as a memory theatre.

A third feature that aligns Camillo and Joyce is their attempts to capture the whole of what is known through their respective systems. Camillo wants to do so for magical and occult purposes. To hold everything in one's mind at one time, with the help of the memory system, would be tantamount to being God and may well grant divine powers to man. Joyce's aim is less mystical, but equally comprehensive. As he said in the letter to Linati that accompanied his second schema, *Ulysses* is also an encyclopedia. Almost any part of Joyce's novel can testify to its encyclopedic scope. On a couple of random pages from the 'Oxen of the Sun' episode there are references to Anglesey; cancer of the stomach; the feast of the Holy Innocents; the use of rare or archaic words such as 'wanhope', 'cautels', 'avis' and 'mandement'; stylistic pastiches of *Everyman* and Mandeville; allusions to Job; meditations on menstruation; and asides about the Mater Misericordiae Hospital, Mahoud or Mohammed and ancient Chaldea (Joyce, 1990: 386–87). Such profligacy of knowledge is present throughout the novel.

So, Camillo's memory theatre and Joyce's third schema have several things in common, as we have seen. Both feature a vertical axis governed by classical figures and a horizontal axis that runs through seven categories of knowledge. The memory theatre of Camillo is rationally ordered into tiers, with the most important features first. The rows of this theatre move from the elements, through objects, man's faculties (intellect, baviour, emotions) to the arts, sciences and crafts. Joyce's schemas lack this rigorous categorisation of knowledge and experience, but nevertheless retain some vestige of it in the importance given to the arts and sciences and the human faculties. Both Camillo and Joyce arrange their material in a way that is consistent with the classical rules of memory. By making strong associations between place and image, people and events, they bind together the elements of knowledge to be recalled.

VI

Having established an isomorphism between Camillo's memory theatre and Joyce's schema, it is time to look at some specific examples of how Joyce's *Ulysses* embodies mnemotechnic principles. According to the Gorman-Gilbert schema, the second chapter has the following schematic features:

Scene: School
Hour: 10 a.m.
Organ: none
Science/Art: History
Colour: brown
Symbol: horse
Technic: catechism (personal)

In this chapter, or 'adventure' as Joyce calls it, Stephen is at the Summerfield Lodge School in Dalkey (place), teaching a history lesson (science/art) between 9 and 10 a.m. (time). The subject is that of Pyrrhus of Epirus and his famous fight against the Romans, a battle hardly worth winning due to the casualties sustained (hence the phrase 'pyrrhic victory'). Stephen's pedagogical style can clearly be described as a type of catechism (technique), in which multiple questions are posed, to which memorised answers are required:

—You, Cochrane, what city sent for him?
—Tarentum, sir.
—Very good. Well?
—There was a battle, sir.
—Very good. Where?
The boy's blank face asked the blank window.

...

–I forgot the place, sir. 279 B.C.
–Asculum, Stephen said, glancing at the name and date in the gorescareed book.
(Joyce, 1990: 24)

After the lesson, Stephen goes to the study of headmaster Mr Deasy
where he is to be paid. Deasy's walls are decorated with framed pictures
of racehorses (symbol) from the past. The chapter is named after Nestor
(title and imaginary agent), the elderly statesman in Homer from whom
Telemachus seeks advice at Pylos about how to find his father, Ulysses.
Nestor is a bit of a windbag and somewhat self-regarding: much like
Deasy himself, in fact, who treats Stephen to a harangue about the virtues
of saving money, a treatment for foot-and-mouth disease and a joke in
poor taste about anti-semitism in Ireland. Although the colour brown is
not directly mentioned in the chapter, it is implied by the pictures of the
racehorses. Also, Stephen could be said to be in a 'brown study' in both
a literal and metaphorical sense of the term (i.e. a state of deep thought)
throughout these events. The chapter does not correspond with a named
organ: as Joyce notes cryptically in the Linati schema, this is because in
the first three chapters Telemachus does not bear a body. However, most
of the relevant schematic elements are easily discernible in 'Nestor' as
they are in the other chapters.

As mentioned earlier, Joyce formulated the schemas originally for
compositional purposes, but then circulated them privately for purposes
of analysis and comprehension.[9] The homologies between Joyce's system
and Camillo's theatre suggest another way in which the schemas of *Ulysses*
can be employed: as memory aids for the novel itself, the Dublin it tra-
verses and the wealth of knowledge it hosts. If readers wish to recall the
salient business of Joyce's second chapter, they can refer to the schema's
categories as loci, and associate them with relevant material to memorise.
The schema thus becomes a blueprint for Joyce's memory theatre. What

9   There has been much debate about whether or not Joyce's schemas were, in fact,
     instrumental to the composition of the novel or whether they were a late addition
     to the making of *Ulysses*. A persuasive argument in favour of the former can be
     found in Fludernick (1986).

about the page-by-page detail, though, of *Ulysses*? Are the principles of the art of memory operative here? Let us approach this issue from a different angle, concentrating not so much on the schema but Joyce's stream-of-consciousness method.

The classical writers on memory (Cicero, Quintilian and others) had recommended that the subject should visualise themselves moving through their imaginary spaces for the purposes of remembering. Joyce's characters do something very like this. As Bloom and Dedalus traverse Dublin, they mimic the wanderings of Homer's Ulysses and Telemachus. Different places, and the people, objects and events they encounter there, trigger different memories. Therefore knowledge is associated with movement and remembering. The essential difference between Joyce and the Renaissance mnemotechnic is that in the memory theatre constructed by Camillo, the journey is a rational progression through ordered stage-posts. This helps the mind to order its material as the parts of the system exhibit a great deal of synergy with the whole. With Joyce, however, the journeys of Bloom and Dedalus through Dublin have a much more peripatetic, disordered quality, reflecting the chaotic state of modern urban existence.

This difference would seem to diminish the appropriateness of applying mnemonic ideas to *Ulysses*, as recall is usually bound up with logic and sequence: usually, but not always. A digression into myrmecology will help to address this issue. The study of ants suggests that memory is not always dependent upon internalised patterns of recall. It has long puzzled scientists how ants are able to build complex anthills. Do they have a 'memory' of what to do stored inside them? Or are they able somehow to communicate with each other about how to construct the anthill? The answer turns out to involve neither of these options. What happens is that each ant moves at random until it finds a suitable piece of material. On its way back to base, it leaves a pheremone trace. This can then be followed by subsequent ants as a marker for where to go to find what they need. The more ants that follow a particular trace, the stronger the path becomes, until the source is exhausted – at which point the pheremones are allowed to fade. The ants therefore access a distributed memory that is activated through movement and is situated in the environment. This process is called 'stigmergy' – it is a word coined from the combination of the Greek words 'stigma', meaning sign or mark, and 'ergon', meaning work. The idea is that the mark itself triggers a particular action.

Applying this to Bloom and Dedalus, we can venture the proposition that their mnemonic journeys are also stigmergic. As they move through Dublin in a seemingly haphazard manner, their movement takes them to places that prompt other memories, actions and anticipations. These places act like pheromones: perhaps we should call then 'pheromnemones'. The cluster of actions and thoughts is associated with a particular place, as advised by the classic mnemotechnic, except that in the novel the environment itself (i.e. the bars, shops and streets of Dublin) acts as a form of 'distributed memory' in these encounters. There are thousands of examples of pheromnemones in *Ulysses* – indeed, it is the very *modus operandi* of the stream-of-consciousness method that Joyce perfected in the novel – but two will suffice to convey the flavour.

In the 'Lestrygonians' episode, Bloom pauses by the shop window of Yeates and Son, located on Grafton Street on the corner of Nassau Street. He looks at the field glasses displayed there and this reminds him that he must fix his own pair of binoculars. He wonders whether or not he would be able to find a suitable replacement pair at the railway lost property office. Still musing on such matters of optics, he tries a little experiment. He stretches his right arm at full length and blots out the sun with the tip of his little finger. The image (and its associations) recurs in 'Circe' (as does much of the rest of the novel) when Bloom hallucinates that he is atop Nelson's Pillar and 'eclipses the sun by extending his little finger' (Joyce, 1990; 166). The place, or shop window, has therefore activated Bloom's memory (of his old binoculars); prompted the anticipation of a possible future activity (getting them fixed or finding a replacement pair); and motivated a specific action in the present (the sun experiment).[10]

10   The passage accrues a further significance when we take into account the observation that blotting out the sun with the finger was, to the druids, a symbol of man's divinatory powers. There are also links here with recurrent themes of Joyce's *Ulysses*, such as parallax, the setting of the 'Home Rule' sun and the limitations of one-eyed visions.

This whole sequence of shop window-binoculars-lost property office-sun experiment forms a pheromnemone that is easily remembered by the reader, who is able to associate place with images in the classic mnemonic fashion as a means of recalling the novel's events.

Similarly, in the 'Proteus' episode when Stephen wanders along Leahy's Terrace in Sandymount after finishing his morning's teaching, he spots two midwives. He recognises one of them as Florence MacCabe and is intrigued by the bag she carries. His thoughts move as follows:

> One of her sisterhood lugged me squealing into life. Creation from nothing. What has she in the bag? A misbirth with a trailing navelcord, hushed in ruddy wool. The cords of all link back, strandentwining cable of all flesh. That is why mystic monks. Will you be as gods? Gaze in your omphalos. Hello! Kinch here. Put me on to Edenville. Aleph, alpha: nought, nought, one. (Joyce, 1990: 37–8)

So the gruesome picture of a dead foetus in a bag leads to a complex stream of thought that touches upon the umbilical cord; the common ancestry of humanity; meditative navel-gazing; and a fantasy about telephoning Eve with a number composed of sacred letters (the first letters of the Hebrew and Greek alphabets) and digits signifying creation out of nothing. This last flourish is presumably incited by a mental switch between navel cords and telephone cords, and the notion we are all linked together like a vast telephone exchange. This pheromnemone tells us much about Stephen's thought processes and is fixed in the reader's mind by associating place (Leahy Terrace) with images (navels, cords, telephones).[11] The 'Lestrygonians' passage operates in this way, too. The stream-of-consciousness technique can therefore be construed as conforming to the art of memory. Not only does it render convincingly everyday thought processes, it also binds together material in ways that enhance recall. It

11   Again, the passage acquires further depth if we accept the suggestion that the omphalos, the Greek word for 'navel', was a name given to the Delphi oracle, the source of prophecy in Ancient Greece. Other themes from *Ulysses* flicker throughout this passage: the mystery of birth, the interpenetration of phenomena, the fascination with modern technology and so on.

is by such means that Joyce provides the building blocks for the reconstruction of the Dublin of 1904.

VII

Renaissance magic, anthills and a masterpiece of Modernist literature: it is almost like one of Stephen Dedalus's riddles. These diverse topics have been brought into contact to explore further Rickard's proposition that the Dublin of Joyce's *Ulysses* can be viewed usefully from a mnemotechnical perspective. The parallels I have suggested between Joyce's schemas and the memory theatre of Giulio Camillo corroborate Rickard's notion of thinking about the novel (and the city) as a memory space. Analysis of selected passages of the novel has revealed how the stream-of-consciousness narrative method also conforms to mnemonic principles. The conclusion reached is that Camillo's memory procedures are synergistic, whilst Joyce's are stigmergic.

The evidence for considering *Ulysses* as a memory theatre is mainly analogical: no claim has been made that Joyce knew of Camillo and his theatre, though it is surely a possibility. What cannot be doubted is Joyce's familiarity with other Renaissance thinkers who created memory systems. He owned a copy of Tommaso Campanella's *City of the Sun* (1602), a text that offers an entire imaginary city as a memory space, much as Joyce does with Dublin. Campanella was directly influenced by Camillo. Moreover, Joyce was intimately acquainted with the work of the greatest memory artist of all, Giordano Bruno, a man whose ideas saturate Joyce's oeuvre. But these are matters for later deliberation.

As a final thought, consider that every sixteenth of June, readers of James Joyce walk through Dublin to retrace the routes taken by Stephen Dedalus and Leopold Bloom. They commemorate Bloomsday, the fabled date in 1904 on which Joyce set *Ulysses*, by reminding themselves through the powers of association and image of what Dedalus and Bloom thought,

spoke and did in each location. Whether they realise it or not, these literary tourists are participating in a form of remembrance that has its roots
in the world of the ancients and which flourished during the medieval
period and the Renaissance. They are remembering the city in Joyce's very
own city of remembering.

Works Cited

Bonabeau, E., Dorigo, M. and Theraulaz, G. (1992), *Swarm Intelligence:
From Natural to Artificial Systems*, Oxford University Press, New
York.
Ellmann, R. (1972), *Ulysses on the Liffey*, Oxford University Press, Oxford.
——(1982), James Joyce, New and Revised Edition, Oxford University
Press, New York.
Fludernick, M. (1986), '*Ulysses* and Joyce's Change of Artistic Aims', *James
Joyce Quarterly*, 23, pp. 173–88.
Gilbert, S. (1930), *James Joyce's Ulysses: A Study*, Faber and Faber,
London.
Gunn, I., Hart, C. and Beck, H. (2004), *James Joyce's Dublin: A
Topographical Guide to the Dublin of Ulysses*, Thames and Hudson,
London.
Joyce, J. (1990), *Ulysses*, Vintage, New York.
Radcliff-Umstead, D. (1972), 'Giulio Camillo's Emblems of Memory',
Yale French Studies, 23, pp. 47–56.
Rickard, J.S. (1999), *Joyce's Book of Memory: The Mnemotechnic of Ulysses*,
Duke University Press, Durham and London.
Robinson, K. (2004), 'Power and Persuasion in the Theatre of Camillo',
in Szulakowska, U. (ed.), *Power and Persuasion: Sculpture in its
Rhetorical Context*, Institute of Art of the Polish Academy of Sciences,
Warsaw, pp. 37–48.
Yates, F. (1966), *The Art of Memory*, University of Chicago Press,
Chicago.

Sexual Dissidents and Queer Space in Northern Irish Fiction

CAROLINE MAGENNIS

The ways by which Northern Irish society has preserved its boundaries and cohesion in the maintenance of certain forms of sectarian identity are in unnerving correspondence with the ways in which it has repressed homosexuality through law, protests and intimidation. For each subversion of the norm, it seems, there is a tactic of marginalisation against those who dare dissent. Space is a critical issue for the study of both ethno-sectarian conflict and the queer experience. This essay takes a number of theoretical cues from the work of the sociologist Rob Kitchin, whose essay 'Sexing the City', (2002) describes Belfast as having a 'homophobic hyper-hetero masculinity' (2002: 215). Kitchin, working with Karen Lysaught, employs the term 'sexual dissidents'[1] remarks that:

> It is clear that Belfast, as expressed through legislation and political policy, and institutional and public attitudes and practises, is on the whole a sexually conservative and homophobic society. (2000: 11)

Space is a critical issue for both gay activists and for queer theory. As Kitchin and Lysaught note, there is a growing academic interest in the provision and maintenance of 'queer space' and debate on the necessity of a separate space. These debates, in Northern Ireland, are inflected with political consequences.

---

[1]   Kitchin and Lysaght use this term to 'represent all those people who do not perform as "good" heterosexuals' (23) in the formulation set out by Gayle Rubin (Rubin, 1989).

This essay will focus on the representation of homosexuality and homophobia in Northern Irish fiction, with particular reference to Maurice Leitch's *The Liberty Lad* (1965) and Glenn Patterson's *The International* (1999). Both of these novels are set in pre-troubles Northern Ireland, where bisexuality appears to correspond with an ambivalent attitude to sectarian politics. Patterson's novel was published in 1999, over thirty years after *The Liberty Lad*, and so allows a more knowing glance at the era's sexual politics. There will be an emphasis on the spatial tensions in Northern Irish gay life rendered in fiction, particularly the inscribing of a sexual status to space, and how this intersects with sectarian violence.[2]

Representations of homosexuality in Northern Irish fiction are notable by their absence. The work of Forrest Reid, particularly *Uncle Stephen* (1931) explores the potential for quasi-Hellenistic relations between man and boy. Tom refers to his uncle as 'his master' and understands his role as a 'pupil' (Reid, 1931: 268). After this, one of the earliest mentions of homosexuality in Northern Irish fiction is in the prolific Brian Moore's novel *The Emperor of Ice Cream* (1965). Gavin and Freddy meet Maurice Markham, a friend of a poet whom Freddy admires. When Freddy implies that there is homosexuality in their local community a shocked Gavin retorts 'You mean they're *fruits*?' (Moore, 1996: 96) Freddy acts nonplussed, nonchalantly cleaning his glasses and asking Gavin if he had never met an actual 'fruit' in a Catholic school. Gavin retorts that boys often tried to 'grab you in the jakes' but they weren't 'real pansies' (Moore, 1996: 96). His 'good' side, manifested in the novel by the 'white angel', is shocked and sees Freddy as introducing him to deviants and degenerates. He muses:

> What did homos *do*, anyway? What repulsive couplings took place between Reverend McMurty and Maurice? There was something about the thought which made him physically sick. O God, he did not want to be like Maurice or Matthew. How could he have ever admired those effeminate twerps? *He* had never felt homo,

2   It must be noted at this juncture that this essay deals with male-authored fiction; with a few notable exceptions such as Deirdre Madden and Lucy Caldwell, it seems Northern Irish novels are rarely written by women.

never. Still, if you lusted after girls but had never actually slept with one, then how could you be sure you mightn't be homo at a future date? (Moore, 1996: 96)

It is important, though, to note the critical voice with which Moore addresses the Catholic Church and the prejudices it has instilled in him, in this novel and others. This passage, written as the gay movement began to gain consciousness, can be read as a satire on heterosexual panic. The Belfast-born singer Brian Kennedy has written two novels, *The Arrival of Fergal Flynn* (2004) and *Roman Song* (2005) about a young homosexual man growing up in war-torn 1980s Falls Road. These present us with a loose fictionalisation of Kennedy's own upbringing. Also featuring a gay sexually active priest is Damian McNicholl's *A Son Called Gabriel* (2004), set in the sixties and seventies in a working class Catholic community in Northern Ireland. This novel centres on the adolescence and sexual awakening of Gabriel Harkin. It is worth noting, though that while the gay male experience has been under-represented in Northern Irish literature the lesbian experience is almost completely absent from Ulster writing.

So, why this barely audible queer Ulster voice? Northern Ireland has a long history of homophobia, the apex of which was Ian Paisley's Save Ulster from Sodomy Campaign, which was launched in 1977. This was a response to the decriminalisation of homosexual acts between men in England and Wales in 1967 and subsequent attempts to extend the laws to Northern Ireland. The European Court of Human Rights ensured that this campaign failed in 1982 as homosexual acts were decriminalised. However, Alan Bairner, drawing our attention back to issues of space, notes that

when a young policeman was shot dead in a Belfast pub during the final stages of the conflict, more attention was paid to the fact that he had been drinking in a gay bar than that he had been killed. Similarly, one of the main complaints levelled at the film *Resurrection Man* ... was not that the leading character was portrayed as a sociopath but that homosexual tendencies were ascribed to him and one of the other loyalist paramilitaries. In a climate, which allows such attitudes to persist, it is by no means only women who should be frightened of hegemonic masculinity. (Bairner, 1999: 136)

These attitudes are evidenced by Martin's father in David Park's *Swallowing the Sun* (2004) as he tells his sons 'It's fuckin' dresses they ought to be wearing. It's handbags they should be carrying. Bloody nancy boys the pair of them' (Park, 2004: 1). A more progressive picture emerged in a survey conducted by Ipsos-Mori on behalf of the Lesbian Advocacy Services Initiative, and reported in *The Observer* (McDonald, 2006). According to this survey, three-quarters of the Northern Irish people say they are tolerant of gay men, lesbians and bisexuals, and 88 per cent believe there should be no discrimination against them. However, despite these figures, they still perceive the Province as a homophobic place. Fifty-nine per cent said they considered the North 'either not very or not at all accepting' of lesbians, gay men and bisexuals, yet only 21 per cent of the same people hold such views themselves. Catholics perceive themselves as less homophobic than Protestants do. Eighty-three per cent of Catholics said they were 'very accepting' of gays, lesbians and bisexuals compared with 70 per cent of Protestants. The new mood of tolerance this survey conveys is in sharp contrast to the findings for the Belfast-based Institute for Conflict Research in 2006. Their research found that 82 per cent of gay men had suffered harassment, usually at the hands of young men, reminding us of the five gay men who have been killed in Northern Ireland since 1997, and contrasted this with the fact that only 42 per cent of declared victims had notified the police of the crime committed against them.

In Eoin McNamee's work, references to homosexuality are refracted through the same dark lens applied to all sexuality in his novels. His characters' sexual encounters, whether gay or straight, are joyless and serve as portrayals of hierarchical structures of power. In *The Blue Tango* (2002) the barber, Wesley Courtney, is homosexual and this marks him out as deviant to the police officers who are investigating the death of Patricia Curran. This is an indication how sexuality, or at least the appearance of heterosexuality, is integral to the masculine collective. Due to his deviance, the hairdresser is singled out for investigation by the police over the murder, and is considered to have knowledge of any sexually deviant activity in the area, homosexual or not. There are echoes of Judith Butler's idea on the penalties for not performing your gender as expected by the society in which you live. When Patricia jokes about 'Fruity Wesley's demon barber shop' (McNamee, 2002: 28), his space is marked as queer, therefore taboo and deviant. In *The Blue Tango*, in a similar manner to the work of Italian physiognomist Cesare Lombroso, homosexuality was believed to have physiological manifestations: 'It was widely believed that they could be singled out by their high-pitched effeminate speaking voices, their weak handshakes, their poor eyesight' (McNamee, 2002: 124). In this novel, homosexuality is the rampant, unruly, Other which conflicts with upstanding Protestant Ulster. The 'Sons of Ulster' must always be on their guard.

An interesting account of homosexuality and homophobia in a Northern Irish paramilitary comes from Brendí McClenaghan in his 'Letter from a Gay Republican: H-Block 5'(McClenaghan, 1995). McClenaghan tells his story of trying to be both Republican and gay, and how these two discourses of masculinity at first seemed irreconcilable. In a return to our concern of space, he had been in prison for seventeen years at the time of writing his letter, and was on blanket protest in the early 1980s. These facts point to his participation in Republicanism as severe and bloody. In prison, he was ostracised and contemplated moving to a non-paramilitary wing and even suicide. The leader of his wing was made aware of the situation and offered his full support; McClenaghan then published an article 'Invisible Comrades: Gays and Lesbians in the Struggle' in *An Glór Gafa*, the Republican prisoners' quarterly magazine. The response was diverse, as he notes: 'Reactions to the piece were many and varied, ranging from blatant homophobia to solid support' (McClenaghan, 1995: 128). Vincent Quinn has drawn more specifi parallels between the politics of sectarian and gay identity in Northern Ireland:

> If gay space exists what does it look like? Shops and houses marked with emblems? Banners bearing provocative slogans? Marches? Demos? Clubs and bars with particular clienteles? Flags? Bodies declaring their allegiance via dress codes and styles of personal adornment? Resistance? Pride? A statement of identity in the face of public hostility? (Quinn, 2000: 258)

Like Brendí McClenaghan, Quinn asks if one can both be homosexual and accepted as a member of a Loyalist or Republican community. Quinn also asks important questions about the gendering of the conflict in Northern Irish literature, and the consequences this has for non-traditional sexual identities.

Both McNamee and McClenaghan examined the reaction to homosexuality in a Northern Irish paramilitary organisation. However, there is also some representation of non-violent gay men in Northern Irish novels, even if they are rarely protagonists. *Eureka Street* (1996) by Robert McLiam Wilson features a number of interesting depictions of the ways in which men function together in social settings; in homosocial rather than homoerotic groupings. Jake's group of friends is one of his few stable relationships in the text. The sincere affection this cross-community group of men has for each other is palpable, despite their ribald banter. This novel features a small number of 'out' gay characters. When Jake's friend Donal announces that he is gay, his friends are remarkably accepting of both him and his new partner. Jake muses that: 'Donal was there with his new boyfriend. Pablo seemed a nice young man, if pointlessly good looking and well muscled' (Wilson, 1997: 353). While this is a discussion of male sexuality, it is worth pointing out that this text also features a lesbian relationship between two older women, Chuckie's mother and her neighbour. Jake's romantic tendencies are also applied to men, as an acne-ridden youth who works in the local corner shop incurs his reveries: 'This kid just blushed because he thought he was generally a crap idea, a big mistake. It made me want to kiss his lumpy neck. It made me want to die of love' (Wilson, 1997: 171). It is only Roche, the abused child who befriends Jake, who brings any real homophobia into the text. 'You're not going to fruit me up, are you? You're going to try and fuck my bum, you dirty poof' (Wilson, 1997: 166). While the boy states 'No handjobs, remember?' (Wilson, 1997: 247) Jake wryly tells Roche: 'You're much less sexually attractive than you believe' (Wilson, 1997: 301). This child is abandoned by his parents, and his tough exterior masks his ill treatment and abuse.

Maurice Leitch's *The Liberty Lad* centres on a young teacher, Frank, and the fractured relationship he has with the place in which he has grown up and still lives – rural Northern Ireland. His best friend is a gay man, Terry, with whom he has a number of encounters and whose lifestyle fascinates him. Frank begins a flirtation with a local married woman whom he later chides for lack of imagination whilst being drawn to the furtiveness of the encounter: 'Wonder would she perform, extra-maritally, as they say in the News of the World?' (Leitch, 1985: 80). Belfast, for Frank, represents erotic potentiality, with the rural figured as a parochial, non-sexual site. However, the homoerotic elements of Frank's experience provide the most telling comment on the relationship between sex and space in Northern Ireland. The youthful play between Frank and Terry arouses conflicting feelings in Frank. One August afternoon while wrestling with Terry they point 'mockingly at the bulges that had suddenly appeared in our trunks. And I suppose before that there must have been other times too when we fumbled innocently with each other. Just how *normal* was our relationship anyway?' (Leitch, 1985: 27).

Frank's education leads him often to theorise in depth about the nature of his encounters with Terry. He is aware of psychoanalysis and is fascinated by the erotic: 'A clear case of fetishism of erotic symbolism', I said. 'If you'd read your Krafft-Ebing you'd know that' (Leitch, 1985: 29). Frank has obviously read extensively into the psychology of sexuality, which at this point was booming after the Kinsey Reports. One would consider this unusual reading for a primary school teacher in rural Northern Ireland. When Terry and Frank visit the Isle of Man, it is the first time out of the safely regimented space of Northern Ireland for either of them. Having booked a double room in order to save money, Frank wakes up with Terry lying behind him, pressed into his back, with Terry's hand on his genitals:

> Everything left my mind except the pleasure that came from the deft fingers ... I was turned round and pulled roughly towards him. His arms went round me and I felt the rasp of his male face against the side of mine. I think it was that which brought me to my senses. (Leitch, 1985: 39)

This leads to a frank exchange between the pair that begins with Frank asking him 'point-blank if he was a homosexual' (Leitch, 1985: 39). Terry is remarkably candid about his previous sexual escapades and offers Frank a glimpse into a world he hardly dared think of:

> The flood-gates were up, all the secrets and private feelings he had been guard-
> ing for years he poured out for me and I listened, fascinated, by the strange new
> underground world of an in-between sex. Many of the things he told me I had
> read about, tantalisingly in novels or clinically in textbook, but there were other
> things that struck me with a hammer-like force. (Leitch, 1985: 39)

Frank is surprised when Terry recounts the names of men he has been
intimate with and men he knows to be homosexual: '(H)e listed me film
stars, actors, writers and celebrities he knew about and some he had slept
with, and he told me of local men, some of whom I knew and some of
them married' (Leitch, 1985: 39). Frank is fascinated by these new codes
of behaviour, admitting that 'it was a new world for me, with its own
languages and laws, and I was greedy for knowledge' (Leitch, 1985: 40).
After Mona rejects his attempts at a sexual encounter in a house for sale
he goes to a bar named Delargy's in the Docks Area of Belfast with Terry
and some of Terry's friends. Frank begins the evening unsettled by the
effeminate manner in which these men are acting, and slowly comes round
to the idea that he is drinking in a bar frequented by homosexuals. He
notices the shift in Terry's behaviour: 'Here he was with his own kind.
Before that night I'd always thought of *him* as being different ... but now
it was me who has out of place' (Leitch, 1985: 160). Bradley, Terry's MP
friend, is a predatory gay man, despite being a married father. When they
first meet, Bradley and Terry leave Frank at the end of the evening with
a few pleasantries that barely conceal their intentions. Frank is disconcerted by Bradley's charm and charisma, believing his personal traits to
be studied. Frank remarks that: 'I became aware for the first time of his
trick – if it was a trick – of concentrating all his attention on the person
he was speaking to at the time, and when he shifted to someone else it
was like being deprived of the glow of a powerful searchlight' (Leitch,
1985: 53).

In a comedic scene, Frank offers himself up to Bradley. Frank is being
considered for the post of head-teacher of the school where he works, and
Bradley is on the interview panel. Frank is reluctant at the beginning to
give himself to Bradley in return for his influence but he changes his mind,
and it is not clear whether he is career or sexually motivated. Bradley is

in full control of the situation, which plays like a seduction scene from a
bad movie. Leitch again feminises the homosexual figure, casting Frank
in the role of supplicant: 'And so now I was to be the fatalistic pea-hen
awaiting king cobra. The desire to squawk arose in me' (Leitch, 1985:
184). The licentiousness is temporarily halted by Bradley's young son, but
carries on with Frank, terrified and reluctant, unfamiliar with the codes
of homosexual seduction. In his encounters with women in the text, he
endeavours to be the aggressor. This role reversal troubles his masculine
sense of self. However, when Bradley reaches to feel if Frank is aroused,
he finds that Frank is not and their encounter ends with both parties
covering their obvious embarrassment with pleasantries. When Frank is
driving home, he feels sexual stirrings, which are couched in euphemism:
'I felt a sudden delayed tightening and stirring between my legs. In the
words of our local delicate turn of phrase I was "touching cloth"' (Leitch,
1985: 190). His body fails him again at his father's funeral when he cannot
cry: 'My eyes were like two cinders. Truthfully, I was obsessed more with
the fact that people might notice my absence of external grief than any
personal worries' (Leitch, 1985: 194).

Glenn Patterson's *The International* tells the story of Danny, a bisexual barman in a Belfast hotel. Patterson's collected non-fiction writing,
Lapsed Protestant (2006), describes the hostility to any behaviour that
deviates from hegemonic masculinity. On returning home from university in England, local 'hard men' loyalists refer to him as 'Glenda' due to
his appearance, which was presumably the height of new wave fashion
at the time:

> I had taken to wearing nail varnish while I was away, dyeing my hair and crimping
> it. I had taken to wearing tight black leggings and carrying a shoulder bag (hand-
> bag, these people preferred to think of it as), sometimes black, sometimes pink.
> I kept my hairspray in it. (Patterson, 2006: 30)

This could be a description of an early sartorial creation of Patrick Brady
from Patrick McCabe's *Breakfast on Pluto* (1998). In a Northern Ireland
consumed with extreme violence and a Save Ulster from Sodomy campaign it is not hard to see why this performance can be read as so subversive

and disruptive to normative Northern Irish masculinity. Patterson offers his opinion on the derision he receives:

> Of course, back then, their ridicule didn't bother me. I invited it. Their ridicule was a measure of the difference between us and I was determined to be as different as I could possibly be from the people I had left behind. (Patterson, 2006: 30)

Patterson maintains the importance of identity markers as he grew up during the troubles: 'I had spent most of my late teens trying to distinguish myself from the people in had grown up with, the place I had grown up in' (Appendix). This performance alienates Patterson from a sectarian identity, aligning him with a third category of Northern Irish identity, one that disrupts both communities' sense of self. This category is populated by those who, like Stephen Dedalus in *A Portrait of the Artist as a Young Man* (1916), decide that '*non serviam: I will not serve*' (126).

In Patterson's *The International*, Danny's first homosexual experiences are marked by shame and lead to rebuke and censure. He is also the subject of homophobic abuse in the street, as men call after him '"Fruit!"... "He's not denying it. Bum boy!"' He kisses another boy while he is still in school (Patterson, 1999: 47), who claims Danny got him drunk and forced his affections. Danny is expelled from school and his parents refer to the incident as 'the unpleasantness' (Patterson, 1999: 47). One must bear in mind that the novel sets these instances in the 1960s long before homosexuality was decriminalised. Patterson cites part of his inspiration for the novel to be a gay actor he worked with on his monologue play *Monday Night Little Ireland North of England* (1994). According to Patterson, he 'was gay, in his fifties and had told me something about going to a bar, about the gay scene in the late 1950s'. Patterson speaks about 'camp' as a subject position outside of normative sexuality, one could, of course, substitute 'queer' for 'camp'. Camp allows Patterson to step outside of the Northern Irish mainstream and commentate. It is an authorial decision, with camp/queer as a vantage point: 'I am interested in 'camp'; there is a sort of positioning of yourself, a stepping outside. A positioning of yourself in a place where you can commentate'. There is a 'stepping outside' inherent in Patterson's choice to set this novel in pre-troubles Northern Ireland, the vantage point of history.

In *The International*, Danny has sex with a girl (Patterson, 1999: 45) while thinking about a classmate Gregory, who he has a crush on and who, Danny notes, plays the tuba. Danny finds the subversive nature of his sexuality exhilarating.

> Some part of me even enjoyed the subterfuge. That what I was doing was illegal did cross my mind, but it was the Sack, not the Law I most feared, Anyway, I had grown up in a place where all sex was considered dirty; furtiveness seemed a necessary part of it. (Patterson, 1999: 100)

This clandestine approach to sex may be a contributing factor to Patterson's comment in *Lapsed Protestant* that 'Were you aware that, despite our old fashioned attitudes to sex, there are men on the London gay scene who will *only* sleep with men from here?' (Patterson, 2006: 13) Patterson, by his own admission a 'white heterosexual male', uses a character with ambiguous sexuality as a metaphor for his belief in the fluidity of identity. That is, in employing a bisexual leading man he queers Northern Irish identity. Patterson states that:

> I don't feel like it's fixed, I don't feel our identities are fixed, and I think that most identities are limiting positions. In *The International*, Danny is simply who he is, you know, he doesn't really even call himself gay; he was alive to anything that went on ... I deliberately didn't make an issue of it because I didn't want it to be an identity. (Patterson, 2008: 117)

Patterson is aware of homoerotic moments in his fiction: 'I am aware that there are other bits and pieces right through the fiction, like the scene in the toilet in *Black Night at Big Thunder Mountain*. It's 'speeded' up, but there's something there. There's also in *Number 5* a 'homo-fascinated' thing going on'. Danny gains employment at a hotel in Belfast city centre, and his allows him to be promiscuous with the hotel guests. He becomes '...champion of the one-night hand-stand' (Patterson, 1999: 101) and admits, wryly, that there 'had been women as well, the odd time' (Patterson, 1999: 101). In their study, Kitchin and Lysaught detail their interview with a young Belfast gay man called Anthony, discussing how 'the dominant heterosexuality of the bar can be subverted by using it as a place to pick up sexual partners' (Kitchin and Lysaught, 2000: 18). His conquests, of both sexes and religions, signify a pre-troubles pre-AIDS innocence and naiveté.

The so-called swinging sixties never quite made the impact in Belfast that they made elsewhere. Two politically yet equally morally conservative traditions in Northern Ireland ensured that Danny's sexual liberation was a rare thing indeed. Danny states: 'In those days in Belfast the Sabbath was kept wholly. This was the town where swings were chained to their frames on Saturday night and not let down till Monday morning' (Patterson, 1999: 15). Although the sexually permissive sixties, cultural myth or not, never quite made the same impact in Northern Ireland as elsewhere, Patterson allows Danny no small amount of erotic freedom as prospective partners take his eye with a surprising regularity. Danny considers why he is so successful in his conquests, admitting '...there was nothing attractive about me, save this one thing: I worked in a hotel and I looked as if, were you to ask me, I wouldn't say no' (Patterson, 1999: 101). Like the protagonists in Robert McLiam Wilson's novels *Ripley Bogle* and *Eureka Street*, he is prone to romantic reveries, falling in love with both genders in the course of one day: '...In any case I had worked a fourteen-hour shift the day before and had fallen in love twice and twice been rebuffed' (Patterson, 1999: 9). Danny ends up having a threesome with an older but attractive American couple who are staying at the hotel. There is extreme awkwardness when Danny bumps into the couple the next day. The scene at the hotel is decadent: '...I didn't know suddenly whether I wanted to push him aside or her aside or push them both together but I was over by the bed myself and Natalie's hands were tugging my belt and Bob said shit and fuck and baby and Natalie said shush, over and over again' (Patterson, 1999: 115).

When space is inscribed with violent and sectarian resonances, as it has been in Northern Ireland, it limits the possibility of that space being gay. As Anne Enright states in her endnote to the novel:

[*The International*] says that there are different ways to describe people's lives – different maps, if you like – and those maps can be stolen. And so the man who describes himself as gay becomes a Catholic gay or a Protestant gay, but only if he wants his knees capped for deviant sexual behaviour. ... So it was another heist to make your narrator gay – and easily, naturally gay; like a wildflower growing from the cracks in concrete; gay without anguish or blame. It is another insistence on things being as they are. (in Patterson, 1999: 258)

When space is inscribed with violent and sectarian resonances, it makes it more difficult to queer. There is the oft-used public/private, male/female dichotomy to be considered. Public houses and betting shops offered almost 'legitimate' targets for paramilitaries, so imbued were they with sectarianism and masculinity. Bars were often strongly aligned with a community, and seen as non-neutral space. Doorstep shootings were seen as an utter violation as they broke down the barriers between home and violence. Peter Ward, whose job the fictional Danny gets, was one of the first civilian victims in the wrong part of the city at the wrong time. A making sectarian of space had begun which, during the troubles, left little possibility for a queering of space in Northern Ireland. When other cities were developing their own gay areas with the decriminalisation of homosexuality, every inch of Belfast was carved up along ethno-religious lines. Gay Belfast would always be in the divided city.

The International is set at a time when these spatial divisions are becoming more fixed. The novel represents a pre-troubles moment when a bar could be seen as a decent cross-section of Northern Irish masculinity. The pre-eminence of space in gender and sectarian relations offers us an interesting dynamic in *The International* where a hotel offers both public space (the bar) and private space (guests' rooms) and Danny performs differently in both. In their analysis, their 'queer reading of the city' Lysaught and Kitchin 'posit that all space is queered, that the sexing of space is always partial and contested, always in the process of becoming; that heterosexist spatiality, for example, is profoundly unstable, consciously engaged in the process of reproducing itself' (Lysaught and

Kitchin, 2000: 3).³ Their study found that, like Danny, most of their interviewees 'lead double or compartmentalised lives, 'out' in some spaces ... but 'closeted' in others' (Lysaught and Kitchin, 2000: 11). Thus, in *The Liberty Lad* the split between the erotic and the repressed is fundamentally along city lines, whereas *The International* explores the possibility of space to be inscribed with sexualised meaning, and how sectarian conflict stems the fluidity of a gendered subjectivity. Both texts, with their rejection of the violent and embracing of the erotic, offer new potential for Northern Irish masculine identity. They point to the ways in which the queer landscape of Belfast is changing, and one can only hope Northern Irish fiction can represent these changes.

Works Cited

Bairner, A. (1999), 'Masculinity, Violence and the Irish Peace Protest', *Capital and Class, Northern Ireland Between Peace and War*, 69, Autumn, pp. 125–44.
Binnie, J. and G. Valentine (1999), 'Geographies of Sexuality – a Review of Progress', *Progress in Human Geography*, 23, pp. 175–87.
Kennedy, B. (2004), *The Arrival of Fergal Flynn*, Hodder Headline, Dublin.
——(2005), *Roman Song*, Hodder Headline, Dublin.
Kitchin, R. (2002), 'Sexing the city, the sexual production of space in Belfast, Manchester and San Francisco', *City* 6(2), pp. 205–18.
—— and K. Lysaght (2002), 'Queering Belfast, Some thoughts on the Sexing of Space', *NIRSA Working Paper Series*, NIRSA, Maynooth.
Leitch, M. (1985), *The Liberty Lad* (1965), Blackstaff, Belfast.

3   Jon Binnie and Gil Valentine offer a helpful review of studies in queer geography, Binnie and Valentine, 1999: 175–87.

McCabe, P. (1998), *Breakfast on Pluto*, Picador, London.

McClenaghan, Brendí (1995), 'Letter from a Gay Republican: H-Block 5', in *Lesbian and Gay Visions of Ireland: Towards the Twenty-First Century*, ed. Í. O'Carroll and E. Collins, Cassell, London: pp. 122–30.

McDonald, H. (2006), 'Hain moves to outlaw prejudice against gays', *The Observer*, 30 July 2006, London.

McNamee, E. (2002), *The Blue Tango*, Faber and Faber, London.

McNicholl, D. (2004), *A Son called Gabriel*, CDS Books, New York.

Moore, B. (1966), *The Emperor of Ice Cream* (1965), Deutsch, London.

O'Carroll, Í. and E. Collins (1995), *Lesbian and Gay Visions of Ireland: Towards the Twenty-First Century*, Cassell, London.

O'Flaherty, L. (1999), *The Informer* (1925), Wolfhound, London.

Park, D. (2004), *Swallowing the Sun*, Bloomsbury, London.

Patterson, G. (1995), *Black Night at Big Thunder Mountain*, Chatto & Windus, London.

——(2006), *Lapsed Protestant*, New Island, Dublin.

——(1999), *The International*, Anchor, London.

——(2008), 'Interview with Glenn Patterson', *No Country for Old Men*, ed. Paddy Lyons and Alison O'Malley-Younger, Peter Lang, Bern, pp. 115–21.

Quinn, V. (2000), 'On the Borders of Allegiance: Identity Politics in Ulster', *Decentring Sexualities*, ed. R. Philips et al., Routledge, London: pp. 258–77

Reid, F. (1931), *Uncle Stephen*, Faber and Faber, London.

Rubin, G. (1989), 'Thinking Sex: notes for a radical theory of the politics of sexuality' in *Pleasure and Danger: Exploring Female Sexuality*, ed. C. Vance, Pandora, London.

Walshe, É. (1997), *Sex, Nation and Dissent in Irish Writing*, Cork University Press, Cork.

Wilson, R. (1997), *Eureka Street* (1996), Minerva, London.

Futures Past: The Science Fiction of Bob Shaw and James White as a Product of Late-Industrial Belfast

PATRICK MAUME

James White (1928–99) and Bob Shaw (1931–96) were the most prominent Northern Irish science fiction writers of their generation; they are pretty well unknown outside genre circles and less remembered even there as the genre becomes increasingly cinematic and visually-oriented.[1] I came across them in research for the *Dictionary of Irish Biography* and decided that they give an interesting perspective on the post-war Irish relationship with international popular culture – all the more so as their close friendship crossed the division between the two communities in the North. This paper is an attempt to discuss them and their work on a larger scale than possible in their *DIB* entries, through a brief account of their lives and milieu and a discussion of their attitudes to religion and political power. I try to explore how far they can be seen as representative figures – from a generation which grew up just too early to benefit from the post-war expansion of education, seeing the creation of the NHS in quasi-religious terms, working in technical employment while looking to science-fiction as an outlet for social and intellectual expression. Their cultural terms of reference derived as much from the journalistic markets of North America (both men lived for some time in Canada) and from

[1] White's tribute site http://www.sectorgeneral.com/ which contains much useful bio-bibliographical information, does not appear to have been updated since 29 April 2002. (accessed 14 May 2008) and some links – notably an interview between White and Brendan Ryder, formerly at http://homepage.eircom.net/~albedo1/ interview-white.html – have ceased to function. The Ryder interview (published in *FTL* 11 – winter 1991 as 'an Encounter in Bewley's: James Whyte Interviewed') is the source of much of the White information in this piece.

the industrial North of England (where Shaw moved in 1973 to take his
family away from the Troubles) as from the Irish hinterland (though their
Belfast could be seen as an outpost of North British culture based around
proud, drab and somewhat tatty heavy industry – both men worked for
Harland and Wolff for a time). Specific Irish references are very rare in
Shaw, whereas several of White's novels directly or indirectly address the
Northern Ireland Troubles, but as products of Belfast they both come
within the ambit of Irish Studies. I would add that this is an outsider's
exploration; if any real science fiction buffs, or any acquaintances of Shaw
and White, read this paper, I hope they will pardon its shortcomings.

James White was born in 1928, the son of a West Belfast Catholic draper.
White's parents moved to Canada in 1930 but returned to Belfast in
1935; White lived in Andersonstown for most of his working life. White
began reading science fiction at the age of ten after discovering H.G.
Wells's novels. He was educated at St John's Primary School (1935–41)
and in 1941 won a scholarship to St Joseph's Technical High School,
which was destroyed in an air raid a few weeks later. White's experience
of the Belfast blitz gave him a lifelong hatred of war. The school then
moved to Cushendun, Co. Antrim. White spent a year there as a boarder
(1942–3), acquiring an abiding love of the North Antrim coast, to which
he moved after retirement. His first novel, *The Secret Visitors* (1957) is
partly set around the dowdy resort of Port Ballintrae, and includes several references to local landmarks in its story of the struggle against a
plot to rule the galaxy by a ruthless tourist agency (which markets Earth
as an intergalactic beauty spot while organising wars to keep down the
indigenous population).

White dreamed of becoming a doctor but had to leave school aged
fourteen to become an apprentice tailor. Tailors appear in several of his
stories (one, 'Custom Fitting' describes in considerable detail the making
of a hand-fitted suit for the first alien ambassador to the Court of St James,
who resembles a centaur in appearance). On leaving school White began
to collect second-hand American science fiction magazines (sold by some
of the numerous American GIs stationed in Ulster during the preparations for D-Day to shops in Smithfield market in central Belfast). Until

its destruction by firebombs in the early 1970s Smithfield was a central focus for Belfast antiquarians and booklovers (and in the 1950s – and probably earlier – the American comics sold by some stallholders gave rise to moral panics in which both nationalist and unionist Stormont MPs joined.) He was particularly influenced by the space-opera *Lensman* series of the American writer E.E. Smith, saying it taught him that there could be good as well as evil aliens. (The stories feature members of an intergalactic police corps who are, unknown to themselves, being used in a millennial conflict between ancient and super-advanced good and evil civilisations.)[2] His hobbies included ballroom dancing, model aircraft flying, and building homemade radios. In 1947 he founded the Irish Fandom science-fiction group with Walt Willis (1919–99, later a Northern Ireland civil servant). In 1950 the group was joined by Bob Shaw.

Shaw was born in East Belfast in 1931, eldest of three sons of a policeman. He was educated at a technical school. He was an atheist in later life but probably had some exposure to Protestant religious education; a nondescript character in his novel *A Wreath of Stars* (1976) recalls passages from the biblical *Song of Songs* (a favourite recourse of bored and prurient boys in Sunday school) when mentally contemplating a classy and obviously uninterested woman. On leaving school aged seventeen Shaw became an apprentice draughtsman at a London structural engineering firm, then an airplane designer with the Belfast aerospace firm Short and Harland. As a child he developed a lasting enthusiasm for science fiction as 'an escape from the dullness of suburban Belfast'.[3] Like White, he collected American science-fiction magazines in Smithfield Market. In 1950 Shaw discovered Irish Fandom, which maintained a clubbish existence centred on Willis's house in the Upper Newtownards Road. Here the eight members (including Shaw's future wife Sarah ('Sadie') Gourley and Margaret (Peggy) Martin who married White in 1955) played 'ghoodminton', a ball game of their own invention. (They also hiked in

2   Graham Andrews 'Dr Kilcasey in Space: A bio-Bibliography of James White' at http://www.sectorgeneral.com/biobiblio.html (accessed 14 May 2008).

3   Dave Langford 'A wreath of stars: Bob Shaw remembered' at http://www.ansible.co.uk/writing/bobshaw.html accessed 14 May 2008.

the hills around Scrabo Tower, which overlooks Newtownards). The group played a disproportionately important role in the social aspect of subculture of UK and US science-fiction 'fandom' (centred on conventions and 'fanzines' – amateur magazines, not as commercialised as it later became and involving only a small band of aficionados) until c.1960; it produced the fanzines *Slant* (1948–53) and *Hyphen* (1952–65).[4] Shaw contributed stories, cartoons and a humorous column describing its proceedings, adventures and travels to conventions elsewhere (written as 'BoSh') to *Hyphen*. Shaw's first professionally published story appeared in the *New York Post* in 1951; several others (which he later regarded as juvenilia) appeared in *Nebula Science Fiction* and *Authentic* magazines. He also wrote (with Willis) *The Magic Duplicator* (1954) adapting *The Pilgrim's Progress* to the search of 'Jophan' for 'the Tower of Trufandom' (modelled on Scrabo).[5]

White was slower to develop as a writer and initially produced woodcut illustrations for *Slant*. His first published story appeared in the British science fiction magazine *New Worlds* in 1952. White's dislike of the militarism prevalent in much science fiction of the period (such as R.A. Heinlein, whose engineering mentality, creation of a wider historical framework joining up numerous short stories, and use of 'ordinary people' as protagonists White greatly admired) initially hindered him in the American market by antagonising the xenophobic John W. Campbell (1910–71), the most influential contemporary science fiction magazine editor.[6]

The group's activities slackened as the members married and began families; it was finally dissolved in 1965. Years later, during the Troubles, White published a story in which those members of the group still living

---

4   *Slant* is available online at http://www.fanac.org/fanzines/Slant/ (accessed 14 May 2008); *Hyphen* is partially available at http://www.fanac.org/fanzines/ Hyphen/.

5   Available online at http://www.dcs.gla.ac.uk/SF-Archives/Misc/The-Enchanted-Duplicator (accessed 14 May 2008); http://www.dcs.gla.ac.uk/SF-Archives/Misc/ tedcopy.html.

6   http://www.sectorgeneral.com/biobiblio.html.

in Belfast are called back to the house by the authorities and discover that it is haunted by the happy memories of that more peaceful time.[7] In 1956 Shaw moved to Canada, seeking broader experience; he stopped writing for several years. His novel *Vertigo* (1978; aka *Terminal Velocity*) is set in Alberta, whose vast flat expanses also seem to have influenced his *Orbitsville* trilogy, which describes the effects on human civilisation of the discovery of a vast habitable sphere whose dimensions. The effects are decidedly ambiguous (the sphere turns out to have been created as a sort of collecting bottle by arrogant and non-empathetic godlike aliens who wish to seed an uninhabited universe with intelligent life) and the manner in which the unlimited availability of land is described as causing the reversion of human civilisation to an uniform level of unadventurous small-town provincial hickdom may also say something about Shaw's view of his Canadian experiences. The Shaws returned to Belfast in 1958; he joined the Publicity Department of Short and Harland. He polished gemstones as a hobby, and twice represented Ulster at archery.

White spent 22 years working for different Belfast tailoring firms; eventually becoming apprentice manager of the Belfast Co-Operative department store. By 1965 White's income from writing became financially essential to his family; he moved from the Co-Op to a technical clerkship at Shorts aerospace factory, which gave him more time for writing. Eighteen months later he joined the Public Relations department, citing his novels as proof of writing ability; White was publicity assistant 1966–8 and publicity officer 1968–84. Until Shaw's departure for England in 1972 they co-operated in the Belfast Science Fiction Group which met on Thursdays in White's Tavern. (The BSFG was severely disrupted when White's Tavern was destroyed by a bomb in the early 1970s.)

At this time they established their literary reputations within the genre. Unlike the wild narrative leaps (verging on self-parody) of Shaw, White excelled at a sense of development over time, in which conceptual breakthrough is the climax of a slow and often painful cumulative

---

7   'The Exorcists of IF' reprinted in *The White Papers* (Framingham, Massachusetts, 1996).

process. White's novels were translated into Japanese, Portuguese, Polish, Swedish, French, German, Dutch and Italian. In the 1960s and 1970s his novels appeared in paperback editions of 50,000 in Britain and 100,000 in America.

Although White wrote a variety of novels, he is best known for his *Sector General* series, beginning with a 1957 short story and continuing until just before his death in 1999. (White eventually produced twelve *SG* novels, the last of which were only published in America.) The earliest novels have human protagonists, the later ones centre on a variety of aliens. The novels depict a large hospital in space treating hundreds of alien species; as the backstory developed, it was presented as having been developed (by human and Orligian[8] veterans of a particularly bloody interplanetary war which turned out to have been caused by a misunderstanding) to promote peace and mutual understanding between the myriad alien races of the galaxy on the basis that medicine and healing constitute an universal language. Advised by a friend who was a lecturer in animal reproduction, White imagined an amazing variety of possible alien biologies, together with an elaborate classification system where mankind was carefully inserted in the middle rather than at the top.[9] *Sector General* is often called the best example of medical science fiction. It reflects White's frustrated medical ambitions (he obtained a First Aid certificate), his wife's experience as a nurse at the Mater Hospital, and his own medical problem. White developed diabetes in his early twenties, and for the rest of his life had to inject himself with insulin twice daily. One of the earliest and most popular of the Sector General stories grew out of his reflections on how diabetes might be treated in a species with an exoskeleton (here a giant intelligent crab), whose shell could not tolerate repeated injections. (The story concerns the problem faced by a human

8   A martial species resembling teddy-bears in appearance, extremely afraid of an animal resembling humans which preys on their young. The first human astronaut to encounter them decided the most obvious way to indicate friendship was to kiss the nearest Orligian infant; his instantaneous evisceration was similarly misinterpreted by humanity.

9   Gary Louie 'The Classification System' in Thew White Papers op. cit and online at http://www.sectorgeneral.com/articlesclassification.html (14 May 2008).

surgeon, Dr Conway, trying to find a solution with the assistance of some crab medical students; for technical reasons he has been implanted with the memories of a distinguished and lecherous crab surgeon, incurring the unfortunate side-effect of physical attraction to a female crab medical student. Although his colleagues mockingly comment that nobody can call him a pervert because it's a female crab, they counteract the effect by assigning the shapely human Nurse Murchison to the crucial operation. Surgeon and nurse – they later marry – move up the hospital hierarchy during the series, both eventually achieving senior posts.) White must have been acutely aware that had he developed his disease before insulin became available he would have died in early adulthood, and that without the NHS his insulin requirements would have brought a significant financial burden.

Shaw's mature literary production dates from 1965; his reputation was established by the 1966 story 'Light of Other Days' depicting glass which slows light and reflects past events. (This was later incorporated into a novel-length collection, *Other Days, Other Eyes* (1972), in which stories about the marital difficulties of the substance's inventor alternate with depictions of the practical consequences of the glass's increasingly widespread availability.) His first novel *Nightwalk* (whose hero learns to see through telepathy after being blinded by a theocratic regime, resembling the mediaeval Papal monarchy but with modern secret police and tactfully described as Lutheran) appeared in America in 1967; he targeted US audiences, and his first novel published in Britain (1970) was a cut version of his fourth US novel *Shadow of Heaven* (1969). Much of Shaw's work has a preoccupation with physical dismemberment and disintegration – a recurring image is an eye forced out of its socket – and, as with White, this form of physicality had roots in his own experience as well as in an adolescent male audience's love of splatter. As a boy Shaw saw a friend lose his eye in an accident (he fell on a building site and impaled his eye on steel reinforcing rods protruding from concrete)[10] and himself experienced an eye infection; this gave him a morbid fear of blindness

10   This experience is recycled in Shaw's novel *Ground Zero Man* (1971; also known as *The Peace Machine*).

(reinforced by chronic hemiplegic migraine, whose visual hallucinations gave him an interest in the mediaeval visionary Hildegard of Bingen – believed to have suffered the same complaint; in one Shaw novel migraine is harnessed to allow time-travel)[11] and a lifelong preoccupation with perception, reminiscent of Philip K. Dick. As with much genre fiction, it is unclear how far his recurring themes of paranoia, entrapment, telepathy and hidden powers reflect the concerns of his adolescent audience and how far they reflect Shaw's own inner drives and insecurities.[12]

Between 1967 and 1970 Shaw was science correspondent for the *Belfast Telegraph*, when that paper was the foremost voice of the O'Neillite programme of technocratic liberalisation, he also wrote that paper's 'Chichester' social column. After briefly struggling as a full-time writer, Shaw became Shorts' Public Relations officer in 1970. By the early 1970s his work sold over a million copies in several languages (including pirated Russian, Polish, and Lithuanian editions). In April 1973, fearing the impact of the Troubles on their children, the Shaws moved to Ulverston, Cumbria; Shaw became publicity officer with the Vickers shipbuilding group in Barrow-in-Furness. Several of his novels in this period feature aliens in shabby Northern English surroundings; hiding in the cellar of a lodging-house (*Dagger of the Mind* (1979)) or abducting humans to Mercury from the Lake District (*Fire Pattern* (1984)) The move, and Shaw's transition to full-time authorship in 1975, created enduring financial problems.

Intense productivity in the late 1970s (including the humorous pastiche *Who Goes Here?* (1977) and *A Wreath of Stars* (1976) which imagines the discovery of a planet occupying the same space as Earth within an alternate universe composed of antineutrinos) gave way to personal and literary breakdown in the early 1980s. Shaw was much more of a humorist than White, drawn to chaos as White was drawn to order. (During his

11   *The Two-Timers* (London, 1968); Steve Langford 'Me and Hildegard of Bingen' http://www.ansible.co.uk/writing/ft115.html acessed 14 May 2008.
12   Christopher Priests obituary in *Ansible* 104 (March 1996, available online at http://news.ansible.co.uk/a104.html – accessed 14 May 2008) portrays Shaw as an archetypal melancholy clown.

residence in Ulverston, where Stan Laurel was born, he regularly took visiting friends to see the birthplace and complained that 'the funniest man who ever lived' had been forgotten by his townsfolk.)[13] Shaw had a considerable fondness for parodying certain literary genres; like other contemporary British science fiction writers he possessed a strong streak of absurdism, contrasting the grandiose adventures imposed on his protagonist with their shabby provincial settings and implying space colonies will spread suburban ennui across the galaxies. Shaw believed in rigorous extrapolation from fantastic starting-points, so that even many of his self-consciously tall stories were also 'hard SF', based on scientific speculation. (He thought the film *Star Wars* damaged science fiction by reinforcing its image as 'space opera' in futuristic settings.) Shaw himself did some early script work on the Stanley Kubrick project (originally based on Brian Aldiss' story 'Supertoys Last all Summer Long') later filmed by Stephen Spielberg as *AI*.[14] (He had been suggested to Kubrick by Arthur C. Clarke. It may be relevant that Shaw handled an 'artificial child' theme in his story 'Dark Night in Toyland' where the first-person narrator, a religious believer, faced with increasing evidence of the artificial creation of life, declares that this is not 'really' life and anyway human life can never be duplicated by such means; his son, who is dying of cancer, is an infant prodigy and is revealed after his death to have created a duplicate of himself; the narrator dismantles it, professing to believe it was never 'really' alive.)[15]

Shaw's activities as a travelling Irish entertainer within the expanding international scene of science fiction fandom were arguably as significant as his more conventional authorial ventures. (His two Hugo awards, in 1979 and 1980, were for fan-writing rather than fiction.) His wit (which made him a popular speaker and raconteur at the worldwide

13   Christopher Priest obituary for Shaw, op.cit.
14   http://www.scifimoviepage.com/art_kub_2.html; Ian Watson 'Plumbing Stanley Kubrick' http://www.ianwatson.info/kubrick.htm (accessed 14 May 2008). Shaw's work on the science fiction convention circuit proved incompatible with Kubrick's demand for total dedication.
15   It is reprinted as the title story of *Dark Night in Toyland* (1989).

fan conventions around which his social life centred) was accompanied
by alcoholic melancholia and lack of confidence. Shaw recovered to produce the *Ragged Astronauts* trilogy (1986–9). This is set in an universe
where pi=3 and a non-metallurgical civilisation travels by hot-air balloon
between twin planets with intersecting atmospheres; it draws on his professional knowledge of the mechanics of flight. The significance of this
trilogy as a deliberate attempt at stabilisation is highlighted by the fact
that Shaw did not centre his career on a recurring series in the way that
White did. (Shaw's other series are the more sporadically undertaken
three-volume *Orbitsville* trilogy, and two humorous volumes centred on
the bewildered and shiftless antihero Warren Peace.)

Around this time the Shaws moved to Bootle. The sudden death of
Sarah in 1991 triggered further heavy drinking. In late 1993 Shaw under-
went a major cancer operation. In December 1995 he married an American
fan activist, Nancy Tucker (1928–2000) in Michigan. They returned to
Britain the following February. Bob Shaw died in his sleep in Manchester
on 12 February 1996.

White remained in Andersonstown and was deeply affected by the
post-1969 Troubles in the streets around him and in his wife's hospital
work, as well as by the general 1970s sense of social breakdown which is
also reflected in Shaw's work of the period (Shaw's *A Wreath of Stars*, for
example, published in 1976 and set in the mid-1990s, imagines a future in
which Africa has undergone massive political fragmentation, many states
have achieved nuclear weapons and engage in atmospheric testing, Europe
and America are beset by strike waves, it is almost impossible to obtain
an edible fish, low-level warfare is endemic in Africa and South America,
and even the rich rarely travel outside their home countries.) He remained
locally and internationally active in science fiction fandom, where he was
extremely popular because of his gentleness, courtesy and willingness
to help young writers. In 1984 White took early retirement because of
slowly-developing diabetic blindness; he moved from Andersonstown to
Portstewart, on the North Antrim coast. His popularity declined slightly
in later life and several 1990s novels only appeared in America (though
Underkill, which I'll go into more fully later, only appeared in Britain as
it was considered too dark for American audiences). A certain amount of

recycling is noticeable in his later work; his last novel, *The First Protector* was a tie-in for the Gene Roddenberry-inspired TV series *Earth: Final Conflict* and recycles material from earlier novels (though the series' theme of the difficulties caused by contact between human beings and advanced aliens tied in with White's characteristic concerns).[16] White remained active in the science fiction subculture as a council member of the British Science Fiction association and President of the Irish Science Fiction association. James White died of a stroke on 23 August 1999 and is commemorated by the James White Award short story competition.[17]

Now we will take a more detailed look at their specific images of Northern Ireland in relation to their wider portrayals of political power and religious belief. Shaw's specific references to Northern Ireland are easily dealt with because there are very few. His stories never have Irish settings, but East Belfast placenames sometimes appear; *The Two-Timers* features a rural resort called 'Silverstream', while *Orbitsville Judgment* (1990) depicts a frustrated hero in a backwater called Orangefield. Some depictions of the Northern English industrial towns where Shaw spent much of his working life share a frame of reference with Northern Ireland. For example, in his last novel *Warren Peace* (1993, aka *Dimensions*) the anti-hero spends much of the story in the Northern England of an alternate universe where the speed of light is not an invariant and the development of electro-magnetic power has consequently been much slower and more sporadic. Along with a certain amount of northern humour about pea-souper industrial fogs, greasy breakfasts, and the landlady's nymphomaniac daughter, Shaw incorporates apparent parodic memories of his post-war apprenticeship as a draughtsman (using skills outmoded by the time he wrote) in describing Warren Peace's work experiences in the Manchester firm of 'A&W' whose labour-intensive techniques in manufacturing armour-plated battleships sound suspiciously reminiscent of the shipbuilding techniques used by

16   http://en.wikipedia.org/wiki/Earth:_Final_Conflict (accessed 14 May 2008; note that this site is subject to unpredictable changes by users) summarises the series; Shaw's novel is a 'prequel' set in fourth-century Europe.

17   http://www.jameswhiteaward.com/

Harland and Wolff (in contrast to the more streamlined operations of its American and Asian competitors.)

Local Ulster in-jokes occur in some of White's novels. In *All Passion Fled* (1968), astronauts travelling out to meet a vast alien ship which has appeared beyond Mars are briefed in stupefyingly boring lectures by the Professor of Mathematics at the University of Coleraine – the University of Ulster having just been opened when White wrote; *The Watch Below* (1966), which depicts amongst other things the survival underwater of a small number of sailors and WRENS and their descendants in unflooded compartments of a specially-designed tanker sunk during World War II, contains the exchange 'Who made the world?' 'Harland and Wolff'. (The American edition substituted the Brooklyn Navy Yard.) White, however, also wrote stories with specific Northern Ireland themes and settings, introducing the genre into quotidian surroundings; a story 'Sanctuary' (reprinted in *The White Papers*) where an injured alien crashes in Portstewart harbour and takes refuge in the local convent (as visitors will know, its distinctive battlemented walls are one of the most prominent features of the seafront) produced the first-ever portrayal of a nun on the cover of the magazine *Astounding Science Fiction*.[18] *The Dream Millennium* (1974) features cryonic colonists fleeing the earth to escape from (inter alia) the Northern Ireland Troubles, images of which are played to them as they sleep to condition them against bringing the violence of Earth to their new home.

Shaw's writings often play with themes of popular fiction (such as the private eye in 'The Gioconda Caper' who discovers that the Mona Lisa was painted as part of a proto-cinematic peepshow, which is promptly destroyed by an outraged Italian patriot) and these can include tinges of ironic imperial nostalgia of a type often found in 1960s popular culture. In the short story 'The cosmic cocktail party' (*Tomorrow Lies in Ambush* (1973)) an old imperial adventurer whose brain has been preserved in a storage facility takes it over by force of personality; the other distinguished persons in the facility find themselves being subjected to elaborate

18   http://www.sectorgeneral.com/articleslocusinterview.html.

big-game hunts through a virtual reality which he has created, until the system operators persuade him that he is needed elsewhere to defeat the conspiracies of socialist aliens led by Harold Wilson. *A Wreath of Stars* features a corrupt East African dictator co-existing uneasily with his violent, racist army Chief of Staff (they appear to be modelled on Milton Obote and Idi Amin), and a scene where the leading female character (who is white) is threatened by black soldiers might be seen as having unfortunate undertones, though the novel also features a sympathetic black engineer who gives his life for the protagonists, and the regime is disposed of by an uprising of black workers which is expressly compared to the 1960 Sharpeville uprising. One or two stories feature African states which react against previous regimes by adopting a neo-British official culture, but this is basically a joke rather than a serious suggestion.

A 'sidelight' in *Other Days, Other Eyes* revolves around the imprisonment of a British pilot by an Asian communist leader who tries to pressurise him into signing a confession to crimes against humanity as a condition of release. The communist delivers a fascination with this obdurate prisoner and holds long conversations with him; when some verses which the prisoner repeatedly recites to himself are identified as 'The Private of the Buffs' by Francis Hastings Doyle (a once-popular patriotic recitation in which a private of the East Kent Regiment captured by Chinese forces during the Second Opium War and summarily beheaded after refusing to prostrate himself before their commander is hailed as a second Leonidas, forsaking the hope of revisiting his native Kentish hop-fields rather than sacrifice Western freedom to Eastern despotism)[19] this becomes the central topic of their conversation. The communist leader makes various comments about the poem's racial attitudes ('Let dusky Indians whine and kneel / An English lad must die') which neither his interlocutor nor Shaw dispute; the prisoner in turn points out that while the nineteenth-century warlord was confident enough to execute the prisoner who defied him, the communist feels he has to convert him or

19   The full text may be consulted at http://en.wikisource.org/wiki/The_Private_of_ the_Buffs (accessed 9 May 2008).

be defeated. As the prisoner's health deteriorates, the communist makes a final attempt to defeat him by forcing him to wear spectacles of 'slow glass' charged with images of imperial atrocities against colonial peoples (again, it is emphasised that these are genuine). Instead of submitting, the prisoner sinks into psychosis and dies believing that he is the Private of the Buffs returning home to Kent. Thus, Shaw implies, however delusional and even malevolent may be some of the views expressed by the Victorian poem, it nonetheless contains something admirable. The spoof of *Beau Geste* in *Who Goes Here* comments on the darker side of empire; the anti-hero joins the Space Legion to forget various crimes which he has inadvertently committed (including inventing the memory-erasure machine used on new recruits to the Legion) and discovers that its principal function is to wage war against disaffected colonies which want to break away from the Galactic Federation and object to buying quotas of inferior Earth-manufactured products.

Shaw's religious views, like his political views, amount to a generalised bloody-mindedness; a sense that the world was a mess and could have been handled better and that if God existed he ought to have smoothed out the world's shortcomings Shaw's most aggressively anti-theistic novel, *The Ceres Solution* (1981), features the discovery that human short life and susceptibility to illness have been deliberately caused by a long-lived alien experimenter, who is finally exposed and humiliated in front of a galactic audience; it is clearly implied, though never expressly stated, that this being, posing as a deity, founded the major world religions. Several Shaw novels feature benevolent godlike aliens and/or the scientific discovery of 'mind particles' through which the human personality survives the death of the body; these happier fantasies, however, are not so much religious as expressions of the belief widespread in science fiction, that instrumental reason may eventually be extended to allow human beings to become gods.

Where Shaw's narrative methods often express a certain perverse delight in cosmic chaos, White was attracted to order. His stories show a strong attraction to the idea of an enlightened elite managing society and forestalling conflict. In part this reflects the technocratic leanings of much science fiction (going back to H.G. Wells's Fabian Socialist vision of a self-sustaining governing elite whom he called 'samurai') but in White's rendering it also has distinctly Catholic undertones. His doctors are distinctly priestly figures, in the *Sector General* novels we are told that on many worlds they are actually celibate and form a distinct class with its own specific dress. (Nursing sisters would have been conspicuous in the Mater Hospital of White's day.) White clearly respected the clerical vocation (the nuns in 'Sanctuary' are eminently capable of handling the arrival of an alien in Portstewart because their missionary experience opened them to dealings with strange cultures); nevertheless, the religious overtones of much of his fiction represent not so much an expression of religion as a substitute for it. It is occasionally suggested that the National Health Service, as well as taking over many of the charitable functions formerly exercised by churches, has acquired much of their former role as social cement and object of reverence; the Sector General novels provide much evidence in support of such a view.

Although White observed the outward practices of Catholicism, he told interviewers that he was to a considerable extent an agnostic and that his religious views were expressed in a Sector General novel *The Genocidal Healer* (1991). The novel depicts a (celibate) alien doctor, Lioren, coming to terms with the knowledge that his administration of emergency treatment to a suffering alien race has killed most of them and that his haste was as much due to arrogance as to humanitarian concern; at the same time he has to counsel a spiritually troubled patient. (Lioren tells the patient, who responds to his honesty, that religion is too widespread not to have some function, but that he does not know and therefore cannot say whether it is transcendental or natural in origin.) Both crises are eventually surmounted as Lioren arrives at self-knowledge, achieves forgiveness and becomes a non-denominational counsellor universally addressed as 'Padre'. White said he was inspired by his wife's observation that ministers of religion were often more effective than other helpers in calming patients.

The Silent Stars Roll By (1991) is an alternate history novel set in a fantasy-mediaeval Europe dominated by a Hibernian Empire. (This supposedly came into existence because an Irish sage visiting Alexandria recognised the potential of the primitive steam engines developed by the philosopher Hero, and because St Brendan made lasting contact with the American Indians – in a characteristic White treatment of contact and reconciliation with the Other – allowing the development of a power-ful Indian civilisation.) In 1492, as the different civilisations of earth co-operate in launching a mission to colonise another planet, the civil service of the Hibernian Empire is staffed by Catholic clerics. (A promi-nent social role is also played by a medical association called the Order of Orla, but though its foundress appears to be inspired by the legendary figure of St Brigid and its members are celibate, it is clearly not a religious order but a medical association of the type found in the Sector General novels. The hero spends much of the novel trying to persuade the heroine, a dedicated medic called Derval, that her vow of celibacy need not be lifelong, and is eventually successful; it is clear from their exchanges that the vow is not a religious obligation but is undertaken from professional dedication and practicality.)

The portrayal of Catholicism here is noticeably ambivalent. We are told that St Brendan eventually broke with Rome (while remaining a Christian) rather than compromise his openness towards the Amerindians. The church's representatives (with the exception of a saintly cardinal who spends most of the novel quietly developing a warp drive, which finally propels the characters into our universe where they are last seen arriving at NASA headquarters and demanding to be taken to the High King) are revealed to be conspiring to ensure the new colony will become entirely Catholic. At the same time, even the most underhand of these clerical intriguers is presented as sincerely religious and unwilling to commit murder in pursuit of their objective.

This moral restraint, which was not universal among real-life medi-aeval clerics, is necessary for plot purposes; if the clerics were prepared to achieve their ends by murder it would be impossible to stop them. It does, however, reflect a broader weakness in White's mindset; like other advocates of technocracy and managerialism, he seems hardly to consider the possibility that the self-policing medical and administrative elites he advocates might develop self-serving behaviour leading to systematic corruption (like Shaw's Space Legion). His loving depictions of conflict resolution through behavioural psychology, if only the psychologists are

sufficiently numerous and efficient (a predictable approach from someone who worked in public relations) have the troubling authoritarian
undertones which are often detected in the Freudian-influenced social
democratic liberalism of the First Cold War era and in some form of
theological liberalism which interpret religion in terms of psychological
health. White's emphasis on the irrationality of xenophobic prejudice
towards the Other makes him implicitly dismiss the possibility of genuine
ideological conflict over the ordering of society and equate discontent
with mental disease. (An aggressive militaristic empire does appear in
Star Surgeon (1963) but it is run by an exploitative elite who keep their
populace in line by xenophobic propaganda, and collapses when its own
soldiers turn on it after they realise the staff of Sector Geenral treat them
on the same terms as their defenders.)

It would not be fair to White to say that he was entirely ignorant of
this blind-spot; it is glancingly examined in the consequences of Lioren's
initial arrogance in *Genocidal Healer*. Furthermore, the ideal of perfect
rationality implicitly raises the question of why such an ideal, if possible,
has not already been achieved. This doubt underlies White's darkest novel,
Underkill (1979).

This is set in a crushingly overcrowded and urbanised Earth where
petrocarbon-based society is breaking down with the near-exhaustion of
oil resources. Electricity is manually generated by a caste of 'power-workers'
who spend their lives working on treadmills or in violent oblivion-seeking;
cars are increasingly replaced by pedal power or horses. Everyone is under
perpetual strain and rush-hour is disrupted by pitched battles. These
miseries are being intensified by terrorist attacks aimed at the systematic
breakdown of society through the destruction of its physical infrastruc-
ture. The protagonists – a husband and wife, both doctors, discover that
these attacks are organised by two factions fanatically convinced of their
own righteousness, whose members are all physically identical and called
'John' or 'Luke'. (There is a third group, all female and called 'Mary').
These factions prove to be clones created and co-ordinated by an alien
super-civilisation who are trying to save Earth from the disasters which
they inflicted on their own planet by reducing the human imprint while
the planet is still able to recover. The 'Lukes' (called after the Evangelist

St Luke, who was said to have been a doctor) believe in drastic 'surgery' to save the planet; the 'Johns' (called after St John the Evangelist), though equally violent when they regard it as necessary, favour persuasion where possible. A previous attempt to save a planet by the Johns' method failed, and alternating the two tactics in Earth's earlier history has not brought the required result, so the Lukes have finally been given the upper hand. (They are described as having orchestrated past conflicts in a way oddly reminiscent of the genocidal tourist agency in *The Secret Visitors*.) This nightmare (only published in Europe; American publishers thought it too negative) extrapolates from White's own experience of the Northern Ireland Troubles in such areas as the portrayal of the competing terrorist factions and a long sequence describing policemen attempting to intercept terrorists who are placing bombs in a public building.[20] (A brief depiction of a school where angry, violent teachers are prepared for menial jobs by mindless rote learning and extensive corporal punishment may also owe something to personal experience.) Here White's benevolent vision of an universe united by reason and the pursuit of healing coexists with Swiftian misanthropy. The doctor-protagonists, whose eventual triumph is virtually guaranteed in the Sector General novels, are reduced to helpless witnesses (though their mega-hospital, with its stockpiles and self-contained power supply, becomes one of the few cities of refuge to be preserved). The destruction and prophesied rebirth of human civilisation by a chosen remnant becomes a secular apocalypse, with the clones as destroying angels (like angels they do not reproduce) and the aliens as fallible, experimenting deities, asking humanity's forgiveness for the necessary cruelties they were forced to inflict in response to humanity's own vices. There is thus less difference between Shaw's anti-theistic rage at suffering in *The Ceres Solution* and White's calm Catholic agnosticism than appears at first sight, though they are still differentiated by White's insistence that suffering cannot simply be meaningless and must have a final purpose, however remote or unpalatable.

20   White described it as 'obviously an expanded Belfast' – http://www.sectorgeneral. com/articleslocusinterview.html.

Shaw and White, then, serve as reminders that Ireland's participation in global culture goes back beyond the 1960s or the 1990s; even in the post-war period of cultural protectionism there were Elvis fans and readers of detective stories in Dublin and Belfast, and they too were part of the Irish story. Where other Irish commentators sought to bridge the divisions of Irish society through empathy based on religiosity, on patriotism, or erotics, Shaw and White look to Wellsian technocracy, managerial rationality and the relief of physical suffering – and in defining themselves against the Belfast of their era they preserve echoes of its less scientific apocalypses and of an era when it could plausibly be supposed that at some point in the future spaceships might be manufactured by Nissan-Vickers of Birkenhead.

Works by James White

The Secret Visitors (1957)
Second Ending (1962)
Deadly Litter (1964) – short stories
Escape Orbit (1965)
The Watch Below (1966)
All Judgement Fled (1968)
The Aliens Among Us (1969) [short stories – the 1970 edition has an additional story]
Dark Inferno (1972) aka *Lifeboat*
The Dream Millennium (1974)
Monsters and Medics (1977) – short stories; material also incorporated in *Second Ending Futurse Past* (1978) – short stories
Underkill (1979)
Federation World (1988)
The Silent Stars Go By (1991)
Gene Roddenberry's Earth: Final Conflict – The First Protector (2000)

PATRICK MAUME

SECTOR GENERAL BOOKS

Hospital Station (1962)
Star Surgeon (1963)
Major Operation (1971) –
(These three were collected in 2001 as *Beginning Operations*, with an introduction by Brian Stableford.)

Ambulance Ship (1979)
Sector General (1983)
Star Healer (1985)
(These three were collected in 2002 as *Alien Emergencies*, with an introduction by David Langford)

Code Blue – Emergency (1987)
The Genocidal Healer (1992)
(These two were collected in 2003 as *General Practice*.)

The Galactic Gourmet (1996)
Final Diagnosis (1997)
Mind Changer (1998)
Double Contact (1999)
The White Papers (1996) – some stories and a taxonomy (by another hand) of the fauna of Sector General.

OTHER MATERIAL RELATING TO JAMES WHITE

http://www.sectorgeneral.com/
http://lacon3.worldcon.org/ww/Text/white2.bio
http://www.ansible.demon.co.uk/writing/odysso1.html
http://homepage.tinet.ie~albedo1/interview-white.html
Belfast Telegraph 7 March 1966, 2 November 1970, 23 July 1971, 2 May 1975
Irish News 23 July 1971

Belfast Newsletter 4 March 1974
Guardian 29 September 1999
Locus March 1993

Works by Bob Shaw

The Enchanted Duplicator (1952) http://www.dcs.gla.ac.uk/SF-Archives/
     Misc/The-Enchanted-Duplicator
Nightwalk (1967)
The Two-Timers (1968)
The Palace of Eternity (1969)
The Shadow of Heaven (1969)
One Million Tomorrows (1970)
Ground Zero Man (1971)
Other Days, Other Eyes (1972)
Tomorrow Lies in Ambush (1973) – short stories
Orbitsville (1975)
Cosmic Kaleidoscope (1976)
A Wreath of Stars (1976)
Medusa's Children (1977)
Who Goes Here? (1977)
Vertigo (1978) – aka *Terminal Velocity*
Dagger of the Mind (1980)
The Ceres Solution (1981)
Orbitsville Departure (1983)
A Better Mantrap (1984) – short stories
Fire Pattern (1984)
Dark Night in Toyland (1989) – short stories
The Ragged Astronauts (1986)
The Wooden Spaceships (1987)
The Fugitive Worlds (1989)

Killer Planet (1989) – children's story
Orbitsville Judgement (1990)
Warren Peace (1993)
Messages Found in an Oxygen Bottle (1996) essays [published in one
    volume with *Between Two Worlds* by Terry Carr]

OTHER MATERIAL RELATING TO BOB SHAW

http://www.ansible.co.uk/writing/bobshaw.html
http://www.fanac.org/fanzines/Slant/
http://news.ansible.co.uk/a104.html
http://en.wikisource.org/wiki/The_Private_of_the_Buffs
http://www.scifimoviepage.com/art_kub_2.html
http://www.ianwatson.info/kubrick.htm
Belfast Telegraph 26 June 1969, 20 March 1972, 2 April 1973, 26 April 1976,
    6 March 1978, 1 December 1980, 13 February 1996
Ulster Commentary March 1971
Independent (London) 17 February 1996

General

There are entries on both writers in John Clute et al. (eds), *The Encyclopedia
    of Science Fiction* (1993).

'Protestant Suspicions of Catholic Duplicity': Religious and Racial Constructs in Le Fanu and Yeats

CLAIRE NALLY

Visions and Vengeance: Anglo-Irish Ghosts

In 1968, Austin Clarke identified a little known but direct connection between Le Fanu and Yeats:

> May I venture to suggest that Yeats owed the expression ['A terrible beauty is born', from 'Easter, 1916'] to a poem by Joseph Sheridan Le Fanu, the Irish writer who is better known as novelist and short-story writer than as poet? It is used to describe a fearful spirit which was sometimes seen in Munster:
>
> Fionula the Cruel, the brightest, the worst,
> With a terrible beauty the vision accurst,
> Gold-filleted, sandalled, of times dead and gone … (Clarke, 1968: 1409)

Indeed, Le Fanu and Yeats share more than the latter's appropriation of a phrase or two. In 'Green Tea' (published as part of the collection *In a Glass Darkly* in 1872), Le Fanu presents the haunted and paranoid figure of Mr Jennings, a middle-aged man of 'high church precision' (Le Fanu, 1999: 6). Like Le Fanu, and in common with Yeats, Mr Jennings is of Anglican pedigree: indeed, he is an ordained minister in the church. Equally the Le Fanus had Huguenot lineage, and their ancestor, Charles de Cresserons, fought on the side of William of Orange in the Battle of the Boyne. The eighteenth-century Le Fanus were bourgeois, Protestant merchants and bankers, whilst Le Fanu's maternal relations were linked to the playwright Richard Brinsley Sheridan (McCormack, 1997: 1).

Equally, Yeats mythologizes himself as part of the Anglo-Irish settler culture, much to the amusement of George Moore:

> [...] we laughed, remembering AE's story, that one day whilst Yeats was crooning over his fire Yeats had said that if he had his rights he would be Duke of Ormonde. AE's answer was: I am afraid, Willie, you are overlooking your father – a detestable remark to make to a poet in search of an ancestry; and the addition: We both belong to the lower-middle classes, was in equally bad taste. AE knew that there were spoons in the Yeats family bearing the Butler crest, just as there are portraits in my family of Sir Thomas More, and he should have remembered that certain passages in *The Countess Cathleen* are clearly derivative from the spoons. (Moore, 1985: 540)

As they gradually lost their powerbase of land, prestige, and authority in the nineteenth and early twentieth centuries, the Anglo-Irish were displaced and disconcerted by an emphatically Gaelic and Catholic majority, something which was a source of major insecurity for both Le Fanu, and Yeats.

Moreover, what Austin Clarke identifies is the 'spirit' of the 1916 rebellion: an eminently noble but cruel and fearful manifestation of the Gaelic spirit which has close parallels with Leo Africanus, Yeats's otherworldly guide who first emerged in a séance on 24 April 1909. Yeats initially identifies him as a Pope (Adams and Harper, 1982: 3), and therefore clearly sees him as representative of the Catholic majority. However, Yeats suggests Leo speaks 'with a strong Irish accent' (Adams and Harper, 1982: 19), but simultaneously aligns him with the historical figure of Leo Africanus, the sixteenth-century diplomat who was born in Granada (then Islamic Spain), and brought up in Morocco. Very much like Le Fanu's demonic monkey in 'Green Tea', Leo is also untrustworthy, and dangerous: as the *Vision Papers* suggest, Leo represents 'sheer malevolence' (Yeats, 1992a: 276–7). In the light of this, I want to suggest that the spirit Leo is a materialisation of Yeats's peculiarly Anglo-Irish anxieties regarding the rise of the 'Gaelic' Irish. Thus Leo has clear affinities with, not only Le Fanu's similar anxieties represented in 'Green Tea', but more broadly, the cultural inscriptions of Gaelic nationalism in the late nineteenth and early twentieth centuries. In the words of Joep Leerssen, 'Gaelic Ireland is excluded, exoticized, rusticated. Anglo-Ireland is domestic, Gaelic Ireland is foreign, alien' (Leerssen, 1996: 50).

As Roy Foster has observed, one clear parallel between Yeats and Le Fanu is through their status as ambassadors of the Anglo-Irish occult (Foster, 1989; 243–66). In 'Green Tea', Mr Jennings engages in studying 'the religious metaphysics of the ancients' (Le Fanu, 1999: 21). In the course of this study, he consumed copious amounts of tea: 'I began to take a little green tea. I found the effect pleasanter, it cleared and intensified the power of thought so. I had come to take it frequently, but not stronger than one might take it for pleasure' (Le Fanu, 1999: 22). The combination of his study with the green tea produces the basis of the story: 'By various abuses, among which the habitual use of such agents as green tea is one... Jennings had inadvertently opened [the inner eye]' (Le Fanu, 1999: 39). This references the Swedenborgian theory of the interior sight (as expounded in *Arcana Caelestia*), which when accessed, allows dialogue with the community of spirits (Le Fanu, 1999: 14). Notably, the tea trade in Britain sustained close affiliations with Empire and the East India Company, with imports (from Burma, India and China) beginning in the 1660s, and reaching their height in the early nineteenth-century. Also, in common with Yeats's experiments with the spirit of Leo Africanus, the ghost Jennings inadvertently summons is a malignant creature:

> [T]wo small circular reflections, as it seemed to me of a reddish light. They were about two inches apart... I began now to perceive an outline of something black, and I soon saw with tolerable distinctness the outline of a small black monkey, pushing its face forward in mimicry to meet mine; those were its eyes, and I now dimly saw its teeth grinning at me. (Le Fanu, 1999: 23)

Jennings is haunted by the spectre of this creature, which possesses a 'stooping gait, on all fours, walking or creeping'. It is 'jaded and sulky', a 'beast', which surreptitiously 'crept ... close to [Jennings'] feet', at turns is 'dazed and languid' or 'sullen and sick' (Le Fanu, 1999: 25–7). At all times, however, it presents a 'character of intense malice and vigilance... [and] an air of menace'(Le Fanu, 1999: 27). Most importantly, perhaps, it is aligned with the demonic: 'It was with me in church – in the reading-desk – in the pulpit – within the communion rails. At last, it reached this

extremity, that while I was reading to the congregation, it would spring
upon the open book and squat there, so that I was unable to see the page'
(Le Fanu, 1999: 29). The monkey thwarts High Church practice, and
in much the same way, Leo Africanus disrupts the occult enterprise of
A Vision. In 1917, he reveals himself as a 'Frustrator', a ghostly presence
which is determined to maliciously thwart the medium's study of the
otherworld (Yeats, 1992a: 276–7). More importantly, like Leo Africanus
who threatens to destroy those who would rend the veil between the
living and the dead, in Le Fanu's tale Dr Hesselius warns 'if [evil spirits]
could flow into the things of his body, they would attempt by a thousand
means to destroy him; for they hate man with a deadly hatred' (Le Fanu,
1999: 14). For this reason, Swedenborg counselled against communion
with spirits (Le Fanu, 1999: 15).

This obvious persecution complex in 'Green Tea' has other important
resonances. As the monkey proceeds to speak, Dr Hesselius asks, 'How
do you mean – speak as a man does, do you mean?' (Le Fanu, 1999: 31).
The subhuman species is not credited with that marker of the civilised –
language (both Leo Africanus, as Latin for *lion*, and the spectral monkey
in Le Fanu, are credited with animalistic characteristics). Of course this
has an overtly colonial dimension. Equally, Dr Hesselius comments that
'I have met with ... fifty-seven cases of this kind of vision, which I term
indifferently "sublimated", "precocious", and "interior"' (Le Fanu, 1999:
38). The apparition of the monkey represents an example of a subconscious self, a doppelganger or Other, a common enough trope in Gothic
fiction. Specifically in relation to Le Fanu, Victor Sage has called this
motif the 'Two Brother Plot', manifested for instance, in *Uncle Silas* (Sage,
2004: 6). The self is confronted with a monstrous Other which is also
disturbingly proximate: 'the Other that is not only a brother but a twin,
born not of man, nor in man, but beside him and at the same time, in an
identical newness, in an unavoidable duality' (Foucault, 1973: 326). Like
the Will's relationship to the Mask in the theory of *A Vision*, duality also
includes a disturbing nearness. Similarly, both Leo Africanus and the
green tea consumed in Le Fanu's story are signs of empire and evidence
of a colonial legacy.

Gothicism's obsession with guilt is also a feature here, as in 'The Familiar', which directly follows 'Green Tea' in the collection, *In a Glass Darkly*. Here, Captain Barton was involved in a 'guilty attachment' with the daughter of a man in the Navy, and she later died of a 'broken heart' (Le Fanu, 1999: 81–2). In 'Green Tea' however, the guilty fear is ancestral and inherited. Published during the Fenian uprisings and the rise of O'Connell, alongside Gladstone's disestablishment of the Church of Ireland, the story of the demonic monkey suggests the underbelly of Gaelic Irishness: stereotypically violent, irrational, bestial, and uncontrollable. It is an image which haunts the Anglo-Irish ascendancy: 'there was some monster in Le Fanu's thought, not too hideous to be shown but perhaps too hideous to be confronted directly.' (Tracy, in Le Fanu, 1999: xiv). In this way, Gothic also becomes a way of reclaiming, or at least partly confronting, suppressed histories and nations: 'In Ireland, one can similarly point to a Gothic tradition that deals with Irish issues in a variety of guises' (Punter, 2002: 107). Recent criticism has highlighted this context in the work of Le Fanu:

> Jennings's monkey may reflect Victorian anxieties after Darwin's unwelcome suggestion that man was of simian ancestry. Crudely popularized versions of Darwin's theory served to argue that certain races – Australian Bushmen, sub-Saharan Africans, the Irish – were still close to their gorilla ancestors. Le Fanu would have been well aware of the simian Irish who were common in Victorian political cartoons, especially in the pages of *Punch*. (Tracy, in Le Fanu, 1999: xiv)

Likewise, what does Yeats's Leo Africanus symbolically represent if not a degenerate spirit? In *Heaven and Hell*, which Yeats read and referred to repeatedly, Swedenborg suggests that the moral state of the spirit is reflected in its appearance:

> [O]ur face changes and becomes quite different. It comes to look like the ruling affection in which the deeper reaches of our minds were engaged in the world, the kind of affection characteristic of the spirit within our body, because the face of the spirit is very different from the face of our body ... People who were engaged in good affections had lovely faces, while people who were engaged in evil affections had ugly ones. Seen in its own right, our spirit is nothing but our affections[.] (Swedenborg, 2000: 346)

The form presented by the spirit in the afterlife is representative of its principles, or conversely, its degeneracy. This is very close to the ideology of colonialism, in which 'the Victorian's faith in physiognomy ... the slope of the forehead, the curve of the nose, the thickness of the lips, or the shape of the chin served as so many skeleton keys to unlock the secrets of the 'real' character hidden within each individual' (Curtis, 1997: xvii). Similarly, Leo Africanus and the simian of 'Green Tea' are indicative of colonial tropes of the late nineteenth and the early years of the twentieth century. Pieter Camper's (1722–1789) theory, influential in the nineteenth century as part of the science of craniometry, proposed a scheme of oppositional facial types, *prognathism*, signifying a projecting mouth and jaw (Curtis, 1997: xix). This idea was easily extended to suggest that the facial characteristics of the individual determined and revealed the nature of the subject (a point further developed in the degenerative theories of Cesare Lombroso and Max Nordau in the latter half of the nineteenth century) – 'small foreheads, short noses, and prognathous mouths were the marks of inferiority, usually found in criminals and Negroes or people of African descent' (Curtis, 1997: xix–xx). Notably, the attribution was common to the native Irish also:

> [S]imian Paddy... longed to use physical force to free his country from British rule. Espousing an Irish Republic wholly separate from Great Britain, this truly 'dangerous' creature looked like a cross between a monstrous ape and primitive man owing to his high and hairy upper lip or muzzle, concave nose, low facial angle, and sharp teeth .... The unforgettable image of simian Paddy, who tried to subvert law and order or English civilization in Ireland, derived in large part from another form of demonization – namely, the construction of a monstrous man-eating ape in equatorial Africa. (Curtis, 1997: xxii–xxiv)

Of course, as evidenced by Charles Kingsley's much quoted comment during his brief sojourn in Ireland in 1860, identifying the Irish with African peoples and both with the simian was common: 'I am haunted by the human chimpanzees I saw along that hundred miles of horrible country. I don't believe they are our fault ... But to see white chimpanzees is dreadful; if they were black, one would not feel it so much' (Curtis, 1968: 84). Kingsley highlights not only the monstrosity of the perceived

Other, but also, the horror at potential affinity: more than the black man, the white Irishman seems disturbingly proximate. The demon-monkey in 'Green Tea' suggests a simianised native Irishman, pursuing and tormenting the Anglican Mr Jennings, much in the same way as on a national scale, the Fenian movement and physical force nationalism, would present themselves as antagonists to the conservative Anglo-Irish section of the community. Similarly, the Negro Irishman, Leo Africanus, clearly represents Yeats's own anxieties about the Gaelic Irish community dominating the Anglo-Irish. Curtis's chronology of the simian Irish in visual representations is apposite here: such pictures surfaced around 1840, with the 1860s serving as a high point in magazines such as *Punch*. However, he also notes that the Irish simian in England and America only died out after 1921, with the Anglo-Irish War and partial independence. In fact, Curtis points out that 'The ape-like Irishman did make a fleeting appearance in *Punch* in the early 1920s during the bitter guerrilla war fought by Sinn Fein militants against the forces of the Crown' (Curtis, 1997: 57). As such, Yeats's own anxieties as to mob rule and fiercely Catholic, Gaelic governmental structures in the Irish Free State contending with his own Anglo-Irish ideologies, closely relate to Leo Africanus, who made his first appearance in 1909 and still remained significant enough to influence *A Vision* in 1925. This orientalised, exoticised spirit suggests Yeats was projecting the threatening aspects of Irish society, the extremity of Gaelic nationalism, as his Other, or alternatively, in the terminology of *A Vision,* Leo is the Gaelic Mask which Yeats's Anglo-Irish Will both desired and despaired at. Leo in the role of Frustrator represents what Luke Gibbons has identified as 'Protestant suspicions of Catholic duplicity' (Gibbons, 2004: 75). As the Mask of the poet, Leo is also the locus of desire, a longing for inclusion in the nation, comparable in some ways to Yeats's earlier appropriation of Celticism.

Following his prioritisation of Anglo-Irishness in the early twentieth century, Yeats carefully and indeed wilfully occluded the Irish nineteenth century and its influences on his work, suppressing any cross-fertilisation with his Gothic predecessor, Le Fanu. This occlusion is represented clearly in Yeats's essay 'Swedenborg, Mediums, and the Desolate Places' (1914). Here he states:

[I]t was indeed Swedenborg who affirmed for the modern world, as against the
abstract reasoning of the learned, the doctrine and practice of the desolate places,
of shepherds and midwives, and discovered a world of spirits where there was a
scenery like that of earth, human forms, grotesque or beautiful, senses that knew
pleasure and pain, marriage and war, all that could be painted on canvas, or put
into stories to make one's hair stand up. (Yeats, 1992b: 312)

Those 'stories', as W.J. McCormack indicates, are undoubtedly an allusion
to Le Fanu's short tales with Swedenborgian influences (McCormack,
1997: 6–7). However, Yeats rejects the nineteenth century in favour of
the earlier Patriot parliament and the more clearly delineated traditions of
the Anglo-Irish in the eighteenth century, and thus he refuses to identify
the short story writer by name. Not only does he reject Le Fanu, but also,
deftly avoids one of the greatest and most tragic events of the century, the
Irish Famine (caused by the potato blight *Phytophthora infestans*), cor-
related by numerous commentators with the aggressive import industry
of the British Empire (having much in common with tea as an imperial
commodity).

Yet, despite Yeats's dismissal, the ghosts of nineteenth-century Ireland
covertly appear throughout his spiritualist work. In her study on twentieth-century spiritualism, Jenny Hazelgrove comments 'The assumption
that individuals were culpable in their own haunting was widespread'
(Hazelgrove, 2000: 30). The idea of guilt resurfacing in demonic form
is also a common Gothic motif: as Victor Sage comments, 'it seems clear
that the story ["Green Tea"] is a pre-Freudian allegory of unconscious
guilt, and that Hesselius's explanations via his theory of "Metaphysical
medicine" are at least in part a form of psychoanalysis' (Sage, 1988: 205).
Unlike the Catholic faith with its adherence to an external confessor,
this idea of an internalised conscience is also very specifically a Protestant
phenomenon (Sage, 1988: xv). Equally, the censorship of Le Fanu's name
in 'Swedenborg, Mediums and the Desolate Places', suggests a tacit avoid-
ance of perceived Anglo-Irish guilt. As Terry Eagleton has commented:
'Where is the Famine in the literature of the Revival? Where is it in
Joyce? If the Famine stirred some to angry rhetoric, it would seem to
have traumatized others into muteness' (Eagleton, 1996: 13). I would
argue the Famine was more covert and less didactic in the literature of

this period: the conclusion of 'The Dead' in *Dubliners* (1914) is but one example (Joyce, 1992: 225). Colm Tóibín notes that those who witnessed the Famine could not and did not remain silent, but that those writers who came directly after the Famine, like Yeats, found its abhorrently premodern quality difficult to relate to (Tóibín and Ferriter, 2002: 28). Corroborating this, the folk record notes that a sixty-six-year-old man from Cork recounted in 1945: 'Several people would be glad if the famine times were altogether forgotten so that the cruel doings of their forebears could not be again renewed and talked about by neighbours' (Ó Gráda, 1999: 211). For whatever reason, this textual repression or amnesia in Yeats's work encourages a ghostly testament, a resurfacing of the 'Gael', through Leo Africanus. As a spirit from the otherworld, representative of the collective spirit of the Gaelic nation, he has obvious allegiances with the Famine dead (Yeats, 1978: 171). And as a sublimated 'other' common to Gothic, he suggests a repressed guilt or perception of transgression in the Anglo-Irish psyche of Yeats himself.

Gaels, Ghouls, and Gorilla Warfare

The task of remembering or recuperating the dead has a twofold role: 'not only events recalled from personal experience but also those inherited recollections that prompt feelings of collective shame, pride or resentment on behalf of our real or metaphorical ancestors' (McBride, 2001: 5). This suggests Leo himself also has a dual role: on a personal level, to figure as Yeats's political and metaphorical other self, and on a collective level, to represent the 'Gaelic' Irish. He is both the Mask, and also the *Spiritus Mundi* or collective unconscious. Leo directly alludes to this idea of ancestral memory: 'When we die [we] have nothing but our memories: we can [no] longer procreate, but those memories our punishment and our reward arrange & measure, & transform in pattern' (Adams and Harper,

1982: 34). This 'return of the repressed' is especially fruitful in terms of occult or 'ghostly' discourse. As Avery F. Gordon remarks:

> The ghost is not simply a dead or missing person, but a social figure, and investigating it can lead to that dense site where history and subjectivity make social life. The ghost or apparition is one form by which something lost, or barely visible, or seemingly not there to our supposedly well-trained eyes, makes itself known or apparent to us, in its own way, of course. (Gordon, 1997: 8)

The ghost as a host or spirit *is* a social being, revealing the lacunae and elisions in official narratives: as Gordon suggests, 'the ghost is a crucible for political mediation and historical memory ... the ghost cannot simply be tracked to an individual loss or trauma' (Gordon, 1997: 183). This effectively politicises the spiritualist project with which Yeats and his wife were involved. At the same time, it is a positive recuperation of a lost event: 'We are in relation to [the spirit or ghost] and it has designs on us such that we must reckon with it graciously, attempting to offer it a hospitable memory *out of a concern for justice*' (Gordon, 1997: 63). Similarly Hazelgrove notes that spirit visitations were commonly associated with 'the righting of injustices' (Hazelgrove, 2000: 33). This spirit-reckoning, the need for justice, suggests Leo Africanus's role in relation to nineteenth-century Irish history. In this way, the subtext of *A Vision* can quite clearly relate to the impetus behind Gothic fiction more generally:

> [T]he rise and currency of literary Gothic is strongly related to the growth of the campaign for Catholic Emancipation from the 1770s onwards until the first stage ends temporarily with the Emancipation Act of 1829; but further, that continuance of the horror novel is equally, if not more strongly, related to the subsequent struggles, doctrinal and political, which flared up between Catholic and Protestant throughout the course of the nineteenth century and well into the twentieth. (Sage, 1988: 28–9)

Apart from this political dimension, the common link between Le Fanu's Gothic and Yeats's occultism is the communion with the dead, crucial in this period of Irish history. The Famine years were also heavily scrutinized in the public imagination during the 1890s and after: 'Ghosts of the Famine victims featured increasingly in the 1890s, in folktales and prohibitions, alongside commemorations of past events' (Kiberd, 2001: 379). In addition, 1897 marked the fiftieth anniversary of the worst Famine years, and Maud Gonne denounced Queen Victoria as the 'Famine Queen.' In a conspicuously Gothic gesture, with James Connolly and Yeats himself, she also organised a demonstration in which a coffin was carried (Yeats, 1966a: 366–8). Most notable, perhaps, was the recurrence of a famine in the 1870s:

> Eighteen seventy-nine brought a third consecutive bad harvest. A combination of bad weather, the poor harvest, and depressed livestock prices precipitated a major subsistence crisis. The small farmers of Connacht and Donegal were particularly hard hit since agriculture in the west had remained heavily dependent on the potato. Supplies of goods and fuel were virtually exhausted by the end of 1879 and it was clear that the winter months were likely to see serious and widespread distress among the poorer classes. (Crossman, 2004: 167)

Although by no means as severe as those terrible years of the mid-century, A.M. Sullivan, the nationalist MP, accused the government of 'wilful murder ... because, though forewarned and forearmed, they were again allowing the people to perish, and were not averting the spread of famine' (Crossman, 2004: 172). However, relief measures were more successful than in the 1840s, combined with less dependence on the potato than in the previous years. Although a repeated Great Famine was averted, the food shortages of 1879–84 do suggest the economic and cultural currency of famine in the late nineteenth century.

Specifically in Yeats's work, the Famine remains partially concealed. In the early *Representative Irish Tales*, Yeats selects a Famine tale written by Rosa Mulholland, entitled 'The Hungry Death', evidently indicating the tragedy of the 1840s. However, in his short editorial introduction, Yeats makes no reference to this context: 'Miss Mulholland is the novelist of contemporary Catholic Ireland. She has not the square-built power of our older writers, Banim, Carleton, and their tribe, but has, instead, much fancy and style of a sort commoner in our day than theirs, and a distinction of feeling and thought peculiar to herself' (Yeats, 1979: 321). His choices from Carleton do not refer to the Famine (Yeats reprints 'Wildgoose Lodge', 'Condy Cullen and the Gauger', 'The Curse' and 'The Battle of the Factions'). In Yeats's introduction to *Stories from Carleton*, the Famine is marked only by its complete absence: he describes Carleton's longer novels as possessing 'a clay-cold melancholy' (Yeats, 1979: 363), which has overt metaphorical associations with the unburied dead, but makes no other allusion to the sombre background of the writer's work.

Despite this editorial elision, *The Countess Cathleen* provides an obvious framework of famine. Yeats is taciturn concerning what famine he represents: this lack of specificity suggests another lacuna in terms of Yeats's Famine portrayal. Of course the worst famine years were remembered as the late 1840s and early 1850s, but famines recurred frequently throughout the nineteenth century. The opening scene of the play details how 'They say that now the land is famine-struck/The graves are walking' (Yeats, 1966b: 5). Yeats problematically provides an idealised feudal vision where Cathleen sacrifices herself for her tenants. Nonetheless, as precursors of Leo Africanus, the Famine dead walk abroad, and as such the suppression of Famine memory re-emerges in ghostly form:

> [T]raumatic events in the lives of individuals – and by extension, communities – are dealt with by an attempt to suppress them, to banish them from consciousness. This is never entirely successful, however, and the memories return in other forms, forms which are usually harmful to the well being of the person. (Ó Cosáin, 2001: 112)

Additionally, the vivid, real experience of hunger reappears constantly as a metaphor in Yeats's occult and spiritual writings. In *A Vision* (B), Yeats states that the spirits forbade him to read philosophy, as it would confuse the transcription of the system, but that they did encourage him to read history. He explains that if he returned too quickly to abstraction, the spirits would claim 'We are starved' (Yeats, 1937: 12 and 239). The Famine 'spirits' seek historical recognition, or remembrance. In 'The Poet and Actress,' the Poet from Fez, undoubtedly Leo Africanus claims, 'every artist is a starving man' (Clark and Clark, 1993: 175). In *A Vision* (A), Yeats also employs the metaphor of hunger: 'There is yet another expiation that follows denial of experience, the wilful refusal of expression. Because of this denial the *Ghostly Self* is famished' (Yeats, 1978: 242). Such metaphors directly relate to Swedenborg's doctrine of the

'correspondences' in the afterlife, which are reiterated in *A Vision*. In
death, we live through the experiences of life. In principle, it relates to
the Hermetic dictum, 'As above, so below,' or as Swedenborg relates: 'in
general there is nothing natural to which something spiritual does not
have an answer' (Swedenborg, 2000: 371). Swedenborg explains these
'correspondences' in *Heaven and Hell:*

> As 'spirit people,' we enjoy every outer and inner sense we enjoyed in the world. We
> see the way we used to, we hear and talk the way we used to; *we smell and taste and
> feel things* when we touch them the way we used to; we want, wish, crave, think,
> ponder, are moved, love, and intend the way we used to ... We even take with us
> our natural memory, since we retain everything we have heard seen, read, learned,
> or thought in the world from earliest infancy to the very end of life. (Swedenborg,
> 2000: 348, my italics)

Yeats later develops this idea for the stage in *Purgatory* (1938) and *The
Dreaming of the Bones* (1921). However, he also discusses it in his essay
on Swedenborg:

> [Swedenborg discovered] the doctrine and practice of the desolate places, of shep-
> herds and of midwives, and discovered a world of spirits where there was a scenery
> like that of earth, human forms, grotesque or beautiful, *senses that knew pleasure
> and pain*, marriage and war. (Yeats, 1992b: 312, my italics)

The doctrine of correspondences, therefore, provides that not only does
the spirit carry the individual or collective memory with it into the afterlife, but that it also bears the trauma of physical experience suffered in
life.

The hungry, emaciated, Gothicised body features prominently in
reports of the Famine: 'The dread *spectre* of famine had already set foot
on the shores of Ireland, and was making ready to *stalk* through the fruitful land, from north to south, from east to west' (Guinan, 1908: 15, in
Morash, 1996: 112, my italics). In Yeats's spiritualist discourse, this figure
emerges as Leo Africanus: he is at once a Gothic emanation, a voice of
Famine and death, an angry retaliator, and representative of the native
Irish people. Leo voices the idea of the ghost as a national emissary in
his dialogue with Yeats: 'We are not indeed solitary for we can share

each memory like souls drifting together – & build a common world'
(Adams and Harper, 1982: 34). He is also Yeats's submerged expression
of ancestral guilt. In the afterlife, through the state called *The Shiftings*,
in order to achieve greater wisdom before reincarnation, the spirit must
confront its opposite to seek understanding, and ultimately, this is construed in feudal terms:

> The victim must … live the act of cruelty, not as victim but as tyrant; whereas the
> tyrant must by a necessity of his or her nature become the victim. But if one is dead
> and the other living they find each other in thought and symbol, the one that has
> been passive and is now active may from within control the other, once tyrant now
> victim … The souls of victim and tyrant are bound together and, *unless there is a
> redemption through the intercommunication of the living and the dead,* that bond
> may continue life after life, and this is just, for there had been no need of expiation
> had they seen in one another that other and not something else … There are other
> bonds, master and servant, benefactor and beneficiary, any relation that is deeper
> than the intellect may become such a bond. (Yeats, 1937: 238–9, my italics)

The recuperation of the spirit of the Famine through spiritualist discourse
promotes healing and renewal, a positive attempt to understand, remember and incorporate the past, whilst attempting to free the consciousness
from the endless cycle of historical repetition. It is both empowerment
and regeneration. The communication of the living and the dead frees
the tyrant and victim, or master and servant, from that cycle of destruction. The ultimate achievement on the individual, as on the collective
level is the harmonising of divergent forces, without the suppression of
concrete particularity. The admittance of the Other promotes greater
unity in both the self in psychological terms, and the nation in political
terms. The attempt at unity, the incorporation of Leo-as-native-Irish, has
obvious resonances with Yeats's own enterprise in the Irish Free State.
Leo is threatening, wronged, potentially dangerous and disconcertingly
Other. He represents a figuration of the 'Gaelic' Irishman just as that
social group were finally attaining political ascendancy. That nation is also
one which, until the relatively recent advent of Catholic Emancipation
and the Free State, were politically disenfranchised. As such, the 'Gaelic'
Other re-emerges with a ghostly testament demanding acknowledgement.

In this way, Yeats's communion with the dead is also giving a voice to those who cannot speak:

> Three times this morning ... I had given up in despair lest I not remember that this task has been laid upon me by those who cannot speak being dead & who if I fail may never find another interpreter. (Yeats cited in Harper, 1981: 15)

As such, Yeats offers to the dead a complex and often highly anxious presence in his literary and spiritual work, much in common with his hesitant, delayed, but insistent eulogy to the heroes in 'Easter 1916':

> I write it out in a verse –
> MacDonagh and MacBride
> And Connolly and Pearse
> Now and in the time to be,
> Wherever green in worn,
> Are changed, changed utterly:
> A terribly beauty is born.
>   (Yeats, 1988: 297–8)

Work Cited

Adams, Steve L., and George Mills Harper (eds) (1982), 'The Manuscript of "Leo Africanus"', *Yeats Annual no. 1*, pp. 3–47.

Clark, David R. and Rosalind Clark (1993, rev. edn), *W.B. Yeats & the Theatre of Desolate Reality*, The Catholic University of America Press: Washington.

Clarke, Austin (1968), 'Yeats and Le Fanu', *The Times Literary Supplement*, 12 December, p. 1409.

Crossman, Virginia (2004), '"With the experience of 1846 and 1847 before them": The politics of emergency relief, 1879–94', in Peter Gray (ed.), *Victoria's Ireland: Irishness and Britishness, 1837–1901*, Four Courts, Dublin, pp. 167–81.

Curtis, L. Perry, Jr (1997, rev. edn), *Apes and Angels: The Irishman in Victorian Caricature*, Smithsonian Institution Press, Washington.

—— (1968), *Anglo-Saxons and Celts: A Study of Anti-Irish Prejudice in Victorian England*, University of Bridgeport, New York.

Eagleton, Terry (1996), *Heathcliff and the Great Hunger: Studies in Irish Culture*, Verso, London.

Foster, R.F. (1989), 'Protestant Magic: W.B. Yeats and the Spell of Irish History', *Proceedings of the British Academy* 75, pp. 243–66.

Foucault, Michel (1973), *The Order of Things: An Archaeology of the Human Sciences*, Vintage, New York.

Gibbons, Luke (2004), *Gaelic Gothic,* Arlen House, Galway.

Gordon, Avery F. (1997), *Ghostly Matters: Haunting and the Sociological Imagination*, University of Minnesota Press, London and Minneapolis.

Harper, George Mills (1981), '"Unbelievers in the House": Yeats's Automatic Script', *Studies in the Literary Imagination* vol. xiv, no. 1 (Spring), pp. 1–15.

Hazelgrove, Jenny (2000), *Spiritualism and British Society between the Wars*, Manchester University Press, Manchester.

Joyce, James (1992), *Dubliners*, Penguin, Harmondsworth.

Kiberd, Declan (2001), *Irish Classics*, Granta, London.

Le Fanu, Sheridan (1999), *In a Glass Darkly*, ed. Robert Tracey, Oxford University Press, Oxford.

Leerssen, Joep (1996), *Remembrance and Imagination: Patterns in the Historical and Literary Representation of Ireland in the Nineteenth Century*, Cork University Press, Cork.

McBride, Ian (2001), 'Memory and national identity in modern Ireland', in Ian McBride (ed.), *History and Memory in Modern Ireland,* Cambridge University Press, Cambridge, pp. 1–42.

McCormack, W.J. (1997, third edn), *Sheridan Le Fanu*, Sutton Publishing, Stroud.

Morash, Chris (1996), 'Literature, Memory, Atrocity' in Chris Morash and Richard Hayes (eds), *'Fearful Realities': New Perspectives on the Famine*, Irish Academic Press, Dublin, pp. 110–18.

Moore, George (1985), *Hail and Farewell*, ed. Richard Allen Cave, Colin Smythe, Gerrards Cross.

Ó Cíosáin, Niall (2001), 'Famine memory and the popular representation of scarcity' in Ian McBride (ed.), *History and Memory in Modern Ireland*, Cambridge University Press, Cambridge, pp. 95–117.

Ó Gráda, Cormac (1999), *Black '47 and Beyond: The Great Irish Famine in History, Economy, and Memory*, Princeton University Press, Princeton.

Punter, David (2002), 'Scottish and Irish Gothic', in Jerrold E. Hogle, (ed.), *The Cambridge Companion to Gothic Fiction*, Cambridge University Press, Cambridge, pp. 105–23.

Swedenborg, Emmanuel (2000), *Heaven and Hell: Drawn from Things Heard and Seen* trans. George F. Dole, Swedenborg Foundation, Pennsylvania.

Sage, Victor (2004), *Le Fanu's Gothic: The Rhetoric of Darkness*, Palgrave Macmillan, Basingstoke.

—— (1988), *Horror Fiction in the Protestant Tradition*, Macmillan, Basingstoke.

Tóibín, Colm, and Diarmaid Ferriter (2002), *The Irish Famine: A Documentary* Profile Books, London.

Yeats, W.B. (1992a), *Yeats's Vision Papers*, vol. 2 ed. Steve L. Adams, Barbara J. Frieling and Sandra L. Sprayberry, Macmillan, Basingstoke.

—— (1992b), 'Swedenborg, Mediums, and the Desolate Places' in Gregory, Lady Augusta, *Visions and Beliefs in the West of Ireland*, Colin Smythe, Gerrards Cross, pp. 317–36.

—— (1988), *Poems of W.B Yeats*, ed. A. Norman Jeffares, Macmillan, Basingstoke, second edition.

—— (ed.) (1979), *Representative Irish Tales*, Colin Smythe, Gerrards Cross.

—— (1978), *A Critical Edition of Yeats's A Vision (1925)*, ed. George Mills Harper, London, Macmillan, London ('A' Text).

—— (1966a), *Autobiographies*, Macmillan, London.

—— (1966b), *Variorum Edition of the Plays of W.B. Yeats*, ed. Russell K. Alspach, Macmillan, London.

—— (1937), *A Vision*, Macmillan, London ('B' Text).

'One of themselves': Class Divisions in Eilís Dillon's *Blood Relations* and *The Bitter Glass*

DEIRDRE O'BYRNE

Eilís Dillon wrote two historical novels directly concerned with the birth of the new Irish state. *Blood Relations* (1993), first published in 1977, deals with the War of Independence, and *The Bitter Glass* (Dillon, 1987), though published in 1958, deals with the historically later period of the Civil War. This article examines the depiction of class in both novels, which feature young upper-class women who, in the course of the narrative, must learn to value the Connemara people amongst whom they live as more than 'ignorant peasants' (Dillon, 1987: 205). However, the texts betray some authorial prejudices in the depiction of the working classes, and it is apparent that the narrative viewpoint is that of the priviliged group to which the author belonged. Dillon was born :

> into ... an old Connaught family which produced several noteworthy nationalist figures .... Her ... grandfather ... was a minister in the first Dáil Éireann .... Her [uncle] ... was executed for his part in the 1916 Rising. Her immediate family was intensely republican, and her father ... was jailed for ... Sinn Féin activities. This background greatly influenced her writing when she drew on family history to recreate the nation's past and the traumas of the country's march to nationhood. (O Ceirín, 1996: 64)

As befits its title, family is an important theme in *Blood Relations,* but the ambiguity of the term is significant. Dillon's text shows how the bloody conflict entangles people in unexpected liaisons. The crucial relationship in this respect is between Molly, a young 'lady' (as we're repeatedly told), and Peter Morrow, born in poverty in Connemara but now a rich Galway-based businessman. Morrow is a man who transcends class. The so-called ordinary people see him as 'one of themselves' (Dillon, 1993: 145),

234 DEIRDRE O'BYRNE

a phrase Molly also uses about him (162), in her case with suspicion, but his money enables him to live in an elegant house and dress well. Only after Peter has been hanged for his political activism does Molly begin to appreciate him, and that encapsulates the didactic purpose of the novel. Peter, as his surname Morrow suggests, is a man of the future, even though he doesn't live to see the end of the conflict.

A stereotypically bad landlord, Molly's father Henry Gould is a man of the past, and the villain of the novel; he blackmails his sister, bullies his daughters and is responsible for the death of his wife. But the author is scrupulously fair to the gentry who are on the nationalist side. When Henry's sister Jack is asked 'What do you think of this rebellion?', she answers 'at once, without thinking: "I'm all in favour of anything that will finish off people like my brother."' To the query, 'You mean the old landlords?' (Dillon, 1993: 118), Jack responds dryly that 'Some people think they all should be shot' (ibid.: 119). Dillon depicts Aunt Jack as progressive in her outlook, but she is not without snobbery. In her younger days, we see her deploring the 'delusions of grandeur' (ibid.: 22) of the Gilmore family, for whom she is governess. Their naming their home 'Castle Gilmore' is condemned by Jack as 'sheer nonsense' (ibid.: 22), and 'Miss Gould' is quick to point out that her family have occupied Woodbrook[1] for 170 years, as compared to the mere 100-years-old inhabitancy of Castle Gilmore (ibid.: 22–3).

Snobbery is not confined to Aunt Jack. Everyone in the text, from horrid Henry to progressive Peter, commends her for bringing up Henry's motherless daughters as 'ladies'. According to Dillon's narrator, she has had a head start; her niece Molly, as well as 'neat wrists and ankles ... [possesses a] narrow head and neck, so that every movement marked her as a lady' (ibid.: 12). However, it transpires that Molly's 'narrow head' encloses a correspondingly narrow mind. She sees her fiancé Sam's nationalist cause as 'crazy rubbish', and thinks 'people had

1   The name Woodbrook is now best known as the title of David Thomson's memoir, first published in 1974, of his time as tutor in a house of that name. Co-incidentally or not, Thomson's Woodbrook is, like Dillon's, in the West of Ireland, in his case in Sligo (Thomson, 1988).

bamboozled themselves with history and songs and poetry' (ibid.: 40). The struggle for independence is shown to be a 'most bitter and tragic struggle', not least within Molly Gould herself. As in *The Bitter Glass*, Eilís Dillon shows that external conflict is mirrored by inner turmoil, with its own opposing factions. Molly is required to grow less like her father and more like her Aunt Jack in order to survive in the new Ireland. In the beginning of the novel she is at loggerheads with her father, yet is shown to be surprisingly like him in opinion. Henry muses that '[i]t was ridiculous to be frightened' of Morrow:

> No matter how rich Peter became, no matter how smartly he dressed in his fine grey suit and shining boots and silk scarf, Henry knew that he would never be anything but an ignorant, backward Connemara Mike. No amount of education could do anything for these people. (Dillon, 1993: 54)

According to Henry, '[t]heir appearance gave [them] away', as 'by midday' they would begin 'to show a black stubble. Strong hair was a sure sign of ill breeding' (ibid.: 54). Although the narrative does not sympathise with Henry, his class-ridden opinions echo those of the narrator: a person can don the costume of the upper classes, but peasant origins will be betrayed by the diameter, if not of one's ankles, neck or wrists, then of the hair.

However, notwithstanding his vigorous hirsuteness, Peter is seen by Aunt Jack as 'one of nature's gentlemen' (ibid.: 42). Molly's fiancé Sam says 'Peter has a knack of mixing with all kinds of people, on equal terms' (ibid.: 30), and Nicholas, whom Molly marries, tells her 'Everyone loves Peter. He does things for everyone' (ibid.: 162). Only Molly and her father cannot see the good in this character. The transcending of class which is praised by Sam is seen by Henry as a threat: 'You never knew where you stood with a fellow like him, neither a gentleman nor a lout – there was nothing to go on. There were upstarts everywhere these days' (ibid.: 55). Dillon explains Peter Morrow's abilities to mingle in all social strata by giving him a tragic back-story befitting his heroic status in the novel. He relates the story of his transformation by a married woman in England, daughter of a 'powerful family'. She 'began to educate me ... She said it would help me to get the better of the bosses if I were a lot smoother, and

she taught me how to speak better and generally licked me into shape'
(ibid.: 241). One assumes that it is this experience that enables Peter to
hope, vainly, that Molly Gould will overcome her class prejudices and
marry him, especially since she is carrying his child.

Dillon's narration constantly highlights issues of class. As a young
governess, Jack is seduced by the son of the house, falls pregnant, and is
of course abandoned by him. Thrown out by her employers, she is taken
in by their coachman and his wife, who take over the rearing of Jack's
daughter (ibid.: 24). When Jack meets her daughter later, Margaret is
thirty-five, and as we might expect, given the narrator's anatomical prejudices, reveals her breeding in her 'small, pointed face and neat hands
and feet' . Jack observes approvingly that she has also had the foresight
to 'have gone to some trouble to rid herself of ... the ugly Dublin accent'
(ibid.: 320). So Jack too judges on outward appearance, though the narrative offers no sympathy to Henry or Molly for doing likewise. Jack is
shown to be very conscious of the nuanced language of class. When her
daughter's foster-mother tells her Margaret is being interviewed for a
'situation', Jack ponders that it is a '[f]oul word, the one they always used
about servants. Her employment as a governess had been a position, not
a situation, a subtle difference' (ibid.: 319).

Aunt Jack's skills include the ability to use class privilege as a means
of getting what she wants. She accompanies Molly and Peter on a train
journey to Dublin to see Sam, who is in Kilmainham, and acts out a
perfect parody of the Anglo-Irish lady, addressing a British officer in 'a
high fluting voice':

> I'm taking my niece to see a doctor in Dublin. I must get through today ... This
> gentleman is coming with us as an escort ... Two ladies couldn't possibly travel
> alone, though I must say the Army has been wonderful, so kind and thoughtful
> and with such splendid manners ... that reminded me of the phrase 'an officer and
> a gentleman'. My mother always said ... 'You can trust a British officer' (Dillon,
> 1993: 105)

The 'outrageous performance' works, so the dissemblance that is seen as
a real or potential fault in Molly and her father is shown to be a useful
tool when deployed by Aunt Jack, as she is on the nationalist side. She,

like Peter Morrow, can transcend class barriers. Like the peasants, she tells fortunes from cards (ibid.: 38), and acts as midwife for the poor women of the district (ibid.: 263), a significant position in that she is fostering the continuation of another class besides her own moribund one.

Unlike her forward-seeing aunt, Molly for much of the narrative appears to be incapable of seeing beyond Peter Morrow's original social class. Despite having fallen into his arms in the height of her distress about Sam, she recoils from marrying him, even though she is carrying his child. She throws herself on the mercy of Sam's cousin, described by her father Henry as 'a gentleman, naturally' (ibid.: 194). Molly tells Nicholas:

> I'm afraid ... I'm suddenly terrified. Of what? I don't know – of all sorts of vague things that may never happen ... Can you stay with me always? I'm afraid. Can you keep me from – from Peter Morrow? ... I'm afraid of him. He'll do me some harm. I don't know what. I'm just afraid ... He frightens me ... I can never marry him .... Can you take me away, anywhere, so that he can never get at me? ... I'm repelled by him. (Dillon, 1993: 168–9)

This presumably is meant by Dillon to represent the less progressive gentry's fear of the man of the future, the 'counter-jumper' who is capable of ousting them from undeserved power.

Money is shown to muffle other prejudices. Henry, who threatens to throw his daughters out if they marry a Catholic, changes his mind when his eldest gains a wealthy admirer: 'After so many generations of poverty, Molly's engagement to young Samuel Flaherty had been a tremendous piece of good fortune', as the Flahertys were one of the few neighbouring families 'of their own class'. Henry's own pedigree is considered suspect by his neighbours: 'Though the Goulds were Protestant gentry who had been given the land in Cromwell's time ... they were always regarded as upstarts' (ibid.: 13). So the term 'upstart' is used both about Henry's family by others who judge themselves to be better placed, and then by Henry when referring to such upwardly-mobile figures as Peter Morrow.

It's not just the gentry who are shown to be concerned with slotting people into social hierarchies. When Peter is travelling around Ireland organising the resistance, an activist asks 'Where did you get that foreign accent you have?' Morrow explains that he acquired it in England,

and adds 'I have to meet all sorts of people in the way of business and it's convenient to be able to speak to them in their own way' (ibid.: 144), which suggests that most business people are of the Anglo-Irish class. Peter then goes on to ally himself with another hero of Irish politics: 'Parnell didn't have Irish, and he must have had a foreign accent too'. However, he is firmly put in his place: 'Ah, but Parnell was born a gentleman'. Peter takes no offence, merely being relieved that the activists recognise him as 'what he was, one of themselves' (ibid.: 145), despite his accent.

The Anglo-Irish as a class marked themselves out by their way of speaking: 'the better-off [Anglo-Irish] aped English manners' (de Vere White, 1972: 18), and, according to Elizabeth Bowen, '[t]o speak with a brogue ... was to be under-bred' (Bowen, 1998: 193). Such attitudes are not confined to the Anglo-Irish community:

> In Ireland, research suggests that we have internalised a stratification system for language and accents which approximates very closely to that of the old core elite. The closer a speaker's accent is in English to that of the English 'Received Pronunciation' standard, the more likely he is to be assumed to belong to a higher status occupation like a solicitor or bank manager, to have qualities of leadership and self-confidence. (Tovey, Hannan and Abramson, 1989: 22)

This statement was published in the 1980s, but fits in well with the attitudes displayed in Dillon's text.

Molly finds it impossible to accept Peter as a life-partner. She tells Sam 'I find him a very strange man', and later comes to regret her moment of passion with him:

> She trembled through her whole body with disgust and loathing of herself. Peter Morrow! He was not even a gentleman, for all his big house with its fine furnishings – none of them chosen by him – though she had to concede that he was a lot cleaner than many of the gentlemen she had met around Galway. How could she have done it? How could she? (Dillon, 1993: 102)

Peter is generally so highly regarded that this repugnance is a sign of Molly's narrow-mindedness, which (like her narrow head), she has inherited from her father. Her regret for what she sees as a moment of weakness echoes an earlier passage in the book when Henry rues his reliance on

Peter, as he has borrowed money from him. Both Henry and Molly are happiest when they can pull rank on Peter, and awareness of their own vulnerability in relation to him makes them uncomfortable.

If Molly and Henry are wrong in their character analysis, they are shown to be equally flawed in their political awareness. Henry, like his daughter, thinks that the Republican cause is born out of ignorance. When he hears of the arrest of his daughter's fiancé, he is disgusted; 'You've ruined us all, my lady' (ibid.: 32). The irony contained in that 'my lady' is biting, as we read that 'from treating [Molly] as if she were already the lady of the manor, he had taken to snapping at her as if she had deceived them all in some way' (ibid.: 13). In conversation with Peter about Sam, Henry pretends sympathy, but exposes his own ignorance in condemning Sam's: 'poor little devil was caught up in this without knowing what he was in for, I suppose' (ibid.: 55). This is close to Molly's opinion that the people are 'bamboozled' (ibid.: 40), even though Sam has tried to make the situation clear to her. When she asks, 'Why must there be a rising?', he tells her, 'Look around you. The people are starving. No one will ever do anything for them until we have a government of our own'. Molly asks if it's a 'rebellion of the poor' (ibid.: 31), apparently forgetting that her own family is so impoverished that they sit in a cold room without fuel for a fire. She cannot identify with the peasant Irish who surround them, and when Peter, in concern for her wellbeing, takes her arm, 'she let[s] him hold it quietly, covering her resentment and anger with the manners of a lady' (ibid.: 104). No wonder Peter tells his sister-in-law: 'She's a lady and you can never tell with them' ibid.: 99). Molly takes a long time to overcome her particular prejudices, and part of the learning process is realising that 'poor people' have something to teach her. The book ends, as does *The Bitter Glass*, with the wealthy young woman thinking: 'She would go back to [the poor people] and find out from them how you reached ... wisdom' (Dillon, 1993, 443).

Molly's redemption comes about when she finally begins to realise, as the narrative puts it, 'What a privilege it was to have been loved by [Peter Morrow]' (ibid.: 443), now safely dead and no longer in a position to claim his rights. She also come to the realisation that, as she tells Nicholas and his nationalistic comrade-in-arms: 'You do the things that need to be done' (ibid.: 445). Her final moment of restitution to Peter comes when she confesses, very close to the end of the book, to her husband that her first-born Sam is actually Peter's child. She tells Nicholas that she didn't marry Peter because she did not love him, but it is clear in the narrative that she did not love Nicholas when she married him either, but he was at least the 'right class'. However, Peter's son, named Samuel after his supposed father, is reared by Nicholas and Molly, so in that respect, the classes are integrated to a degree.

Meanwhile, on the other side of the world, class barriers are also breaking down. Henry, fearful that he will be exposed as a spy, runs away to America with his mistress Nora. Nora worries about her reception there: 'They say everyone is rich there .... Maybe they'd look down on the likes of me' (ibid.: 193), but is reassured by Henry, confident that class privilege will still exist in the New World: 'No, Nora, they would not, especially if I was with you'. When Aunt Jack visits (uninvited and unwelcomed by her brother), Nora confides that she is thinking of taking speech lessons: 'There's a woman here near us, and she said she could teach me to talk better in no time ... This woman said she could give me a bit of an American accent that would cover up everything'. Jack, true to her character, encourages Nora, who admits that 'Henry would like it ... He used to be always asking me to talk right' (ibid.: 193).

Blood Relations opens on 1 May, traditionally a day of new beginnings, and ends in the so-called New World, as Aunt Jack eschews the chance to expose Henry to his wife as the informer she knows him to be. She reflects that 'it must mean that blood is thicker than water after all' (Dillon, 1993: 465), a strange conclusion to a book that seems to suggest that what people need is to forget about is so-called breeding and blood, and integrate with one another in the cause of freedom.

In *The Bitter Glass*, Dillon is also concerned with a society in flux. The story focuses on the privileged MacAuley family and those immediately connected to them, showing how the winds of political change are experienced on an individual and familial basis. Against the backdrop of civil war, various conflicts are played out: traditional cures versus orthodox medicine, passion against coldness, country versus city, and class tensions between the so-called 'ordinary' people – often referred to in the novel as 'the people' – and the wealthy MacAuleys and their friend Colman Andrews. The character of Peter Morrow has his counterpart in this text in Joe Thornton, who is romantically linked to the outspoken Nora MacAuley. As his name suggests, Joe is allied with nature, and is recognised by the Connemara people as 'one of themselves' (Dillon, 1987: 205), a phrase which appears in both novels. Like Peter, Joe is differentiated from the the constraints of his origins by means of education, though in his case it is formalised. He is the son of a schoolmaster (ibid.: 25) and is training to be a doctor.

Sixteen-year-old Brian MacAuley is ostensibly the rebel of the family. He communicates more readily with the Connemara train driver than he does with his family; he dreams of aeroplanes and flights to freedom (Dillon, 1987: 44). When an injured Republican soldier is brought into the house, the stretcher-bearers are, we read, 'piloted by Brian' (ibid.: 64), so it's no surprise when he leaves his family to join the flying column. However, when the Republican Captain Horgan meets Nora, he says 'This is your sister, Brian? ... There's a great likeness between ye' (ibid.: 59), and Nora is actually the character who is shown to be most questioning of unequal power relations. She is 'angry' that their servant Sarah has 'not travelled in the same carriage [as the family] from Dublin' (ibid.: 13), a segregation apparently instigated by Colman, Ruth MacAuley's fiancé, who thinks he doesn't want a nurse for his children to be 'a Connemara girl who never knew her place, like Sarah' (ibid.: 79). Nora is the only one of the family who directly challenges Colman, although his bullying ways with Ruth also irritate her older brother Pat. Colman is very obviously the representation of imperialism in the novel – he is even described by the Republican Captain Horgan as 'that west British yoke', punning on the Irish dialect use of 'yoke', derogatory when applied to a person, and the yoke of colonialism. When Colman prevents Cáit, a red-haired Connemara peasant woman, from getting into their rail carriage, Nora glares at him and says: 'That was a mighty poor joke' (ibid.: 25).

Colman, as his name suggests, appears to be an emotionally cold man. In the opening paragraphs of the book, Ruth calls him to look at Galway as they arrive on the train: 'Come and look Colman, you can't see through that frosted glass window' (ibid.: 9). We are told she is disappointed 'at his

coolness' (ibid.: 9). Throughout the novel, Ruth makes similar attempts
to thaw his frosty outlook. When he eventually runs away, her brother
Pat worries about the effect of the breakup on her, but Joe says:

> I was thinking of something I saw once in Galway. There was a fall of snow early
> in June, caused by icebergs floating in the Gulf Stream, several miles out to sea,
> someone said. The roses were in flower. I saw them covered in snow. They looked
> like frost flowers on glass. When the snow melted it hadn't injured the roses. I
> think it will be like that with Ruth. (Dillon, 1987: 212)

Presumably this is Eilís Dillon's optimistic assessment of English rule in
Ireland, that it did not change the Irish national characteristic of warmth,
any more than Colman changed that of his sometime fiancée.

Daughter of old Republicans that she is, Dillon cannot conceal her
contempt for Colman and his ilk, with her intrusive narrator describing
him as a 'querulous, complaining ... worm' (ibid.: 117). He is represented
as only having gained a good position because he is tall, very good looking, and born into wealth. Pat, also known as Paddy and Patcheen, is
the epitome of the 'decent' Irish man, looks askance at Colman, and we
read that he

> thought that, as he had sometimes thought before now, how he would like to spring
> on Colman and rub his face in the ground. Pat thought of it like this because he
> himself was small, and was not likely to grow any more. (Dillon, 1987: 10)

As the vertically-challenged Pat is contrasted with the taller, impos-
ing bully Colman, the two men rather obviously represent Ireland and
Britain.

The narrative shows Ruth, throughout the few days of the narrative, endeavouring to keep her real feelings in check. She likes the smell
of fair-day, but

> She told herself that it was not very nice ... to have a nostalgic attachment for the
> smell of cattle-markets. She reflected that she must learn to cover up these coarse
> tendencies, lest they might peek out without warning after her marriage to Colman
> and disgrace him. But she felt too a painful sense of restriction, of which she was
> immediately ashamed. (Dillon, 1987: 15)

As the novel opens with the words 'Galway is like a different world' (ibid.: 9), this sets it up as a world Colman rejects, and expects his future wife to reject too. A Galwegian herself, Dillon identifies the county, and in particular rural Connemara, as the site of authenticity.[2] Integrating well into Connemara society becomes the yardstick against which people are measured.

The novel ends with Ruth consulting Sarah's mother for advice. The sensible Mrs Lynch, we're told, has spent time in America and come home to marry a farmer-fisherman. Her daughter 'does not believe in pishrogues and queer old cures' (ibid.: 72), but Mrs Lynch is regarded by neighbour Hannah Franks, who is traditional in her ways, as 'a fine knowledgeable woman [who] gives good advice' (ibid.: 85). Even the medical student Pat respects her as 'almost the only woman in Derrylea who believed in the power of science', and the local doctor remarks that 'her advice is to be found in the text-books too' (ibid.: 107). Thus, like Joe Thornton, and Peter Morrow in *Blood Relations*, she straddles the wider world and that of Connemara. Her voice is the voice of reason and she counsels Ruth not to run after Colman, who is 'kind of puffed-up in himself' (Dillon, 1987: 219). She continues 'You'd have to ask his leave before you'd do every little thing, which would be a queer state of affairs ... You'd be like a person would be working for him, and nothing you'd do would be right' (ibid.: 220). Clearly, this is a pointer to the way forward for Ruth (representing Ireland), to choose autonomy and independence over oppression posing as protectiveness.

As in *Blood Relations*, Dillon's narrator in *The Bitter Glass* reveals class prejudices. The babies' nurse Sarah Lynch is allied in several passages to traditional ways. This Connemara girl is described as moving 'as if she were walking barefoot on a mountain-side' (Dillon, 1987: 14), suggesting a primitive and untamed quality. We read that 'her feet moved in the rhythm of the song that was running in her head ... Her eyes were never quite free of an ancient, hereditary melancholy, like a Byzantine madonna' (ibid.: 14).

2   Of course she's not the only Irish writer to do this. It's a characteristic of many writers, including J.M. Synge, Pádraig Pearse, W.B. Yeats and Augusta Gregory.

There is an echo here of H.V. Morton's voyeuristic account of his personal encounter with a female farm-worker in Connemara, during his travels in the 1920s:

> She was perhaps eighteen years of age, slim, tall, and her fine legs were bare. . . . She stood on an overhanging ledge of rock grasping a long, primitive rake with which she lifted great bunches of dripping sea-weed ... Here, within twenty-four hours of London, was a primitive woman. She was more primitive than Eve. (Morton 1944, 185–6)

This extraordinary piece of prose was first published in 1930. Dillon, like Morton, allies the Connemara female with the primitive. Sarah is described as like 'the widow of an African chief' (88), apparently not capable of attaining chiefdom in her own right. Irish literature and culture are strewn with similar associations of West of Ireland women with a sort of raw primitivism – we have only to look at the depiction of Nora Barnacle and Edna O'Brien (Carlson, 1990: 73).

Later in *The Bitter Glass*, we read a description of the Republican Captain Horgan: 'Above the half-inch stubble of beard, the skin of his face was tanned so dark that the whites of his eyes glittered like a negro's' (Dillon, 1987: 58). Even allowing for the changes in acceptable language since the book was published in 1958, there's a disturbing ambivalence in the narrative's attitude to the so-called primitive. As I said, Dillon associates rural Connemara with authenticity, but it is also allied to something more sinister. In the beginning of their stay at Derrylea, Pat and Nora perceive the night-time at Derrylea in very different ways. When Pat and Joe walks about the house after dark, they feel that 'even at night it was a friendly house' (ibid.: 41). By contrast, Nora imagines 'long thin black hands clutch[ing]' at her nightdress. 'She always saw the hands as black ones' (ibid.: 44). Thus the narrative presents an association of blackness with a threat to female safety.

As I have said, the narrative is equivocal in its presentation of the peasant culture of Connemara. Unsympathetic characters are scathing about local people; the drug-addled Doctor Kenny says 'I was never meant for this place ... the ignorant, primitive people' (ibid.: 110), and Colman's consciousness of Joe's 'humble origins' (ibid.: 147) is only another facet of his lack of understanding. Nora, who has some heroic characteristics in that she faces up to the villain Colman, and hates injustice, starts out by saying that she 'hate[s] ... the primitive life', but we are told she says this 'savagely' (ibid.: 32), and the thought of the fastidious Colman travelling in his 'beautiful clean clothes' in a smelly fishing-boat brings a 'savage, primitive smile' to her face (ibid.: 163). The narrative suggests that Nora needs to come to terms with that wild side within herself, and by extension the Connemara people, who recognise Joe Thornton as 'one of themselves' despite his education.

Despite the equivocal nature of these texts, they are ground-breaking in their depiction of class relations. Dillon makes a valiant effort to valorise traditional Irish culture, and if, like Lady Gregory before her, she risks accusations of Kiltartanism, her historical novels make a good case for the integration of classes in the embryo Irish state.

Works Cited

Bowen, E. (1998), *Bowen's Court*, Collins, Cork.

de Vere White, T. (1972), *The Anglo-Irish*, Victor Gollancz, London.

Dillon, É. (1987), *The Bitter Glass*, Poolbeg, Dublin.

——(1993), *Blood Relations*, Souvenir, London.

Luddy, M (ed.) (2002), 'Women and Politics in Ireland, 1860–1918' in Bourke, A., Kilfeather, S., Luddy, M., MacCurtain, M., Meaney, G., Ní Dhonnchadha, M., O'Dowd, M., and Wills, C. (eds), *The Field Day Anthology of Irish Writing*, vol v, Cork University Press, Cork, pp. 69–119.

Ó Ceirín, K. and C. (1996), *Women of Ireland: A Biographic Dictionary*, Tír Eolas, Newtownlynch.

Thomson, D. (1988), *Woodbrook*, Vintage, London.

Tovey, H., Hannan, D. and Abramson, H. (1989), *Why Irish? Language and Identity in Ireland Today*, Bord na Gaeilge, Dublin.

'Dressing Up In Ascendancy Robes': The Big House and Brian Friel's *Aristocrats*

ALISON O'MALLEY-YOUNGER

> A greater, more gracious time has gone;
> For painted forms or boxes of make-up
> In ancient tombs I sighed; but not again
> What matter?
>
> —W.B. YEATS, *The Gyres*

It is a critical given that the Big House belongs to a predominantly Anglo-Irish, novelistic genre, in which it is a repository of traditional values, its decline evoking a contrast between golden, glory days in the past and the deprivations of the present. According to critics such as Seamus Deane and Vera Kreilkamp, the decaying Big House symbolises a failing Protestant hegemony beset with fears of genealogical extinction, usurpation, and miscegenation: shabby gentility threatened by what is perceived as the barbarism of the natives who reside beyond the walled demesnes. The inhabitants of such houses await death, listening to the ancestral voices of ghosts, in a state of suspended animation as the edifice crumbles, while what Yeats termed 'the filthy modern tide' of modernity threatens to engulf them. Isolated, world-weary, and interred in the decomposing remains of a past world of gentility and affluence, the largely Protestant inhabitants of these feudal edifices fixate on what once was, endure what is, and fear what will be.

Thus, the Big House has a symbolic function, metonymically representing the Protestant Ascendancy class. However, as the American academic Tom Hoffnung points out in Brian Friel's play *Aristocrats,* there

also existed in Ireland 'a Roman Catholic big house – by no means as thick
on the ground [as the Protestant] but still there' (Friel, 1969: 39). Pariahs
twice over, the Catholic inhabitants of these houses were perceived as
'seonin' culture – and viewed as 'copies of copies', and neither Anglo-Irish
nor indigenous Catholic Irish. They occupied an uncomfortably liminal
position, 'mimicking' an Ascendancy culture, which in turn was seen as
an imitation of English culture. This double mimicry is, I will argue, the
central thematic focus of *Aristocrats,* and it is my intention to discuss how
the play offers a catachrestical rereading of the Big House genre to foreground the ineluctably discursive nature of identity, the past, and myth.
Vestigial cultural traditions, superstitions and memorable (though possibly apocryphal) magical episodes are fused in the 'memories' of Casimir,
the storyteller figure who interjects throughout with his own version of
events. The mythic past is preserved and translated into a present that is
on the surface rational and 'real', in a practice that mediates and hybri-
dises the traditional and the modern, the indigene and the settler – a
process analogous to the cultural history of the Protestant Ascendancy
class rewritten in a contemporary Catholic setting. Such an approach
challenges the singularity of the 'Story of Ireland' (singular) by offering
'Stories of Ireland' (plural).

My contention is that in *Aristocrats* Friel breaches the apparently
insuperable divides between class and caste commonly found in the Big
House novel by locating his characters in the interstices – in the border-
lands between constructed identities, equally plausible versions and possible histories – in order to unsettle the facile and static binarisms which
have historically operated across the colonial divide. Such an approach
is inherently critical of polarised notions of what it is to be 'Irish'. For
Friel, 'Irishness' is hybrid, double, processual and performative. It is based
on syncretism, and forged in the chiasmic spaces between binarisms. In
Aristocrats the wreck of the past – and its disabling cargo of myth, and
sectarian bias – is revisited in the light of its dual inheritance. To read
the past thus renders rigidified binary oppositions irrelevant, and opens
a space for new conceptions of 'Irish' identity.

'Study that House'[1]

In *Inventing Ireland* Declan Kiberd notes that 'the theoretical self-image of the Anglo-Irish was aristocratic and gentlemanly, but in practice, as Edmund Burke sarcastically noted, they were a middle-class masquerading as an aristocracy'; he continues: 'the Big House contained no culture worth speaking of' and he quotes from Louis MacNeice, ('one of them') to suggest their scorn for all who resided beyond the big house walls was: 'nothing but obsolete bravado, an insidious bonhomie and a way with horses'. (Kiberd, 1995: 449). Whether or not it was supported by such unequivocal disdain, the core suggestion is that 'masquerade' was characteristic of the Ascendancy class. This implies they undertook what could be described as a form of colonial and class-based cross-dressing, adopting the clothing, manners, mien and rituals of the English Aristocracy, while relying on the native Catholic population for sustenance. They were, to adapt an ironic couplet from Daniel Defoe's *The True Born Englishman*, 'in speech an irony, in fact a fiction' (Defoe, 1997: 36). It is fair to say that, despite Yeats's later protestations of Anglo-Irish exceptionalism and essentially aristocratic provenance, the Ascendancy did not constitute an 'aristocracy' but a feudal class which occupied a vacillating social position in Ireland during the eighteenth and nineteenth centuries. Denounced by Fenians as 'coroneted ghouls' and 'cormorant vampires', for some – such as Michael Davitt – they occupied a parasitic role in Ireland, threatening the very people they claimed to govern. Yet, the Anglo-Irish were both victimisers and victims, governors and governed, colonisers and colonised trapped in a liminal state between identities, listening to ancestral voices and using the crumbling walls of Big Houses as a symbolic bulwark against their own degeneration and decline. Ghosts haunt the Ancestral Homes of the Anglo-Irish, robbing the living of vitality. The walls close in and fall down, as the world beyond them shrinks and decays. Identities without borders or foundations coalesce and dissolve. In a world of continuous re-enactment and eternal return – paradoxically obsessed with

---

1   Yeats, in Cave, 1997b: 255.

transmission, dynastic line and inheritance – the living dead of the Big
Houses are forced to live and re-live their inevitable demise: 'horseman
pass by' (Yeats).

'In The Midst of Life We Are In Death'[2]

Ballybeg Hall, the Big House in Friel's *Aristocrats*, is like its literary and
historical precursors in decline. The House is dilapidated and falling
into ruin: the floors are rotting, the gazebo is falling down, the seats are
rusted, the roof leaks, and buckets are distributed around the crumbling
rooms to catch the water when it rains. Its decaying state echoes the Big
House in Yeats's *Purgatory* where the roof and the walls have fallen in,
leaving the interior exposed to the elements:

> The floor is gone, the windows gone,
> And where there should be roof there's sky,
> And here's a bit of egg-shell thrown
> Out of a jackdaw's nest (Yeats, in Harrington, 1991: 34)

There is a harmony of dissonance about the dissolution of this manse
as the landscape effectively reclaims it. It is open to but also part of its
natural surroundings. In Friel's play we enter the world of greasy tills and
mortgages. Money not myth-making is the only solution for Ballybeg Hall
and the occupants are without the necessary lucre. The house, according
to Margaret. has become a 'liability' (Friel, 1980: 317), its wiring dangerous, its land and contents worthless and its repairs short-term and
unreliable: 'polythene sheets nailed to the rafters' (Friel, 1980: 317). This
is Friel's catachrestical re-reading of the Big House – a reading in which
he takes the symbol of the manse and empties it of traditionally ascribed
meaning, making it a sign for emptiness and hopelessness rather than
a bulwark against the incursions of a bourgeois modernity. Here the

2   *The Book of Common Prayer*, cited in Bowen, 1998: 11.

ruinous feudal edifice of the Big House evokes not the sublime pleasure of horror or terror but a sense of impending calamity, isolation, ennui and world-weariness as the inhabitants live in a quasi-inert state of fear of their own extinction.

In *Horror Fiction*, Victor Sage discusses the gothic function of the Big House as: 'a perfect emblem of the ravaged body, the dead sight of the world's insults: yet sinister and aggressive, as if this dross might resurrect itself in a frightening, attenuated form of life' (Sage, 1988: 17). This reading is surprisingly appropriate to Friel's play as the decaying state of Ballybeg Hall echoes the 'ravaged body' of Father, paralysed from a stroke, emotionally and physically incontinent, and fixated on the past; rendered thus by shameful family secrets. At the mercy of the world's insults is the figure of Father, who is 'sinister and aggressive' as *in absentia* he controls the action of the 'attenuated lives of his family', each of whom is living in altered states, unable to communicate with either each other or the outside world.

The O'Donnell's of Ballybeg Hall all suffer from an inability to engage with reality: Mother O'Donnell is dead without even the wraith-like echoes of the Mother in *Purgatory*; Father is 'petrified' (Friel, 1980: 258) and reduced to incoherent ramblings over a baby alarm; Anna is a child-like voice over a tape recorder, in a state of arrested development – battening herself to the past and all its glories; inebriate Uncle George gestures frequently but says nothing until he is given the option of escape; Alice also has taken to drink; Claire is manic-depressive and given to bouts of hysteria and melancholy; spinster Judith is the imago of Irish womanhood in her long-suffering and fortitude, and is generally heard in the wings, negotiating the business of day-to-day survival; Casimir by his own admission is 'different'; a perpetual recounter of half-truths, myths and apocrypha. Together they are a liminal, interstitial entity, in an uncertain world wherein the past persists into the present as both promise and threat.

As is often the case in Friel's plays the action revolves around dysfunctional or absent family relationships. The most striking of these are the father/son dynamic between Father and Casimir and the impaired marital/romantic relationships that are prevalent in the play. I will discuss the latter first. All of the O'Donnell's have either not married or have married outside of their class, caste or both. Father it transpires married Mother O'Donnell, a travelling show-girl, after a five day courtship; Alice is unhappily married to Eamon, grandson of a servant at Ballybeg Hall; Judith and Anna have never married – the former is the mother of an illegitimate son whom she has had adopted, the latter is a nun in the Missions in Zambia. As the play begins Claire is about to embark, with little relish, on her marriage to Jerry, a fat, balding, middle-aged green-grocer with a domineering sister and a plastic banana on the top of his delivery van. Casimir is married – or perhaps is not – to 'Helga the Hun', and from his descriptions she seems a German Spritualist amalgamation of Eva Braun and Madame Blavatsky, and communes with spirits but doesn't answer the phone to her husband.

There are no ghosts in *Aristocrats*: indeed the only spectral aura in the play comes from Helga's 'table-rapping, séances, all that stuff' (Friel, 1980: 301); but there is Casimir's recollection of Yeats with his 'cold, cold, eyes' (Friel, 1980: 267) spending three nights sitting on Daniel O'Connell the chaise-longue because he had been told the Hall was haunted. It isn't as Casimir states, 'because Father wouldn't believe in ghosts'. (Friel, 180: 267). The uncanny atmosphere which pervades Ballybeg Hall – the ghostly presence which haunts the living – is no revenant or undead wraith, but results from a combination of Father, the characters' memories, and the past – either real or imagined – which returns incessantly to disrupt the present. Repeatedly, Friel's characters attempt to inoculate themselves from their problematic presents with large doses of nostalgia, myth and reminiscences, only to have the present reassert itself with disastrous consequences. One such event is the death of Father, who dies of shock when the present, (in the form of the tape-recorded voice of Anna), irrupts into his recollections – themselves a composite of delusions, bias, half-truths, wish-fulfilment and inaccurate memories – causing him to confront the purgatorial here-and-now of Ballybeg Hall. It is too much for him, and he dies, yet he still continues to haunt Casimir's thoughts, 'changed, changed utterly' from a tyrannical spectre who stifled his family to the essence of Ballybeg Hall without which it cannot survive. Though emotionally crippled and later forgotten by his father, Casmir cannot exist as an autonomous being without him. When Father collapses, Casimir (named ironically after a Medieval Polish prince who was canonised for defying his father) is stupefied; when he imagines he hears Father's voice *in articulo mortis* over the baby alarm he is petrified. Damaged thus he creates a new Father and a new past, rejecting the official version. To paraphrase Edna Longley, Father attempted to 'father history, to sire the future on images of the past' (Longley, 1994: 159). He has set out to be the fixater of meanings – a purveyor of unimpeachable 'truth'. Casimir's catachrestical re-readings challenge the 'legitimate' version of history authorised by Father. For Casimir, the past is not discoverable or discovered; rather it is made or constructed in narrative and memory. 'The key', according to Willy Maley, commenting in another context on constructed histories, is to view matters in terms of 'variety rather than verity', (Maley, in Brewster et al. 1999: 21). This is what Casimir does. To him and to his creator history is something that is made; and if it is made it can be re-made in a different context. In *Aristocrats* as in most of Friel's works, there are no historical absolutes or unqualified truths.

In Yeats's *Purgatory* the family is brought low by the aristocratic mother engaging in inappropriate sexual union with one not of her class. This initiates a cycles of recrimination and atonement which results in the dissolution of the family as the 'sins' of the mother are visited upon her son. In *Aristocrats* not only have the sins of the father been exacted upon his family, but the sins of the children have come back to haunt the father. Judith's involvement in the civil rights movement and her sexual liaison with, and subsequent pregnancy by a Dutch journalist apparently caused the stroke which trapped him in a nightmare life in death. His actual death (and perhaps release) occurs when he hears the voice of the absent Anna on the tape recorder. Repeatedly there is a play on the presence of absence and the absence of presence as the half-presence of the largely absent father motivates much of the action in the play; and it is the apparent, (though quasi-fictional) presence of the absent Anna which ends his physical life in it. However, even when absent in physical form, Father still exists in the memories of his family, haunting those who survive him.

Siobhan Kilfeather makes a compelling argument in her *Origins of the Irish Female Gothic* to the effect that the tropes and traps of the Gothic

– and by extension, Big House fictions – relate to a failing Ascendancy hegemony under threat from possible insurgency on the part of the native Irish: 'the possibility of a native rebellion was to be most strongly denied as it contradicted a developing theory of cultural transmission in which the Protestant Irish were constructing themselves as the true legatees and preservers of Irish culture and identity' (Kilfeather, 1994: 42). This fear of a native insurgent population is absent in *Aristocrats* because these 'aristocrats' are not Protestants any more than their Protestant (figurative) progenitors were aristocrats. The O'Donnell's of Ballybeg Hall are in fact 'West Brits' – descendants of the Redmondite 'Castle Catholics', mimics of the Protestant ruling elites who supported the British constitution. In *Aristocrats*, as Elmer Andrews argues, 'it is as if Friel was dressing up the Catholic middle class in the borrowed robes of the Ascendancy' (Andrews, 1995: 149). The irony is of course that these latter-day pseudo-aristocrats are more entitled to the title than the Ascendancy elite who supplanted their Gaelic ancestors and preceded them. The O'Donnells of Tirconnail, (Donegal) were one of the last of the Gaelic aristocracy that was eroded and deracinated during the Plantation of Ulster in 1607. The present days 'aristocrats' are thus the usurped who have become usurpers fearing their own usurpation. They have chosen to discard their 'birthright', their hereditary robes, in order to dress up in robes that neither fit nor belong to them, and which have become faded and threadbare over time.

    This is a play in which mimicry is central – thematically it mimics Anglo-Irish Big House fictions, the context changed from Protestant to Catholic and prose to drama. From the point of view of characterisation it is a hall of mirrors in which the O'Donnells are copies of copies, attempting to maintain a status quo that has gone, and to re-enact the decline of a class that is not their own. Venal and degenerating now, the glamour of their glory days has gone, leaving them debilitated, weakened and apropos to the genre, haunted by spectres of a past they cannot understand and a future they cannot contemplate.

    Friel's (re)interpretation of Big House culture is undoubtedly catachrestical: the metonymic function of the Big House redeployed in the service of Catholic nostalgia can only be seen within an Irish context as a misapplication. However, a misapplication, or an inappropriate use of a concept or word implies the existence of its opposite, an original concept to which the concept or word is apposite. The Big House is no doubt a singularly appropriate genre for the embattled Ascendancy classes of the early nineteenth century. However, as I have indicated, the Anglo-Irish Ascendancy could not itself be viewed as either sufficiently originary or pure to label it an 'original concept'. Indeed, any sense of a source or origin is mimicked in Friel's play, and emerges in the final analysis as insubstantive, illusory, or both. The O'Donnell's are 'seonins' (shoneens), sycophantic and disingenuous imitators of English culture. Theirs is a disintegrating pedigree, as Eamon ironically remarks to Tom Hoffnung:

> The O'Donnell forebears; Great-Grandfather – Lord Chief Justice; Grandfather – Circuit Court Judge; Father – simple District Judge; Casimir – failed solicitor. A fairly rapid descent; but no matter, no matter; good for the book; failure's more loveable than success. D'you know Professor, I've often wondered: if we had children and they wanted to be part of a family legal tradition, the only option open to them would have been as criminals, wouldn't it? (Friel, 1980: 295)

The nexus of concerns here cohere around the concepts of identity and patrilineage, leitmotivs of nationalism (and imperialism). Now, however, this is a family that is like the culture because it is in terminal decline, imitating a culture which has itself declined beyond resuscitation. These 'aristocrats' are anachronisms in twentieth century Ballybeg, yet the threat of barbarity outside the walls of the Big House remains. To the Ascendancy Landlords the threat was from 'unruly tenants', here it is from the encroaching present – political insurrections in the North (which, with the exception of Judith they choose to ignore). Indeed, Father refuses to acknowledge the conflict in Ireland precisely because it is 'across the border in the North', (Friel, 1980: 272). That the O'Donnells have chosen to isolate themselves from engaging with this, and with life beyond the confines of their ancestral home, is made clear by Alice who points out to Tom Hoffnung that Father O'Donnell finds politics 'vulgar' (Friel, 1980: 272) and by Eamon when he suggests to Tom that he write:

A great big block-buster of a gothic novel called Ballybeg Hall – From Supreme Court to Sausage Factory; four generations of a great Irish Catholic legal dynasty; the gripping saga of a family that lived its life in total isolation in a gaunt house on top of a hill above the remote Donegal village of Ballybeg; a family without passion, without loyalty, without commitments; administering the law for anyone who happened to be in power; above all wars and famines and civil strife and political upheaval; ignored by its Protestant counterparts, isolated from the mere Irish, existing only in its own concept of itself, brushing against reality occasionally by the cultivation of artists; but tough – oh, yes, tough, resilient, tenacious; and with one enormous talent for – no a greed for survival – that's the family motto, isn't it – Semper Permanemus. Don't for a second underestimate them. What do you think? (Friel, 1980: 294)

The isolation of the O'Donnell's is both physical and emotional. Historically it is clear that they have attempted to imitate the lifestyle of the aristocratic Protestant classes by cultivating artists and living in a Big House. However they have had no real interaction with their 'Protestant counterparts', and meanwhile the 'mere Irish' peasantry are remote to them too. Just as they are either unwilling or unable to communicate with one another – no more can they communicate with the outside world. This is made evident in Casimir's inability to get a telephone connection because they cannot get a line past the Letterkenny exchange. This isolation again mimics what was seen as the tendencies of the Anglo-Irish gentry to absent themselves from Ireland (spending most of the year in London, apart from the Dublin season). With Father's death the 'aristocratic' line of the O'Donnell's will possibly end, as we are never entirely sure whether Casimir's wife Helga and family exist at all. As Eamon remarks:

EAMON: Casimir pretending she's calling Helga the Hun. All a game. All a fiction.
ALICE: Oh shut up!
EAMON: No one has ever seen her. We're convinced he's invented her. (*Tom laughs uncertainly*)
TOM: Is he serious, Claire?
EAMON: And the three boys – Herbert, Hans and Heinrich. And the dachshund called Deitrich. And the job in a sausage factory. It has the authentic ring of phoney fiction doesn't it? (Friel, 1980: 278)

Even if they do exist, Casimir will return to live in Germany; and the big house culture of Ballybeg Hall, even in its decaying form will cease to exist other than in his imagination. As F.C. McGrath suggests 'Casimir's mythmaking about the O'Donnells is convincing because its impossibilities are probabilities within the context of the myth, whereas Helga and the sausage factory are possibilities outside of the range of probabilities contained by the O'Donnell myth and so they have the 'authentic ring of phoney fiction' (McGrath, 1999: 155). In short, context is all – catachreses are inevitable in the wrong context, but the ambiguity they evoke is no bad thing in a world based on certainties, absolutes and rhetorics of origin.

The origins of the O'Donnell's are spurious, as are their final ends. They are only able or willing to trace their lineage back to 'Great Grandfather' – except in the realm of fantasy wherein distinguished visitors to Ballybeg are translated into items of furniture. What has come before this is conveniently forgotten. Their future is equally uncertain, left in the hands of a peripheral neurotic (Casimir) who, by his own admission, is 'peculiar':

> I made a great discovery when I was nine...I suddenly realised that I was different from other boys ... That was a very important and a very difficult discovery for me ... But it brought certain recognitions, certain compensatory recognitions. Because once I recognised – once I had acknowledged that the larger areas were not accessible to me, I discovered – I had to discover smaller, much smaller areas that were. (Friel, 1980: 310)

The implication here is that Casimir is different. In the context of Ballybeg Hall, under the auspices of the autocratic Father, it is hardly surprising that he chooses to invent other (less frightening) narratives of his life. The past is made up for him of a combination of imaginative yearnings and subjective recollections which cannot be rationally explained or empirically tested, irrespective of the fact that Tom Hoffnung attempts to do just that. 'There are' as Eamon asserts, 'certain things, certain truths ... that are beyond Tom's kind of scrutiny' (Friel, 1980: 309–10). Like Father, Hoffnung impedes the circulation of multivalent meanings with his insistence on the verifiable, the absolute. Casimir challenges this in his reminiscences and ponderings, and he resists enclosure within a fixed identity, an embodied catachresis in which the sign and the referent don't collide. As a copy of a copy taken out of context, he eschews insuperable binarisms. and undermines any notions of an absolute or authentic identity.

Casimir is an inveterate 'storyteller'; an interstitial figure who contextualises the past and the present in mythic recollections of what could have been. In contrast to the monologic certainty of Father, or the data-digging of Tom Hoffnung, Casimir purveys a variety of versions and catachreses which may or may not contain germs of truth. For example, while he is attempting to assist Hoffnung in his search for relevant information on the O'Donnell dynasty, he finds a cross which he says is from:

> Cardinal O'Donnell; present from Salamanaca. No relation just a great family friend. And a Donegal man, of course; a neighbour, almost. Remember him Alice? (Friel, 1980: 261)

Alice, of course, doesn't remember this Cardinal, suggesting that 'He must be dead seventy years'. (Friel, 1980: 266). Casimir, unperturbed, then moves on to an elaborate ritual of naming through association, whereby he reasserts the past in his terms. The footstool is named after G.K. Chesterton who, when giving an imitation of Lloyd George, fell over it across the fender. The chaise longue is 'Daniel O'Connell, The Liberator' who left a mark on it with his riding boots. The bible is Hilaire Belloc, the candlestick is George Moore, a book is Tom Moore, and the cushion on Daniel O'Connell is Yeats whom Casimir 'remembers vividly' (irrespective of the fact that the play is set in the 1970s):

> On one occasion he sat up three nights in succession, just there on Daniel O'Connell, with his head on that cushion and his feet on Chesterton, just because someone had told him that we were haunted. Can you imagine! Three full nights! But of course we weren't haunted. There was never a ghost in the Hall. Father wouldn't believe in ghosts. And he was quite peeved about it; oh, quite peeved. 'You betrayed me Bernard', he said to Father. 'You betrayed me' and those cold eyes of his burning with – (Friel, 1980: 267)

Casimir's claim that the house couldn't have been haunted because 'Father wouldn't believe in ghosts' suggests an absolute, logocentric power wielded by Father, the rational empiricist. Casimir's tale, when viewed in this context, becomes a complex discursive performance in which he resists received representations by reducing canonical figures to inanimate objects based on association. His definitions subvert conventional narratives, and rational empiricism. His very approach challenges epistemology: with Casimir, nothing can be known, and everything is thrown into the arena of speculation. He creates a 'new world' by approximating and recoding what has gone before, and offering tangible symbols reduced to insignificance, to subvert the notion of empirical, ratifiable facts. He uses words to evoke, rather than to signify and categorise. He is dissonant: a *Sean chaithe*; a storyteller who forces us to perceive the narrative through the eyes of the Other.

Casimir's propensity for narrating, links him to other Frielian storytellers and to wider traditions of storytelling in Ireland. As Elmer Andrews remarks:

> The problematics of narrative have always intrigued Friel. His plays are full of writers, chroniclers, history-men, stage directors, and translators, storytellers and artists, whom we watch in the very process of constructing their narratives. (Andrews in Peacock, 1993: 29)

This describes well the anti-foundationalist dimension of Friel's philosophy. However, I would argue that there is another element to his use of storytellers within his fictions which is pertinent to the post-colonial condition. that of uniting traditional modes of discourse with contemporary (and often fictive) narratives thereby inaugurating the hybrid moment. Casimir embodies the historical propensity attributed to the Irish people to tell stories in order to connect tradition with contemporaneity, thereby ensuring a sense of continuity of culture. As Robert Welch observes:

> The sovereignty of Ireland has always been a problem from the very earliest times. And the Irish mythographers, Poets and lawgivers, who often combined in the same person in the traditional Gaelic world, had an interesting way of dealing with this problem .... (telling) many interesting and entertaining stories. (Welch, 1993: 271)

Storytelling was thus an affective measure which recognised the alterity
of the Irish in a performative act of cyclical repetition, which by its very
nature denied closure. Irish heroes were literally re-cycled and modified according to the demands of context. For example Yeats summons
Cuchulainn to the side of Pearse at the Post Office in The Statues in order
to suggest a continuity of resistance. As Yeats puts it:

> The Irish stories make us understand why the Greeks call myths the activities of
> daemons. The great virtues, the great joys, the great privations come in myths,
> and, as it were, take mankind between their naked arms, without putting off their
> divinity. Poets have taken their themes more often from stories that are all or half
> mythological, than from history or stories that give one the sensation of history,
> understanding, as I think, that the imagination which resembles the proportions
> of life is but a long wooing and that it has to forget them before it becomes the
> torch and marriage bed. (Yeats, 1991: 59)

This is catachrestical re-insciption of Irish mythical figures, the 'purity'
of whom is challenged due to their constant re-readings within different
contexts. The imaginative and context specific re-enactment of mythical events is, for Yeats – and Friel – far more important than efforts to
establish the historical 'truth'. Here, Yeats recognises the importance of
enunciating archetypal 'traits' or imprints that bear little relations to
realism but are nevertheless important to the constitution of an 'Irish'
character. Friel adopts a similar approach. Irishness may be based on fictive accounts from the past, just as it may be based on a sense of not-
Englishness, (or at least not-quite-Englishness); nonetheless, all of these
constitutive elements must be taken into account under the rubric that
they are all apocryphal.

Casimir voices the rural/mythical as opposed to the urban/rational
espoused by his Father. The Father's symbolic function is as an exem-
plar of urban/rational discourse, his actual senility marking this as itself
perhaps fundamentally irrational. Thus, Casimir can be linked to a long
line of Irish storytellers originating with the Druidic *filid*. His inability
to function satisfactorily within the confines of a solely rationalistic discourse, (which why he dropped out of the legal profession of his family),
allows two arguments to be advanced. The first and more negative of the

two is that he is incapable of dealing with the modern world, and thus uses myth as a form of sterile escapism. The second is that he voices the incommensurable aspect of colonised culture: that which cannot be fully assimilated. This is not an immutable essence but comprises discursively constructed traits from his 'racial' memory bank. Theoretically, Friel's conception of character here parallels Spivak's notion of 'strategic essentialism' in which she argues that the construction of essentialist forms of identity is legitimate for cultural self-respect (Spivak, 1995: 214). However, uncritical deployment of these terms is dangerously addictive and it results in a binary dialectic based on fixity and stasis. The purpose of strategic essentialism is to interrogate the application of essentialist terms within a post-colonial context by particularising the narrative of the colonised as something other than an imperfect alter-ego of the coloniser. In other words strategic essentialism recognises alterity and highlights the impossibility of absolute assimilation without suggesting that identity is based on an abstract pre-given and unchanging (unchangeable) essence. Difference between cultures exists; it cannot be fully erased. The recognition and construction of this difference is a necessary tool for cultural survival.

This paradoxical notion of a constructed essence is central to both Spivak and Friel. Friel finds creative latitude and inspiration in examinations of subject formation that Homi Bhabha would describe as 'in between, or in excess of the sum of the parts of difference' (Bhabha, 1994: 155). Casimir is such a subject: an ambivalent compromise of Anglo-Irishness and Gaelic-Irishness who is unbounded. His propensity to oral tale-telling suggests that he is partially constructed out of historico/racial narratives of Celtic provenance. There is a trace memory, albeit fictive, that links him to a pre-colonial past. Yet he exists in a post-colonial present and has adopted many of the conventions of the English (and Anglo-Irish) aristocracy. He is however, neither one thing nor the other; an inhabitant of the margins, residing in a Bhabalian liminal space, betwixt and between designated conceptions of identity.

Friel's *Aristocrats* begins with preparations for a wedding and ends in the wake of a funeral. Father is dead but not forgotten; Claire still looks forward to her nuptials with a mixture of excitement and revulsion; Judith, freed from the torment of devoting herself to father, intends

to stay at Ballybeg Hall, and to retrieve her illegitimate child from the
orphanage in which she was forced to place him; Alice and Eamon will
take Uncle George back to London as a surrogate child-cum-keepsake.
For one who is silent throughout the play his response to their invitation is proof that this Ireland is no country for old men. He is, as he says
'about due another visit' to London' ... 'I'll pack' (Friel, 1980: 322). It is no
country for young men either, nor for that matter for young women, but
for Casimir it is the ancestral home of his memories and fantasies, hence
his unvoiced desire to stay, and his acceptance that he go. Ballybeg Hall
is falling down but Casimir's will continue to exhume it in his memories
– these residual traces in which the past is dead but won't lie down. Yet,
like himself his memories are mobile, and the culture of Ballybeg Hall
will continue, *semper permanemus*, in different countries and different
forms – in parties in Hamburg or Vienna – in memories which in Paul
Ricoeur's terms are 'directed towards the future and not the past' (in
Whelan, 2003: 93).

Works Cited

Andrews, E. (1995), *The Art of Brian Friel*, Macmillan, Basingstoke.
Backus, M. (1999), *The Gothic Family Romance: Heterosexuality, Child
   Sacrifice and The Anglo-Irish Colonial Order*, Duke University Press,
   Durham.
Bhabha, H. (1994), *The Location of Culture*, Routledge, London.
Bowen, E. (1998), *The Last September*, Vintage, London.
——(1950), *The Big House*, reprinted in Collected Impressions, Longmans
   Green, London, pp. 195–200.
Brewster, S., Becket, F., Alderson, D. and Crossman, V. (eds) (1999),
   Ireland in Proximity: History, Gender, Space, Routledge, London.
Defoe, D. (1997), *The True Born Englishman and Other Writings*, ed.
   P.N. Furbank and W.R. Owens, Penguin, London.

Foster, R. (2001), *The Irish Story: Telling Tales and Making it up in Ireland*, Penguin, London.

Grene, N. (1999), *The Politics of Irish Drama: Plays in Context from Boucicault to Friel*, Cambridge University Press, Cambridge.

Harrington, J. P. (1991), *Modern Irish Drama*, Norton, London.

Kiberd, D. (1984), *Anglo Irish Attitudes*, Field Day Pamphlet 6, Field Day, Derry.

——(1995), *Inventing Ireland*, Jonathan Cape, London.

Kilfeather, S. (1994), 'Origins of the Irish Female Gothic', *Bullán: An Irish Studies Journal*, (Autumn 1994, 1.2: 35–45).

Krielkamp, V. (1998), *The Anglo-Irish Novel and the Big House*, Syracuse, New York.

Longley, E. (1994), *The Living Stream: Literature and Revisionism in Ireland*, Bloodaxe, Newcastle Upon Tyne.

McConville, M. (1986), *Ascendancy to Oblivion: the Story of the Anglo-Irish*, Quartet, London.

McCormac, W. (1991), *Irish Gothic and After*, (1820–1945) in S. Deane (ed.), *The Field Day Anthology of Irish Writing, Vol II*, Field Day Publications, Derry, pp. 831–54.

O'Grady, S. (1918), *Selected Essays and Passages*, Ernest Boyd, Dublin.

Peacock, A. (ed.) (1993), *The Achievement of Brian Friel*, Colin Smyth, Gerrards Cross.

Punter, D. (1999), *Ceremonial Gothic: Spectral Readings Towards a Gothic Geography*, St Martin's, New York.

Sage, V. (1988), *Horror Fiction in the Protestant Tradition*, Macmillan, Basingstoke.

Spivak, G. (1995), *The Spivak Reader*, (ed.) Landry and MacLean, Routledge, London.

Welch, R. (1993), *Changing States: Transformations in Modern Irish Writing*, Routledge, London.

Whelan, K. (2003), 'Between Filiation and Affiliation: The Politics of Postcolonial Memory' in *Ireland and Postcolonial Theory*, ed. Carrol, C, and King, P., University of Notre Dame Press, Notre Dame.

Yeats, W.B. (1961), 'Debate on Divorce' in *The Senate Speeches of W.B. Yeats*, ed. D.R. Pearce, Faber & Faber, London.

——(1997.a), 'The Gyres', in *The Yeats Reader: a Portable compendium of Poetry, Drama and Prose*, ed. Richard J. Finneran, Scribner Poetry, New York, pp. 252–9.

—— (1997.b), *Selected Plays*, ed. Richard Allen Cave, Penguin, Harmondsworth.

No Man's Land:
Irish Women Writers of the First World War

TERRY PHILLIPS

Recent developments in Irish Studies consequent upon changing political circumstances – as well as a move towards 'postnationalism' (Graham, 2001: 81–102) – have allowed a breaking of the silence about Irish involvement in the Great War. The last decade has seen the publication of a number of historical studies and there is an emerging interest in aspects of the literary engagement with the War. One might cite as an example, Dermot Bolger's recent play, *Walking the Road* which deals with the life of the soldier poet, Francis Ledwidge. Bolger, and critics such as Fran Brearton and Jim Haughey enter a space created by recent critical challenges to the predominant and monolithic nationalist narrative (Bolger, 2007; Brearton, 2000; Haughey, 2002). Parallel with this new interest is the slightly earlier emergence in the early 1990s of British interest in women's war writing, an attempt to move away from what Claire has described as a 'men only construction of the Great War'. Such a move, an inevitable if delayed consequence of second-wave feminism, has enabled a range of critics such as Tylee, Suzanne Raitt and Trudi Tate to recover not only women's poetry but a range of fictional writing, notably in the subgenre of 'home front' writing.

To extend such critical analysis to Irish home front writing is to enter a more complex critical arena, not least because national identity was a shifting phenomenon in the period, allowing a much greater range of positions from Unionist through to Republican than historical retrospection tends to allow as, for example, Thomas Hennessey (Hennessey, 1998: 235–9) argues in his analysis of the link between the First World War and partition.

A second complexity is the continuing debate about the relationship between gender and nationalism, in a postcolonial context generally, and more specifically in an Irish context. The work of the subaltern studies group on subalternity, and more particularly of Gayatri Chakrovorty Spivak in highlighting gender as a distinct category of subalternity, opens up the possibility of challenging the concept of both gender and nationalism as monolithic categories. In Spivak's words, the colonised subaltern subject is irretrievably heterogeneous' (Spivak, 1993: 79). Alongside this Irish feminist critics have challenged the very particular clashes of feminism and nationalism within an Irish context both in terms of the repression of women by the postcolonial nation, and increasingly in a revisiting of the contribution of women to the revolutionary period, for example in Karen Steele's (2007) recent volume.

The literature of the first two decades of the twentieth century is then the site of complexity and fluidity as the voices of ethnic subcategories of hyphenated Irishness (Anglo-, Scots- and Irish-), combine with those affiliated to various political and cultural versions of Irish and British nationalism, and widely different members of the subaltern category woman. The tendency to read backwards with monolithic concepts of nationalism and gender is to be resisted. It should be recognised, as Colin Graham argues, that 'discourses within the subaltern category ... collide as well as collude' (Graham, 2003: 157). The very particular example of First World War literature cuts across all these colliding and colluding categories, addressing concepts of national identity, cultural affiliation and gender. In this essay I will consider three writers with different and intersecting affiliations.

I begin with a consideration of Pamela Hinkson's *The Ladies Road* (1932). Hinkson was the daughter of the Catholic poet Katharine Tynan and spent much of her time during the war as a teenager at Brookhill House, County Mayo, where her Protestant father was a Resident Magistrate (Jeffery, 2000: 100; and Tynan, 1919) and the novel echoes some of the themes of Tynan's autobiographical account of the war years, *The Years of the Shadow.* Tynan was a nationalist sympathiser, a constitutional Nationalist broadly supportive of the war effort, who was connected to members of the ruling elite such as the Viceroy's wife, Lady Aberdeen.

The Ladies Road may be seen as having similarities with certain kinds of Home Front novels written by British women writers[1] which recount an experience of dreariness and monotony on the home front, contrasted with all-too dramatic events overseas. *The Ladies Road* offers an account of the experience of women during the war which is at once both negative and, more significantly, challenging – a challenge which is conveyed by the implied separatism of the title. It refers to the *Chemin Des Dames*, a ridge which lies to the north and east of Soissons on the Aisne and saw numerous battles in the struggle for the Western Front culminating in the one in which the central character's favourite brother meets his death in May 1918. However the English translation of the name, 'a road before her that seemed to lead nowhere – the Ladies Road' (Hinkson, 1932: 217) evokes a powerful sense of helplessness and loss; the role of woman as bystander and as grieving mother, sister, lover. The narration reveals its modernist influences through a focalisation shared among a number of characters. The chief of these is Stella Mannering, an Englishwoman who spends her time between Winds, her home in England, and Cappagh, her aunt Nancy Creagh's home in Ireland, modelled on Brookhill House. The narrative encompasses the two families and four friends. In the course of the war, Nancy loses her husband and one of her two sons, while Stella loses both her brothers, and one of the three male friends also loses his life. The survivors are scarred and changed.

The novel opens with the convention of the glorious pre-war summer, transferred to Ireland, and disturbed only by talk of Home Rule and the observation of their neighbour Irene, newly returned from London, that she had heard that in Ireland 'they were drilling all over the country' (Hinkson, 1932: 37). War in this text is introduced by an abrupt and sudden transition from the English guest, Edmund rowing Irene back across the lake at Cappagh to the opening of the next chapter, 'When

1   For surveys of such writing, see for example Goldman (1993) Oudit (1994) and Raitt and Tate (1997).

Edmund Urquart met Irene again it was at Victoria Station' (ibid.: 52). As Hinkson's mother, Katharine Tynan, makes clear in her autobiographical account, war comes to Ireland with even greater suddenness and less warning than it comes to England. (Tynan, 1919: 140–2). To women, moreover, it comes as loss and departure and appropriately begins at the railway station. As Irene breakfasts with Philip she thinks back over her last night with George and their fragmented conversation. In fact last conversations become a theme of the novel. Much later, in 1918, when David finally goes to the front, Stella (perhaps taking on something of the narrator's consciousness) reflects:

> Hubert Creagh had talked to Philip before he went out and Philip had talked to Guy. And George had talked slow difficult talk to Irene. Husband and wife, lovers, friends, talked before they parted. (Hinkson, 1932: 175)

Hinkson here points up the separate experience of women. Parting is sometimes the lot of men, but always the lot of women, both the English and Irish women of the text, although perhaps for the Irish women there is a double remoteness.

Deprivations figure strongly in Hinkson's text and form part of what I read as a narrative of resistance. As a schoolgirl, Stella cannot even share the consolations of 'war work', the channel for pent up energies experienced by most women in both Ireland and England (Reilly, 2002: 49–72). At the time of Stella's parting from David in 1918, 'She was less physically fit than he was, because she had been underfed for the last three years ... She had had neuralgia the whole of the last term' (Hinkson, 1932: 176).

The resistance which lurks beneath Stella's account of deprivation is made at times explicit. After the war, Stella is visited by a former comrade of her older brother Godfrey (who had died earlier in the conflict) and realises that he assumes her suffering is less than that of Godfrey's wife, Mary. 'Men were like that' she reflects, 'They only understood the relationships they created. It was part of their vanity ... You could get another husband. But she had lost two brothers.' Stella never quite reaches the level of bitterness and competition in suffering expressed for example in H.D.'s *Bid Me To Live*, but this is the moment when she comes nearest to it. Nancy too reflects on a difference between men and women, when, during the Anglo-Irish war, a local woman, Mrs Murphy, assisting her in clearing her dead husband's and son's belongings, advises her to hide the ceremonial swords, implying though not directly stating that the local rebels with whom her son is implicated might take them. Mrs Murphy's caution causes Nancy to reflect, 'But women were the same the world over when there was fighting.' Here we see a small but significant example of a collision of discourses within the subaltern category. The country-woman allies herself with the female landowner in the common sister-hood of resistance to war, preferring the practical survival of her family to any kind of male ideology such as republican nationalism, just as the landowning woman shows no inclination to take action against her infor-mant's family.

For Stella, David is the greatest loss. After he leaves for the front he is an absence, a ghost who is far more present on the occasion when she kisses another soldier about to leave for the front than the soldier himself. The real separation has however come earlier and is a separation of minds. After the German Spring Offensive and the battle of 21 March, David feels more acutely his exclusion from the comradeship of war shared by returning soldiers.

> It was a war of which civilians knew nothing. But he belonged to the War and the War to him … Like most people of his generation he was not troubled about right or wrong … If he had been twenty-eight or thirty the bayonet practice might have shocked him as it would have shocked a civilian. (Hinkson, 1932: 160–1)

This is a powerful representation of the gulf which separates the home front from the battle front, a gulf which is well attested on both sides, not only by the women writers referred to above but by male writers such as Siegfried Sassoon and Richard Aldington. The shifting of conscious-ness, employed as part of the narrative technique, enables a sympathetic portrayal of David's motivation but nevertheless the prevailing female bias of the narrative is critical.

This profound sense of divide between the home front and the battle front is a common perception in British writing of the war and can be seen also in, for example, the German writer, Erich Maria Remarque's *All Quiet on the Western Front*. A further insight of combatants from both sides is the overpowering sense of disillusion and disappointment which emerges in prose writing of the First World War during the 1920s and reflects an experience of what is sometimes called 'The Lost Generation'. However, here a specifically Irish dimension is added as the novel moves into the early nineteen twenties and two further conflicts reduce the international conflict to the opening, if horrific first act of a three act drama. A gap in the narrative takes us from the winter of 1918–19 to the summer of 1921 and the final months of the Anglo-Irish War. Stella increasingly spends more of her time at Cappagh, sensing that in England there is no place for her. Expressing the sense of the lost generation, she reflects that, because 'she wasn't old enough or young enough' the First World War has left her in a temporal No Man's Land 'with a country on either side that was not hers' (Hinkson, 1932: 313). There is then for the resistant Stella a possibility of seeing Ireland as a place of refuge and escape. However Cappagh occupies a cultural No Man's Land between England and Ireland.[2] Stella's new-found haven is in fact doomed. Hubert and his son Philip, who believed that Home Rule 'has got to come' (ibid.: 25), are dead and in any case their progressiveness has come too late. The emotional exhaustion which visited the survivors, particularly female survivors, of the First World War, is dramatised and writ large by the Anglo-Irish context. It provides some explanation for the extraordinary fatalism which seems to overtake the family at the end of the novel. In the concluding scene of the novel in which Cappagh is burned to the ground, Nancy wonders, apparently without emotion, which of the big houses will burn that night. Stella has met one of the perpetrators earlier and guessing his purpose, says nothing, 'the house knew, she thought.' The burning of several houses in one area is an historical misrepresentation[3] but contributes to an evocation of despair and disappointment which goes far beyond the literal. The novel leaves Stella with her refuge destroyed,

2   For a fuller discussion of this, see Phillips (2007).
3   See Bence-Jones (1993).

leaving her possibilities for recovery to our imagination. Hinkson's novel has elements of resistance to patriarchal domination rather than to the war itself, and may be seen as its title suggests as a distinctly female rather than a pacifist voice. Of the three novels under discussion here it is the closest to British home front novels by women and represents a shared experience across the British/Irish divide. More particularly a shared desire for peace is shared by the female Ascendancy landowner and the servant from the Nationalist family, of which some but not all the members are militant nationalists.

The Fire of Green Boughs (1918) shares with The Ladies Road a mix of Irish and English characters and settings in both countries, although the crucial action takes place in Ireland. The novel was written by Mrs Victor Rickard, who was loosely associated with the Revival, and a member of the establishment, being the daughter of a Church of Ireland minister and whose husband Lieutenant-Colonel Victor Rickard was killed at the Rue du Bois in 1915 while serving with the Royal Munster Fusiliers. Like The Ladies Road, The Fire of Green Boughs explores the gulf between combatants and non-combatants, but is an ultimately more radical novel. Although the novel is framed by the story of Dominic Roydon, returned disabled from the war and ordained in the Church of England, the most memorable character who occupies much of the central part of the novel, is his cousin Sylvia whose disillusion with the role of women is deeper and more marked than Stella's, but who like Stella finds a different and in her case more complete redemption in Ireland.

Sylvia is a classic victim of the patriarchal system, a dependant in the house of Dominic's father Jasper, exploited by both aunt and uncle to whom 'it never occurred … to write her a cheque' (Rickard, 1918: 21) Interestingly Sylvia's battle for some kind of comfort is described in military terms as 'an entente between herself and the hostile army who drew its wages from Sir Jasper and Lady Roydon and disliked them both with silent bitterness' (ibid.: 21). After the death of Lady Roydon, and Sir Jasper's decision to close up the house rendering her homeless, Sylvia, with a survivor's instinct for self-preservation, steals some of Lady Roydon's jewels. Significantly, and unlike Stella she is not interested in making a contribution to the war effort, and rejects work with the WAACS and the Red Cross as uncongenial (ibid.: 87). This form of passive resistance marks her out as a much more overtly rebellious figure than Sylvia.

She is thus exiled to Ireland, forced to take up Sir Jasper's offer of a home in his Irish house, Ballinadree in Kerry. Ireland functions in the novel as a place of escape and resistance, and as a benchmark by which to judge the characters. It is thus significant that Sir Jasper dislikes the house which he had bought some years before, and apparently has himself no Irish family connection. 'Your mother never liked the Irish, nor did I, but I believe you are fond of the house' he tells his idealistic son, Dominic. (Rickard, 1918: 61). Dominic, in spite of his own love for the country, fears that it would not suit his town-bred cousin. Ultimately it proves to be a litmus test for the hitherto distinctly unheroic Sylvia.

In the house she stays in (the former home of an Anglo-Irish family) and in the surrounding area she finds a country of contradictions: a country in which, according to the housekeeper 'now seemingly, all the gentry is Nationalists, and it's the boys are lepping to be fighting the troops'(Rickard, 1918: 119–20). The housekeeper herself has two sons fighting in France but remembers the police coming to her home to arrest her father for hiding ammunition (ibid.: 167 and 168). Willie Kent, the local Nationalist MP whom Sylvia has met in London, is admired by the local gentry for making recruiting speeches but has been imprisoned twice in his career (ibid.: 192). These characters thus highlight the impossibility of equating political views on the Irish question with support or opposition to the war effort. Significantly, Sylvia finds the landscape of Kerry 'tremendous and overpowering' never having seen anything 'more grand and more lonely' (ibid.: 108) and it is here that she performs her life-transforming action, which is both futile and heroic. Here, in the evocation of landscape, its location in the west and its implied link with heroic action are clear echoes of the Literary Revival with which Rickard was associated.

A dying German naval officer who has escaped from a submarine shipwrecked on the coast seeks shelter in Ballinadree and Sylvia, assisted by the housekeeper shelters him from the authorities in order that he may die in peace and dignity. Her motive is her anger at the sufferings of her generation (the title of the novel refers to the premature burning

of still green branches, the young generation sacrificed in the war): 'For
the sake of the young men she determined to let him remain where he
was; and in the name of youth, she challenged any infringement of this
right.'(Rickard, 1918: 165) The apparently shallow young woman, hitherto a victim of patriarchal power, who has appropriated some of her
dead aunt's jewellery and refused the hard work of contributing to the
war effort, finds herself not wanting when her ideals are called upon in
this remote part of Ireland far from the London she has known all her
life:'she did not know that a sudden realisation of a common humanity
with all the wide numbers of her own generation would sweep in over
her like a travelling tide, and carry her out to sea,' the narrator comments,
echoing the symbolic power of the sea in, for example, Synge's *Riders of
the Sea* (ibid.: 179).

In a crucial passage the Head Constable of the local RIC division in
the process of cross-examining her reflects:

> Inwardly he was convinced that the man had been assisted but he was equally
> puzzled to attribute his assistance to the fragile, fine-looking girl, who spoke with
> so fashionable a voice ... There was nothing in her of the wild, devilish subtlety
> ... which had blazed at him out of the eyes of the peasant women in lonely farms
> along the mountain-side. (Rickard, 1918: 173)

The judgement is erroneous. Sylvia's fashionable voice and demeanour are
simply another manifestation of the wild, devilish subtlety of the peasant
women. The English Sylvia, as surely as they do, belongs to a conquered
people, in her case dependent womanhood and therefore must resort to
the devious weapons of resistance, employed by oppressed groups everywhere. Of both it might be said as Willie Kent says of his compatriots:
'It isn't really much fun to grin through a horse collar at an eminently
superior class of beings who own your own country' (ibid.: 280).

For Sylvia, Ireland provides her with a challenge which awakes a
latent heroism within her and her story, unlike Stella's concludes happily
with her rescue from threatened imprisonment for shielding the German,
her subsequent marriage to Willie Kent in London and her escape back
to Ireland. The text is indeed more romantic than *The Ladies Road* and
reflects something of the Revival's romanticisation of rural Ireland, lacking

the brutal and tedious realism of the war experience described in the former novel. *The Fire of Green Boughs* connects nationalism and feminism in a way which challenges the assumptions of both: by establishing a common ground of resistance between the English woman and the Irish woman and their shared concern for the dying German soldier; and between the English woman and the male Irish Member of Parliament. At the same time it connects with the Revival's interest in heroic values, evident not just in Sylvia's protection of the dying German but her determined resistance to the patriarchal values of her society, by whatever means lie within her power.[4]

Margaret Barrington's *My Cousin Justin* (1939) represents almost a reversal of Sylvia's trajectory towards heroism. Barrington, whose first husband was the historian Edmund Curtis is chiefly known for her short-lived marriage to Liam O'Flaherty. Although like Rickard of Anglo-Irish stock (she was the daughter of a District Inspector in the Royal Irish Constabulary), she was much closer to radical republican movements than either of the other two writers and the novel provides an interesting case study of the interaction of feminism, socialism, pacifism and nationalism. Like *The Ladies Road* it deals not just with the First World War but with its aftermath, in this case both the War of Independence and the Civil War. The heroine and narrator, Anne-Louise Delahaie (known as Loulie), is a socialist and an opponent of the war, more analytical, better educated and possessed of more sophistication than Stella or Sylvia but ultimately is less capable of escaping male power. Towards the end of the novel she complains of her cousin Justin, whose power she never quite eludes: 'Why must I always walk behind him, follow in his steps, obey his command? Why did he think that he could turn towards me and away from me at will, always expecting the same obedience when it pleased him to call for it? Who made him lord and ruler over me?' (Barrington, 1939: 272) The answer is not easy to come by. Loulie like her creator grows up in Donegal, in the home of her grandfather, a landowner of Huguenot descent, which she shares with her cousin Justin (with whom

---

4   For a discussion of the relation of women to the Celtic revival see Innes (1993).

she develops a relationship curiously balanced between the platonic and the sexual) and which becomes her Paradise Lost (significantly she and Justin call the local wood Paradise). At the end, after a failed marriage to Justin's childhood antagonist, the local youth, Egan, Loulie returns to the house and to Justin.

The novel offers a socialist and to some extent feminist perspective on war. The First World War is the conflict whose after effects dominate the mood of the novel and in which both Justin and Egan take part. Later Egan becomes caught up in both the War of Independence and the Civil War. Loulie's Dublin friend, the journalist Tom Hennessey holds the view that it is love of women that drives men into danger so that women become essentially possessions to be fought over. He says of the dockers and foreign sailors they pass by Dublin's North Wall: 'They hate you because they can never possess you. They look at your fine clothes, your gentle appearance and compare you with their own women'(Barrington, 1939: 148).

In keeping with Tom's analysis of war in terms of power relations between men and women, neither Justin nor Egan offer any explanation for joining up. The novel, reflecting the views of its author, offers a socialist analysis of the First World War: 'Don't think it's any pleasure to me to fight and get killed to bring you and your like fat profits' declares one character.(Barrington, 1939: 124). Loulie is a more independent character than Stella in relation to the First World War, which, in a phrase economically conveying the mood of *The Ladies Road* when war broke out, she says, 'fell on us out of a clear summer sky' (ibid.: 82). She loses contact with Justin and Egan, the latter at this stage being only an acquaintance and shares her liberal father's scepticism about the conflict. Living in Ireland, she does not experience the pressures that Sylvia experiences, and records the growing disillusion of her neighbours in the Lagan who as the war progresses begin to ask why our men should die fighting against 'Protestant Germany for Catholic Belgium and infidel France' (ibid.: 23). Thus she undertakes the role neither of grieving/anxious lover nor frustrated war worker. However it is at the time of the War of Independence that the ultimately oppressed nature of Loulie's position becomes clear. Hennessy gives her the role of shelterer and protector of a rebel whose identity she does not know, though it turns out to be Egan, keeping her as much in ignorance as possible, so that her participation reflects the passivity of the traditional female. At the outbreak of the Civil War, Loulie expresses disillusion with both sides in the conflict, 'Free State or Republic, what does it matter? ... the worker will go to the wall' (ibid.: 173). Egan takes the Republican part and is forced to flee the country. Loulie, in spite of her political disillusion, plays the traditional woman's role, accepting his offer of marriage and fleeing with him. In the years that follow she accepts without question his transient life style and his unfaithfulness.

In the final section of the novel, Justin and Egan become involved in a vicious conflict back in the old house, after which Egan leaves and Loulie returns to Justin. Loulie comments:

> As I watched my husband and my cousin, I realized for the first time, that though they had all their limbs intact, though the only sign of war on Egan's body was a scar on the leg and here and there blue marks, each was as badly mutilated as if he had lost an arm or leg. (Barrington, 1939: 263–4)

She makes this comment after a violent quarrel in which they each recount something of their wartime experience. Although they speak of the horrors of encountering death, much of their dialogue focuses on female degradation, on exposed genitals, women exposing themselves and the inevitable encounters with prostitutes, rather confirming Hennessy's diagnosis of war (ibid.: 260–2).

This offers a coherent feminist analysis of war and is quoted on the back cover of the Blackstaff Press edition of the novel, but it is not quite the novel's ultimate analysis. After Justin has hurled a clock at Egan and nearly killed him, for the second time in his life (he has also hurled a rock at him as a child), Loulie reflects: 'Why had he changed from that gentle, sensitive boy? The war? Perhaps. But had he changed? – I thought. Had he not always had this bitter enmity towards his fellows' (Barrington, 1939: 270). Loulie declares that she loathed him, and yet despite her clear-sighted analyses, she returns to him. Perhaps, the novel suggests, the violence of men creates wars, rather than wars creating dehumanised and violent men. In any event Loulie's surrender represents a retreat from a public world in which women have apparently no part other than to serve, as the faithful servant Bella, the most consistent presence in the novel, who serves faithfully their grandfather and aunt and then the way-ward heirs. Loulie has never taken up an overtly feminist position but she has acted independently and taken up a socialist position. Now, she seemingly retreats from the political field to her private paradise, 'The house itself gathered me close to it, a warm, safe place' (ibid.: 287–8). It is almost a retreat into the womb, or in Kristevan terms into the semi-otic. Alternatively, since the novel was written in 1939, it may be read as a retreat from the monstrosity of the new Ireland which Egan and his like have created. Loulie never embraces the celebrated activism of some feminine revolutionaries of the time; at best she is a supporter on the sidelines. Her socialism and her republicanism do not have a developed feminist dimension and indeed tend to confirm the view that revolution-ary movements often contribute to the repression of women.

Much recent criticism in the field of early twentieth-century Irish Studies has illustrated the repression of the active contribution made by women to the nationalist struggle, and in so doing has contested an active/passive gender construction. Two of these novels of the First World War subtly contribute to such a contestation, although not directly in terms of the nationalist struggle. Stella in *The Ladies Road* is at one level an embodiment of passive suffering and loss, but she finds a voice to resist the role. The most heroic character is Sylvia, who sees in Ireland a landscape of resistance from English patriarchal society, which enables her to make her own stand for higher values, although even she is ultimately rescued by an embodiment of male political power, even if in a nationalist guise. The heroines of these novels often express a sisterhood of collusion across the categories of nationalism and colonialism (retrospectively seen as rigid), in the tacit alliance of the Home Rule sympathiser in the Ascendancy household with the local woman from a Nationalist/Republican family and in the more active collaboration of the Englishwoman and the local Irish servant, both in their different ways subtle and devious resisters of authority. The limits of female power are marked by the benevolent use of patriarchal power across the English/Irish divide by the constitu-tional nationalist politician. The exception is the isolated Loulie who does seem to express the loneliness and isolation of woman in a violent male world. While Loulie acts independently if only at the intellectual level, and makes a contribution to the nationalist struggle, it is a passive contribution and she retreats from its results, perhaps recognising the inevitable corruption of nationalism by its accession to power. Thus it is the nationalist woman who succumbs most easily and completely to male power. The two English women, only tangentally sympathetic, assert independence, and find in Ireland a place more in tune with their ideas and their resistance. Nevertheless *My Cousin Justin* does offer a distinctly feminist analysis in suggesting that war of any kind is a specifically male responsibility, taking up rather the position adopted by some feminists of the time such as the Swedish Ellen Key that war is a consequence of specifically male aggression.

Linda Connolly has commented of the early years of the twentieth century that 'the Irish women's movement combined nationalism and unionism with other important "isms" that have been eclipsed in the writing of mainstream Irish Studies (such as socialism, pacifism, internationalism and religious differences)' (Connolly, 2004: 153). These three novels by Irishwomen of different political views and cultural backgrounds all writing of the effects on the lives of women and others of the First World War provide an illustration of this comment and a small opportunity for the '(female) subaltern' to 'speak when *spoken about* in Irish Studies' (ibid.: 154).

Works Cited

Barrington, Margaret (1939), *My Cousin Justin*, Blackstaff Press, Belfast.
Bence-Jones, Mark (1993), *Twilight of the Ascendancy*, London, Constable.
Bolger, Dermot (2007), *Walking The Road*, New Island Books, Dublin.
Brearton, Fran (2000), *The Great War in Irish Poetry*, Oxford University
    Press, Oxford.

Connolly, Linda (2004), 'The Limits of Irish Studies' in *Irish Studies Review*, 12, (2), pp 139–62.

Goldman, Dorothy (1993), *Women and World War I*, Palgrave MacMillan, Basingstoke.

Graham, Colin (2001), *Deconstructing Ireland*, Edinburgh University Press, Edinburgh.

—— (2003), 'Subalternity and Gender' in Connolly, Claire (ed.), *Theorizing Ireland*, Palgrave Macmillan, Basingstoke, pp. 150–9.

Haughey, Jim (2002), *First World War* in Irish Poetry, Bucknell University Press, Lewisburg.

Hennessey, Thomas (1998), *Dividing Ireland*, Routledge, London.

Hinkson, Pamela (1932), *The Ladies Road*, Penguin Books, Harmondsworth.

Innes, C.L. (1993), *Woman and Nation*, University of Georgia Press, Athens, Georgia.

Jeffery, Keith (2000), *Ireland and The Great War*, Cambridge University Press, Cambridge.

Ouditt, Sharon (1994), *Fighting Forces, Writing Women*, Routledge, London.

Phillips, Terry (2007), 'No world Between Two Worlds: Liminality in Anglo-Irish Big House Fiction 1925–1932, in Kay, Lucy, Kinsley, Zoe, Phillips, Terry and Roughley, Alan (eds), *Mapping Liminalities*, Peter Lang, Bern, pp. 69–90.

Raitt, Suzanne and Tate Trudi (1997), *Women's Fiction and The First World War*, Oxford University Press, Oxford.

Reilly, Eileen (2002), 'Women and Volutary War Work' in Gregory, Adrian and Pašeta, Senia (eds), *Ireland and the Great War*, pp. 49–72.

Rickard, Mrs Victor (1918), *The Fire of Green Boughs*, Duckworth, London.

Spival, Gayatri Chakravorty, 'Can the Subaltern Speak?' in Williams, Patrick and Chrisman, Laura (eds), *Colonial Discourse and Postcolonial Theory*, Columbia University Press, New York, pp. 66–111.

Steele, Karen (2007), *Women, Press, and Politics During the Irish Revival*, Syracuse University Press, New York.

Tynan, Katharine (1919), *The Years of The Shadow*, Constable, London.

Contributors

JOHN COYLE is Head of the Department of English Literature at the University of Glasgow. His interests include modernist and postmodernist literature and culture from an international perspective, specifically, Anglophone responses to Proust. He has published on a range of writers from John Ruskin to Don DeLillo.

TOM HERRON is Lecturer in English and Irish Literature in the School of Cultural Studies at Leeds Metropolitan University. He is the co-author (with John Lynch) of *After Bloody Sunday: Representation, Ethics, Justice*. His collection of poetry, *The Harrowing of the Heart* (co-edited with Julieann Campbell) was launched in Derry's Guildhall on 30 January 2008 to mark the thirty-sixth anniversary of Bloody Sunday.

JOSÉ LANTERS is Professor of English at the University of Wisconsin-Milwaukee, where she also serves on the advisory committee of the Center for Celtic Studies, and on the editorial board of the electronic interdisciplinary journal *e-Keltoi*. Her numerous publications in the field of Irish literature and culture include *Unauthorized Versions: Irish Menippean Satire, 1919–1952* and *The 'Tinkers' in Irish Literature: Unsettled Subjects and the Construction of Difference*. She is currently president of the American Conference for Irish Studies.

BARRY LEWIS took his BA in English and Philosophy at King's College, Cambridge, and his doctorate in postmodernist American fiction at the University of Sunderland. He is Senior Lecturer at the University of Sunderland, and he also has held posts at the University of Newcastle, the University of Trondheim, and at Stavanger College, Norway. He is the author of *Kazuo Ishiguro* and *My Words Echo Thus: Possessing the Past in Peter Ackroyd*.

PADDY LYONS teaches at the University of Glasgow, where he is convenor for Irish literature; he also holds a personal professorship at the University of Warsaw. He has published extensively on Restoration theatre, on literary theory and twentieth-century fiction, and on Irish literature, most recently on the playwright Brian Friel, and on the nineteenth-century Dublin novelist May Laffan. He also writes on psycho-linguistics, and is a translator of Louis Althusser. His books include *Congreve's Comedies, Female Playwrights of the Restoration*, the Earl of Rochester's *Complete Poems and Plays* and Mary Shelley's *Frankenstein: the 1818 text*, and he has co-edited several international collections of literary essays.

CAROLINE MAGENNIS gained her PhD from Queen's University, Belfast, in 2007. Her doctoral work focused on the representation of masculinities in contemporary Northern Irish fiction. She is currently a Post-Doctoral Researcher for University College, Dublin.

WILLY MALEY is Professor of Renaissance Studies at the University of Glasgow, and Visiting Professor at the University of Sunderland. He is the author of *A Spenser Chronology, Salvaging Spenser: Colonialism, Culture and Identity*, and *Nation, State and Empire in English Renaissance Literature: Shakespeare to Milton*. He is editor, with Andrew Hadfield, of *A View of the Present State of Ireland: From the First Published Edition*. He has edited many collections of essays: with Brendan Bradshaw and Andrew Hadfield, *Representing Ireland: Literature and the Origins of Conflict, 1534–1660*; with Bart Moore-Gilbert and Gareth Stanton, *Postcolonial Criticism*; with David J. Baker, *British Identities and English Renaissance Literature*; with Andrew Murphy, *Shakespeare and Scotland*; and with Alex Benchimol, *Spheres of Influence: Intellectual and Cultural Publics from Shakespeare to Habermas*.

PATRICK MAUME is a graduate of University College, Cork, and of Queens University, Belfast; he has previously taught history and politics, and he is now a researcher for the *Dictionary of Irish Biography*. He has published numerous books and articles, including biographies of Daniel Corkery and D.P. Moran, and a survey of early twentieth-century Irish nationalist political culture. He has a strong interest in the political and cultural history of Northern Ireland, and has lived in Belfast for the last thirteen years.

MATT MCGUIRE teaches at the University of Glasgow. He has published widely on both Scottish and Irish literature including essays on Northern Irish poetry, fiction and the cultural aesthetics of devolution. His work has appeared in the *Edinburgh Review, Scottish Studies Review* and *The Edinburgh Companion to Contemporary Scottish Literature*. He is the author of *The Essential Guide to Contemporary Scottish Literature*. Forthcoming projects include *The Edinburgh Companion to Contemporary Scottish Poetry*. He primarily lectures on twentieth-century literature, poetry and prose, and on Marxist, feminist and postmodernist approaches to the text.

CLAIRE NALLY currently works at the University of Hull, where she is a lecturer in English. She previously worked at the University of Manchester, where she completed her PhD. She is completing a book project, entitled *Envisioning Ireland: Occult Nationalism in the Work of W.B. Yeats,* which addresses the poet in relation to nationalism and identity formation and is to be published by Peter Lang. She has published in *The Irish Studies Review, The Canadian Journal of Irish Studies,* and also writes on the topic of feminist Burlesque.

BRITTA OLINDER is Professor Emerita of the English Institute of Gothenburg University. Her books include: *Literary Environments: Canada and the Old World; Breaking Circles:* and *The Links of a Curious Chain: studies in the act and scenes of John Dryden's tragedies and tragic-comedies.* She has edited and co-edited many distinguished collections of essays, and has been particularly active in the field of Irish Studies.

DEIRDRE O'BYRNE lectures in English at Loughborough University. Her main area of research is twentieth-century and especially Irish prose fiction. She has recently published on 'Scandalous Women' in relation to the writings of Edna O'Brien and Mary Lavin. She is currently chair of the Nottingham Irish Studies group.

ALISON O'MALLEY-YOUNGER is Senior Lecturer in English and Drama at the University of Sunderland. She is a founder of the annual Irish Studies conference at Sunderland, and is Director of the North East Irish Culture Network (NEICN). She has published in the fields of contemporary critical theory, women's writing in Ireland, and Irish Drama, both contemporary and nineteenth-century. She has edited, with Frank Beardow, *Representing Ireland: Past, Present and Future*, and with John Strachan, *Essays on Modern Irish Literature*. Her current projects include *Essential Criticism: Brian Friel* for Palgrave Macmillan, and two edited collections with John Strachan entitled, *Ireland at War and Peace* for Cambridge Scholars Press and *Ireland: Revolution and Evolution* for Peter Lang.

GLENN PATTERSON was born in Belfast in 1961, and studied on the Creative Writing MA at the University of East Anglia. He returned to Northern Ireland in 1988 as Writer in the Community for Lisburn and Craigavon. He has since been Writer in Residence at the Universities of East Anglia, Cork and at Queen's University, Belfast, where he currently teaches on the MA in Creative Writing. He is the author of eight novels. The first, *Burning Your Own* (1988), won a Betty Trask Award and the Rooney Prize for Irish Literature. *Fat Lad* (1992) was shortlisted for the Guinness Peat Aviation Book. *Black Night at Big Thunder Mountain* (1995), *The International* (1999), *Number 5* (2003), and *That Which Was* (2004) are all set in Belfast; *The Third Party* (2007) is set in Japan. His latest novel, *Over the Hill: Love in Troubled Times* (2008) is part-memoir, part detective-story. *Lapsed Protestant* (2006) collects his non-fiction pieces. In 2006, he was elected to Aosdána, the affiliation of Irish Artists.

TERRY PHILLIPS is Dean of Arts and Humanities at Liverpool Hope University. Her research interests are in the area of Irish literature, particularly of the early twentieth century, and First World War literature. She has published a number of articles in both these areas.

DAMIEN SHORTT is Lecturer of English at Edge Hill University. His interests lie in contemporary Irish fiction and the way in which Irish identity is perceived and represented. At Edge Hill he is a research fellow, with particular focus on exploring the utilisation of computer aided assessment in literature degrees, and the analysis of postgraduate education from a post-structuralist theoretical perspective.

Index of Names and Works

Reimagining Ireland

Series Editor: Dr Eamon Maher, Institute of Technology, Tallaght

The concepts of Ireland and 'Irishness' are in constant flux in the wake of an ever-increasing reappraisal of the notion of cultural and national specificity in a world assailed from all angles by the forces of globalisation and uniformity. Reimagining Ireland interrogates Ireland's past and present and suggests possibilities for the future by looking at Ireland's literature, culture and history and subjecting them to the most up-to-date critical appraisals associated with sociology, literary theory, historiography, political science and theology.

Some of the pertinent issues include, but are not confined to, Irish writing in English and Gaelic, Nationalism, Unionism, the Northern 'Troubles', the Peace Process, economic development in Ireland, the impact and decline of the Celtic Tiger, Irish spirituality, the rise and fall of organised religion, the visual arts, popular cultures, sport, Irish music and dance, emigration and the Irish diaspora, immigration and multiculturalism, marginalisation, globalisation, modernity/postmodernity and postcolonialism. The series publishes monographs, comparative studies, interdisciplinary projects, conference proceedings and edited books.

Proposals should be sent either to Dr Eamon Maher at eamon.maher@ ittdublin.ie or to Joe Armstrong, Commissioning Editor for Ireland, Peter Lang Ltd, P.O. Box 38, Kells, County Meath, +353 (0) 46 924 9285, joearmstrong@eircom.net.

Vol. 1   Eugene O'Brien: 'Kicking Bishop Brennan Up the Arse':
         Interlacing Texts and Contexts in Contemporary Irish Studies
         ISBN 978-3-03911-539-6. Forthcoming.

Vol. 2   James Byrne, Padraig Kirwan and Michael O'Sullivan (eds):
         Affecting Irishness: Negotiating Cultural Identity Within and
         Beyond the Nation
         ISBN 978-3-03911-830-7. Forthcoming.

Vol. 3   Irene Lucchitti: The Islandman: The Hidden Life of Tomás
         O'Crohan
         ISBN 978-3-03911-837-3. Forthcoming.